THE PRIVILEGE OF BEING BANAL

D1593246

CLASS NEW
200 STUDIES
IN
RELIGION

EDITED BY Kathryn Lofton AND John Lardas Modern

THE PRIVILEGE OF BEING BANAL

Art, Secularism, and
Catholicism in Paris

ELAYNE OLIPHANT

The University of Chicago Press

Chicago and London

The University of Chicago Press, Chicago 60637

The University of Chicago Press, Ltd., London

© 2021 by The University of Chicago

Published 2021

Printed in the United States of America

30 29 28 27 26 25 24 23 22 21   1 2 3 4 5

ISBN-13: 978-0-226-73112-4 (cloth)

ISBN-13: 978-0-226-73126-1 (paper)

ISBN-13: 978-0-226-73143-8 (e-book)

DOI: https://doi.org/10.7208/chicago/9780226731438.001.0001

Library of Congress Cataloging-in-Publication Data

Names: Oliphant, Elayne, author.

Title: The privilege of being banal : art, secularism, and Catholicism in Paris / Elayne Oliphant.

Other titles: Class 200, new studies in religion.

Description: Chicago : University of Chicago Press, 2021. | Series: Class 200 | Includes bibliographical references and index.

Identifiers: LCCN 2020020734 | ISBN 9780226731124 (cloth) | ISBN 9780226731261 (paperback) | ISBN 9780226731438 (ebook)

Subjects: LCSH: Catholic Church—Social aspects—France—Paris. | Secularism—France—Paris. | Church and state—France—Paris. | Art and religion—France—Paris.

Classification: LCC BX1533.P3 O45 2021 | DDC 282/.44361—dc23

LC record available at https://lccn.loc.gov/2020020734

For my mother

———————

CONTENTS

INTRODUCTION

The Privilege of Banality

ON THE LEFT BANK OF THE Seine River, at the bottom of a steep hill that leads up toward the heart of Paris's Latin Quarter—just a short walk from the Notre-Dame Cathedral—sits a building known as the Collège des Bernardins. Cistercian monks began construction of the site in 1248. They added a church in 1338. Never fully completed, the church did not survive the nineteenth century, when it was destroyed to make way for one of Paris's central thoroughfares, the Boulevard St. Germain. The Collège's use as a space for monastic learning amid the intellectual and cultural life surrounding the University of Paris had already dwindled when the revolutionary state expropriated it in 1791. In the initial years following the Revolution, the site served briefly as a prison and a warehouse, and then, for nearly one hundred years, as a municipal fire station. In 2001, the Catholic archdiocese purchased the space from the City of Paris and after extensive renovations opened it to the public in 2008, describing it as nothing less than the "renaissance" of the original Cistercian space and project. The French Catholic Church has invested a great deal of money, labor, and ambition in the Collège. Defined as a "space of encounters, culture, and research" it aims to appeal to a broad-based public. Catholic ritual practices take a back seat to lectures and colloquia, theology classes, musical concerts, and contemporary art exhibits. Between 2008 and 2010, I spent countless hours conducting ethnographic research at the Collège, eventually working as a *médiatrice* (the feminine form of *médiateur*), assisting visitors in their encounters with the contemporary art exhibits displayed under its extraordinary medieval vaults.

On a cold December afternoon in 2008, only a few weeks after first discovering the Collège, I hovered near the entrance next to its inaugural art installation. A woman I guessed to be around seventy-five approached me. "Is this something modern?" she asked. I paused, unsure precisely how to respond. "You know about these things then," she observed, pointing to my notebook. "I don't know very much about these things—I'm learning," I replied. Trying to turn the conversation toward her, I asked, "What do you think about it?" She began to articulate a disapproving response and then interrupted herself. "What you should really see is the crypt, down below. That is something spectacular. Perhaps I can take you. But you must be discreet. Discreet, you understand?" I assured her that I understood what she was asking of me. Attendants checking for receipts or badges that would authorize our descent (and which I lacked) blocked the main stairs, so we headed toward a back staircase.[1] At the bottom, we attempted to enter through a door that turned out to be locked. "Perhaps I will just ask," she suggested, shrugging. I followed her back up to the main stairway. "This mademoiselle is a foreigner," the woman—to whom I will refer as my guide—said to the attendant by way of explanation.[2] "I want to show her the crypt, very quickly, for five minutes, and then I will bring her back."

When we finally arrived in what my guide referred to as the crypt, I was taken aback.[3] It was the first time I had visited this level of the Collège and it was indeed beautiful. The low ceiling and floor-level lighting lent a warm glow to the thirteenth-century limestone pillars. The cellar consists of a hallway lined with doors leading to classrooms where theology and seminary classes are taught. As we walked slowly through the space my guide uttered the words "Can you imagine?" again and again in hushed tones, although we were alone in the hallway. "It is so wonderful to learn in this atmosphere," she explained to me. In the weeks that followed, as I attended guided tours of the space, I learned that the monks who built it struggled to stabilize its foundation due to the nearby presence of the Bièvre Canal. Soon after the building's completion, in fact, they had to fill the cellar with dirt in order to keep it standing. Thus, while my guide was clearly moved by the experience of inhabiting a medieval space, the cellar had, in fact, been made accessible only through the very recent renovation.

Returning upstairs, my guide gestured to the art installation. "You see?" now having a comparison with which to make her point. "This is out of place—that's what I think." This final statement was the real reason my guide had approached me that afternoon. Our tour had served as evidence for her claim. The desire to distinguish between the essence of the space of the Collège and matter out of place within it arose time and again in the months and years I spent there. In a remark left in the comment book found next to the contemporary art installation my guide so disliked, a visitor inquired "What would St. Bernard have said?" in order to express the idea that only material forms of which the early leader of the Cistercians would have approved were appropriate in this space. Rarely did it seem sufficient for visitors to keep such opinions to themselves. They had to be declared aloud, angrily asserted, or lamented in the company of those similarly disconcerted. Given my position near the door with a notebook in hand, my guide may have initially mistaken me for an employee, allowing her to assert her critique to someone in a position of authority. Once she realized that I was a "foreigner," the opportunity to clarify what did not belong at the Collège to someone who could not be trusted to fully understand matter's proper place proved equally compelling.

While she was one of the few to so forcefully show me precisely what she desired to see when she entered the Collège, her laments were similar to countless others I encountered. The breathless joy she articulated in her refrain of "Can you imagine?" as we wandered in the quiet intimacy of the cellar powerfully demonstrated a desire for a French medieval Catholic past that many repeated in various ways to me over the months I spent there. Equally common were suspicions and even outrage expressed toward the contemporary art displayed in this space. The contemporary art installations were among the most visible activities undertaken in the newly restored building during its inaugural years. The passionate feelings—both desires for visceral encounters with the medieval and angry dismissals of the contemporary—so often expressed in this space reflect the deep unease and anxieties that surround the complex project underway here.

Given how often "medieval" is used as an accusatory label against Muslims—both in France and around the globe—in order to equate them with all that is irrational, violent, and threatening, the Parisian Catholic Church's ability and willingness to make such positive connections to the medieval past requires our attention. The Collège is certainly not the only space to capitalize on desires for the medieval Catholic past in France today. Rather than an exceptional form of Catholic materiality, I understand the Collège to be a particularly powerful expression of what I call Catholicism's privileged banality in Paris—and indeed in France—today.[4]

When reflecting on Catholicism's privilege, I borrow the term "banal" from the late editor of the satirical magazine *Charlie Hebdo*, Stéphane Charbonnier. In explaining his magazine's relentless publication of images of the Prophet Mohammed that clearly troubled many Muslim French,[5] Charb, as he was known, once declared "we have to keep at it until Islam is made as banal as Catholicism" (Ternision 2012).[6] He clearly used the term "banal" in order to demean both Islam and Catholicism. As he understood it, blasphemous or sacrilegious efforts such as his against sacred images, narratives, and material forms have led Catholics to admit defeat and stop fighting back against the offenses lodged at their objects and images.[7] The fact that some Muslims expressed outrage in response to *Charlie Hebdo*'s cartoons suggested to Charb that the battle with Islam needed to continue until Muslims learned to take their religious materiality less seriously.

Charb's cartoons exemplify a key disciplinary tactic of secularism; they insist upon human mastery over material forms. By transforming religious images from agents of grace deserving of reverence to mere objects impervious to mockery, Charb demonstrated his modernity, contrasting his agency with the inertia of objects and images. His use of the term "banal" to describe Catholicism in France in the twenty-first century suggests that, to his mind, Catholics had developed a more appropriately modern relationship with materiality than Muslims. Slogans such as "Je suis Charlie" used in the demonstrations that followed his murder implied that the true citizens of France must discipline less-than-modern immigrants by demonstrating how blasphemy is key to modern subjectivity and French citizenship.[8]

We should not so readily accept Charb's assumption that banality is a sign of weakness. I complicate Charb's use of the term "banal" by turning to the work of Hannah Arendt (1963). For Arendt, banality was a means of addressing how actions and practices typically deemed reprehensible or unacceptable come to appear as self-evidently unproblematic, both to individuals and collectively. In a country widely admired for its *laïcité* (secularism), numerous Catholic objects, images, and spaces occupy the Parisian landscape in ways that are banal. Generally speaking, the distinction made between laïcité in France and Anglo-American expressions of secularism is that while secularism aims to create a landscape in which people are able to practice their religion freely, laïcité aims to create a space in which people are free from the presence of religion of any kind.[9] It is unsurprising, therefore, that many I met in France insisted that Catholicism can no longer be seen in the nation today. In order to make such a claim, however, they had to overlook how Catholic objects, images, and spaces—from crucifixes to paintings of Christian narratives to neogothic churches—inundate public life in Paris and France alike. Throughout this book, I will use the term "materiality" to refer to these objects, images, and spaces, not to collapse them into sameness but to make clear their shared significance. My guide's breathless delight in the experience of learning in such an atmosphere, or the easy way in which Notre-Dame—particularly its medieval components—was equated with French "culture" when it burned in the spring of 2019 demonstrates the significance of this materiality. Its value in the present resides most prominently in its banality, its capacity to be seen as naturally French, despite widespread claims that religion must always be absent from public life. The banal appears, to borrow Craig Calhoun's account of the secular, as "the normal, natural, tacit context for . . . action" (2010, 38).

Banality—far from a sign of weakness—proffers a series of privileges. Such privilege can most readily be seen in how Catholic materiality moves freely between the unmarked background and marked foreground of public life. Following Linda Waugh, I understand the distinction between the unmarked and marked as expressing "the asymmetrical and hierarchical relationship between the two poles of any opposition" (1982, 299). The concept has been used to explain why certain elements of social life stand out as exemplary of a category and others of the same category do not. In exploring the *Parité* movement—a campaign calling for the equal representation of men and women in French politics—for example, Joan Scott (2005) explains how women were disproportionately absent from representative politics in France because, as the marked category, they were conceived as being sexed and, therefore, unfit for the task of abstract representation in relation to the unsexed and unmarked (male) citizen.

When it comes to religion, Islam stands in relief as the marked against the unmarked secular French.[10] Catholicism, by contrast, is equated with the secular in France through practices that make it isomorphic with the history and culture of France and Europe. Catholic material forms, figures, and practices occupy monumental spaces in Paris. They rise above the skyline, and they provide the names of many of the streets, passageways, and metro stations. Quite often, however, this Catholic materiality goes overlooked. I want to offer just one small example here of the capacity for Catholic materiality to move in the French public sphere in ways that are banal. Debates around the burqa reverberated throughout the mediascape during the two years I spent in Paris.[11] These debates called out from the headlines of newspapers, they were deliberated on radio talk shows, and they were the subjects of many conversations I overheard and in which I participated. This audible racket, however, always contrasted sharply with the absence of these sights on the streets of Paris. As I moved, lived, researched, and worked in the twenty *arrondissements* of the French capital, I never, in fact, encountered a single *niqab*.[12] This spectral omnipresence made me take note when, on two occasions, my eyes caught sight of women dressed in long, dark, flowing robes. Each time, I was surprised enough to want to confirm that my eyes had not deceived me. On both occasions, I pursued the women in order to catch a glimpse of them from the front. After running to position myself ahead of them on the street, however, I realized that the women I saw were not dressed in niqabs but in very similar garb: the nun's habit. Given the violence often enacted against bearers of niqabs during this period, I was struck by how these nuns elicited very little reaction from those around me.[13]

At other times, however—such as when the Notre-Dame Cathedral burned before millions of real and virtual spectators—Catholic materiality is able to exceed the unmarked background and emerge into the monumental foreground. When it does so, the marked visibility of its material forms—in contrast to those associated with Islam—does not invoke outrage. The privilege made possible by banality allows Catholic materiality to occupy public spaces where religion is supposed to be absent in ways both seen and unseen.

The celebration of medieval Catholic materiality I witnessed at the Collège and elsewhere in Paris is another expression of the privilege of banality. So are the virulent attacks against the contemporary art that seemed to threaten the coherence of these medieval forms. As I demonstrate in chapters 3 through 6, in their enraged responses to contemporary art, visitors to the Collège often articulated a notion of enlivened materiality that modern subjects are supposed to abhor. It is these ways in which Catholic materiality pushes up against the interdictions of laïcité—occupying the public sphere in ways both marked and unmarked, offering visceral access to the medieval past, and appearing as enchanted or enlivened forms—without threatening France's celebrated secularity that I understand as the privilege of Catholicism's banality.

Emphasizing the Catholicity of Paris will, perhaps, require readers to look at the world's most visited city in a different light. (And yet, many of the city's "iconic" sights—such as Notre-Dame and Sacré-Coeur—are, indeed, Catholic.) In his exploration of Paris in *The Arcades Project*, Walter Benjamin noted that

> few things in the history of humanity are as well known to us as the history of Paris. Tens of thousands of volumes are dedicated solely to the investigation of this tiny spot on the earth's surface. . . . And at work in the attraction it exercises on people is the kind of beauty that is proper to

great landscapes—more precisely, to volcanic landscapes. Paris is a coun-
terpart in the social order to what Vesuvius is in the geographic order:
a menacing, hazardous massif, an ever-active hotbed of revolution. But
just as the slopes of Vesuvius, thanks to the layers of lava that cover them,
have been transformed into paradisal orchards, so the lava of revolutions
provides uniquely fertile ground for the blossoming of art, festivity, fashion. [1999, 82–83]

I would argue that in the decades that have passed since Benjamin's reflections, Paris has become less of a site of revolutionary eruptions. Today it
stands more frequently as a reliable connection to the past. In attempting to
understand anxious and often enraged responses to modern and contemporary art and architecture, I ask why, in the early decades of the twenty-first
century, a medieval space that seemed to argue for Paris's continuities, rather
than its ruptures, appeared both so enticing and so in need of protection
from menacing and hazardous contemporary aesthetic forms.

The central question driving this book is Why does a space like the Collège appear necessary in France today? If France is celebrated as *the* site of
revolution—the ultimate overthrow of tyrannical power underwritten by
the mythologizing sacraments of an irrational Church—why was it necessary to bring to life a space that celebrates the medieval past? More boldly,
why does secular France still need Catholicism?[14] I argue that France still
needs Catholicism today because it never actually dismantled distinctions
and inequalities in the way that its national myths presume. The vision of
equality imagined and enacted at brief moments during the French Revolution and beyond was never fully implemented, and a number of interests
combine—and continue to recalibrate—to resist moving French social life
toward equality in a fuller sense. A project like the Collège is necessary
because it offers an aesthetic ground for that tenacious inequality. I understand inequality to be tenacious in France both because racial, class, gender,
and religious inequality remain powerfully present, despite the longevity
of declarations of the rights shared by all humans, and because, despite the
fall of feudalism following the Revolution, wealth remains limited to a very
small portion of the French population. The Collège's medieval forms allow
visitors both to take delight in the structures they did overturn and to evade
the need to dismantle the distinctions they continue to reproduce. It allows
them to condone some forms of inequality—between Muslims and Catholics, black and white, or rich and poor—while celebrating the cessation of
others—between priests and the laity, or kings and peasants. In this context,

I see the Collège as, in part, offering Parisians a "cultured" means by which to celebrate the limits of France's equality.[15]

THE COLLÈGE

This book tells the story of the first four contemporary art exhibits displayed at the Collège. In a context where laws and regulations render Islam hypervisible, my focus on the French Catholic archdiocese's decision to display contemporary art in a renovated medieval space in central Paris may seem to distract us from the important questions of inequality central to public life in France today. But, as the political scientist Ruth Marshall (2009) powerfully demonstrates in her research among Born-Again Christians in Nigeria, religious practices are also political practices. I argue that religious practices aimed at reproducing banality and the privilege it proffers are central to understanding inequalities in the present.

Efforts underway at the Collège have the potential to exacerbate particularly exclusionary visions of France and its inhabitants. This exclusion is both race- and class-based. Throughout the twentieth century, a variety of Catholic movements aimed at lay populations explicitly worked to include the poor and the marginalized. In contrast, this site—despite being advertised as a space of *ouverture* (opening)—mostly serves an elite clientele of both practicing and nonpracticing Catholics. This skewed result is not an accident. The primary audience imagined and encouraged by employees at the Collège is a particularly wealthy, white, bourgeois public. In order to reproduce the privilege of Catholicism in Paris in the present, the Collège seeks to attend to those whose connections to their parish church may vary but whose elite status legitimates the project underway here.

I went to Paris to understand the kinds of practices that made Catholicism's banality possible. I wanted to explore the projects in which the French Church was particularly invested, and to see how it attracted and engaged a broader public. I spent the summer of 2007 conducting preliminary research by visiting as many of Paris's Roman Catholic churches as possible to get a sense of how these ubiquitous but often overlooked sites fit into the broader urban landscape.[16] I was particularly intrigued by one of the city's newest churches—Notre-Dame de la Sagesse (Our Lady of Wisdom) in the thirteenth arrondissement.[17] A small, minimalist, modern church, it was built not far from the new location of the national library of France. Its

simple square form made it difficult to identify as a church, given the monumental proportions of its nineteenth-century counterparts that dominate
the cityscape. In addition, the church's programming was unusual, offering
lunchtime lectures on art, literature, and philosophy. As I looked into the
history of the space, I learned that the distinguished French philosophers
Alain Finkielkraut and Paul Ricoeur had given talks at the consecration of
the space when it opened in March 2000.

I made a beeline for the church when I returned for long-term research
in October 2008. Within a few days I discovered a book club at the church
and purchased the group's next selection: a book of poetry by the Pales-
tinian poet Mahmoud Darwish. In my excitement I arrived early but was
soon disappointed to realize that only a very small group would gather that
evening. My questions to the organizer later solidified my impression that
while Notre-Dame de la Sagesse had opened with a great deal of excitement,
its programming had ultimately failed to attract the crowds that had been
anticipated.[18] I continued to follow events in the space but also expanded
my search. I attended a weekend on sacred music at the "artist's church," St.
Roch, near the Louvre museum and began to make a few friends through
these various connections. Three weeks after I arrived, one of these new
friends asked me if I had ever heard of the Collège des Bernardins. The look
he gave me when I shook my head no told me that I had not been searching
hard enough. "You must go to see it immediately," he chastised me. "I think
you'll find it's exactly what you've been looking for."

The renovation of the Collège took longer than planned, but its completion in September 2008 (two weeks before I arrived in Paris for long-term
research) coincided with Pope Benedict XVI's visit to France. While there,
he celebrated its opening with a lecture to seven hundred members of, in the
pope's words, the "world of culture."[19] The fact that, in contrast to the opening of Notre-Dame de la Sagesse, the pope inaugurated rather than consecrated this space speaks volumes about the kind of project the archdiocese
aimed to build here. While capitalizing on desires for a Catholic past, the
building is not, technically, a "sacred" space. It is categorized not as a *lieu de
culte* (a religious space) but a *lieu de culture* (a cultural space). This distinction is significant in France and it may have helped the Collège to access
state support for its renovation, a point I explore in more detail in chapter
2. During the inaugural art exhibition in particular, a number of mediators
would take the time to explicitly make the distinction between the Collège
and a sacred space such as a church when they encountered visitors who
worried at the presence of contemporary art in "such a space."

I was closer in age to the mediators than many employees and most visitors. As I returned to the space day after day, and hovered around the art exhibitions, a number of volunteers and visitors mistook me for a mediator. While I had not anticipated engaging in such a métier when I arrived in Paris, by the spring of 2009, when the most popular art exhibit in the Collège's inaugural years was unexpectedly extended and more mediators were needed in short order, I became a desirable candidate to work there as a mediator myself.[20]

Mediators are nondidactic docents who aim to offer keys with which viewers can engage with artworks on their own terms, rather than limit the precise manner in which an artwork is to be interpreted. In this way, our work was distinguished from that of the "guides," volunteers (mostly women) who gave tours of the building and who had a particular narrative they had been trained to impart. The term "mediation" to describe such labor is not unique to the Collège but instead demonstrates the institute's savvy use of practices found in many spaces of contemporary art display in France. At the Collège (and at many other cultural spaces), mediators tend to be on the lowest end of the institutional hierarchy. Most of us were in our twenties and had been hired through ad hoc means. Charles, one mediator who worked on the inaugural art exhibition referenced above and described more fully in chapter 3, excitedly explained to me that, as someone who had not completed his *bac*, the job was the most interesting he had ever held. The *baccalauréat* is a nationwide exam that French students take at the end of high school and is considered necessary for entrance to postsecondary education and for most middle-class jobs. Those who do not complete it are generally relegated to France's working class. Charles was unique among the mediators with whom I interacted, the vast majority of whom were decidedly middle class. Most of us were in the process of completing some kind of advanced university degree.

Charles also took delight in the job because it was the highest wage he had ever received. The mediators who worked on the inaugural exhibition were indeed well paid. By the end of the exhibit, however, the 2008 financial crisis had settled into France. Everyone who had worked on the first exhibit was dismissed so that a new group of mediators—this time categorized as interns and, therefore, paid significantly less—could be hired to work no more than part-time hours, preventing us from qualifying for additional benefits that accompany full-time employment in France. Along with this shift from well-paid employees to interns came a change in the nationality of the mediators. For the following three exhibitions, I was no longer the only "foreigner" at the Collège. Many of those hired by the Collège were international students seeking an entrance to France's notoriously closed employment system. We came from countries like Spain, Italy, Brazil, and Canada; like the vast majority of visitors to the Collège, we were all white. We received very little training in terms of the ideas we were expected to impart about the Collège or the art we mediated.

As I demonstrate in chapter 1, the Collège both capitalizes on and disavows its Catholicity. According to its website and pamphlets, at the Collège "humanity is explored in all its dimensions: spiritual, intellectual and emotional."[21] Phrases such as these emphasize the supposed universality of the project. Rather than a particularly Catholic space in which to deepen one's faith, the Collège promises to attend to humanity in a broader sense. And yet, it is these very claims to universality that amplify the limited nature of its ouverture. Where do those who do not feel welcome under these vaults fit into the category of "humanity?" That philosophers can participate in the consecration of Notre-Dame de la Sagesse, and a pope can oversee the inauguration of a space of culture, powerfully demonstrates the mobility of Catholic materiality in Paris today. The Collège reflects the extensive cultural work required to maintain the privilege of Catholicism's banality. Here, the French Church is offering up unexpected ways of engaging with Catholicism, increasing the ease with which its material forms are admired in the French public sphere, in stark contrast to the extensive regulation imposed on materiality associated with Islam.

Employees aim to position the Collège not in the context of various religious sites in the city but rather as one of its many spaces of culture. "Art & Culture," "Education," "Research," and "Encounters & Debate" are the menu options found on its website. Programming at the Collège aims to demonstrate the secular modernity of the particularly elite practices produced in this space. And yet, as a renovated medieval site, the space simultaneously serves to fill desires for a Catholic past. It is one of the few buildings left in Paris to boast connections to the medieval period, and as such attracts an enormous number of visitors who come expressly for the visceral experience of encountering its ancient stones. A catalog created for the first exhibition of contemporary art at the space describes it as "at once uniting the beauty of the architecture, the mystical character of a religious building, [and] the intellectual density of an ancient university" (Grenier 2008, 33).

The practices found within this space aim to position Catholicism beyond isolated and privatized beliefs and practices by equating it with a broader French and European cultural history. Such efforts correspond in interesting—and perhaps uncomfortable—ways to current debates within the social scientific study of religion. Such assertions align well with critiques that the modern propensity to malign religion as belief overlooks its expression in social practices. The project underway at the Collège, furthermore, appears perfectly legible in light of studies that question the distinction between the categories of religious and secular. The philosopher Charles Taylor (2007) and the sociologist David Martin (2005) argue that secularism is, in fact, the *product* of theologies and histories in the Christian West. I was struck when interviewing a priest in his office at the Collège by the presence of books by numerous writers popular among American social scientists, such as Peter Sloterdijk, Jacques Derrida, and Pierre Bourdieu. At the Collège, employees can be seen taking up or enacting precisely the kinds of critical analyses scholars have used to dismantle the boundaries between religion and the secular.

In so doing, however, employees at the Collège are aimed at a rather particular end. By asking elite actors to engage in practices of contemporary art viewing under these medieval vaults, the Catholic hierarchy makes use of the ambiguity of aesthetic practices—and the privileged place of Catholic motifs in the European art history canon—to secure its unproblematic place in French public life. Fred Myers has powerfully described the work of "culture making" (2002, 351) by Aboriginal artists in Australia that has shaped the contours of Aboriginal fine art. The contemporary arts project at the Collège similarly engages in many of the "historically and institutionally specific mediations" necessary to authorize its project as a fine arts project (2002, 351). As my guide's skepticism suggests, however, these do not always go smoothly. The arts project invoked the ire of many visitors. Banality proffers numerous privileges, but it also tends to constrain visions of what is possible in the public sphere and limits how Paris "ought" to look. Capaciousness, after all, offers little of value where the reproduction of privilege is concerned.

CATHOLAÏCITÉ OR SECULAR CATHOLICISM?

How is it that Catholic materiality came to enjoy the privilege of banality in Paris? France, after all, is widely celebrated for its secular public sphere, and its numerous laws aimed at reducing the visibility of Islam are often

justified as expressions of the depth of its commitment to laïcité. Many I
met in France insisted that laïcité is actually untranslatable into English.
They tended to make this claim most often when justifying the regulation of
Islamic forms. As an ever-shifting set of legal and social arrangements aimed
at distinguishing religion from culture, and religion from politics, however,
I see secularism and laïcité as occupying the same ground. For this reason,
I use the two terms interchangeably.

As scholars, pundits, and citizens have attempted to explain the refusal
of signs of Islam in public life throughout Europe and the ongoing presence
of a Christianity that had supposedly vanished, two distinct understand-
ings of the present have emerged. Numerous voices have pointed to the
persistence of Christian concepts in nominally secular norms and modes of
governance.[22] Others have highlighted the disciplinary power of the secular
to transform and constrain what religion can do in public life.[23] In other
words, accounts of the religious practices one sees in France and Europe
today—from the widely presumed decline in everyday Catholic rituals to
the increased regulation of signs of Islam in the public sphere—oscillate
between emphasizing the primacy of either Christianity or secularism in
the formation of such paradoxes. In this light, Catholicism's banality could
either be explained as an expression of what some in France have called
catholaïcité (Catholic-secularism) or the result of a secularized Catholicism,
two very different explanations for the same phenomenon.

I first came across the term "catholaïcité" in a footnote to an article by
the French political theorist Étienne Balibar. In it, he argues that recent laws
against Islamic signs reproduce

> a social and political asymmetry, since France has in fact lived for two
> centuries under a regime of catholaïcité (Edgar Morin's very apt pun . . .).
> From the perpetuation of Christian holidays in the republican calendar
> to the state management of the religious heritage, the "national" culture is
> largely defined as Christian and more precisely as Catholic. It is a theolog-
> ical asymmetry because the idea of a "private" religion, located essentially
> in one's heart of hearts, all the more true the more "invisible" it is . . . is a
> Christian theological idea . . . to which Judaism and Islam oppose the idea
> of a social community of mores and rules. [2004, 363, n. 4]

It is fascinating to observe Balibar move from recognizing how Catholic
materiality populates French public life in ways that allow it to be experienced as secular (from holidays to heritage) to then insisting that Catholicism

is, in fact, sign-less. To argue that Catholicism is more easily made invisible because of the value it places on true faith being situated in one's "heart of hearts" requires a remarkable blindness to its dominance of France's visual economy.[2] Rather than the inevitable outcome of Christianity's supposed sign-less-ness, I argue that the uncanny proximity between Catholicism and the presumed neutrality of the secular in France is an expression of Catholicism's banality. Paying attention to expressions of catholaïcité can allow us to emphasize the materiality of Catholic privilege in France, but, as Balibar's slippage suggests, the concept also risks naturalizing the link between Catholicism and French public life. I will demonstrate that the banality of Catholic materiality is the result of a series of actions and decisions—both contingent and strategic—engaged in by the state, representatives of the French Church, and a wide array of groups.

On the other hand, diverse voices point to secularism as key to deciphering present-day inequalities. In light of its similar effects in diverse spaces, various voices might interpret Catholicism's banality as a result of the demands of the secular state. The anthropologist Hussein Agrama (2012) has argued that secularism's power lies in its indeterminacy, or in the never-ending questions it provokes. Where and how does one draw the line between religion and politics, or religion and culture? Such questions are never resolved. These boundaries require continual assertion, renewal, and redrawing. Saba Mahmood argued that such indeterminate questions induce secular states to "become involved in the regulation and management of religious life to an unprecedented degree, thereby embroiling the state in substantive issues of religious doctrine and practice" (2016, 2). Which practices are religious? Which are cultural? How can they be distinguished and separated? Headscarves were banned from schools in France in 2004, with a law describing them as an "ostentatious" religious practice inappropriate in a secular space. This law did not resolve the issue, however. By 2015, conversations had begun surrounding the length of girls' skirts. Were long skirts a cultural practice or a religious innovation seeking to elide the secular's disciplinary power? The secular's indeterminacy continually provokes limitless (and often ridiculous) questions and dilemmas.

In contrast, at the Collège I witnessed the secular state standing at a comfortable remove. As I have described, in order to receive state funding to support the renovation, the creators of the Collège referred to it as a "cultural" rather than a "religious" space. Because the secular state had provided nearly one-third of the renovation costs, a sense that religious rituals would be inappropriate was taken for granted in its early years of operation.

Of course, as Michel Foucault (1977, 1978) has demonstrated, power can be effectively enacted through practices of incitement, rather than oppression. The secular state does not need to impose itself in a draconian fashion in order to effectively discipline the Catholic Church to behave as desired. Indeed, the archdiocese's decision to create a space of culture may well point to how the Church has already been altered by the forces of secularism. It imagined it needed to create a space of culture, rather than religion, in order to be effectively recognized by the state. And yet, over time, the relative distance of the state also had unanticipated effects. When I worked there, for example, no masses were ever held in the space. A small room was dedicated to quiet contemplation and referred to as the oratory. It offered a space for general spiritual reflection, rather than a particularly Catholic ritual or practice. When I returned to the site in the spring of 2018, however, I noticed one of the effects of the state's distance: noontime masses were being held in the oratory, something that would have seemed unthinkable in its early years of operation. The ease by which the cultural could once again become religious without any pushback demonstrates how the Collège has not been the object of the incursions so often described in the anthropological study of the secular. For this reason, the concept of secularized Catholicism ultimately fails to fully account for the privileged banality of Catholic spaces such as the Collège.

The historical entanglements of the Catholic and secular in France prove similarly confounding. Members of the Vatican often refer to France as *l'aînée de l'Église* (the eldest daughter of the Catholic Church).[25] As the state religion of France prior to the French Revolution, and having had many of its rights restored for much of the nineteenth century, the Catholic Church has long held significant power within the country. Under the 1801 concordat signed between Napoléon and Pope Pius VII, Catholicism also began to serve as a model that other religions were required to follow. Over the course of the nineteenth century, various iterations of the French state—empire, monarchy, and republic—worked to encourage particular kinds of religious practices. In 1808, for example, Napoléon created the *Consistoire* to regulate Jewish conduct. Anthropologist Kimberly Arkin describes how, "under the impetus of the reform-minded laymen who controlled the consistorial board [and had been appointed by the government], religious practice was changed to more closely resemble Christianity" (2014, 20), and, in particular, Catholicism. Arkin describes how rabbis were required to wear long black robes clearly inspired by priestly garb, ceremonies in which babies were given their names (as in a Christian baptism) were instituted, and a

Jewish "catechism" was introduced. As other religions were required to more closely resemble the norms of Catholicism, however, the state also expanded its reach over Catholic institutions. The concordat established between Napoléon and the Holy See—and then unilaterally added to by the French state after its signing—gave the state extensive control over French Catholic practices. Some secular voices even resisted the 1905 laws separating church and state in France because of the reduced control over Catholicism this recalibration would imply.[26]

In addressing the complex interplay between Catholicism and the secular, I do not aim to determine whether the secular or the Catholic has played the primary role in shaping the politics of the present. Certain Catholic practices—such as sightings of Mary, or devotion to the Sacred Heart of Jesus—have, at times, been targeted by the state as inappropriate and non-modern. And yet they have also continued to flourish and to benefit from state actions, such as railroad construction.[27] In the twenty-first century, certain elite Catholic practices find expression in the public sphere not only as religious; they also are able to pass as historical, intellectual, artistic, and cultural.

Scholars of religion have provided a number of tools to help make sense of these paradoxes. The French medieval historian Patrick Boucheron (2013), for example, distinguishes between civil religion, civic religion, and secular religion. Following Jean-Jacques Rousseau, Boucheron uses "civil religion" to refer to religious practices that are understood to help maintain an orderly population. For the philosopher Jean-Luc Nancy, Rousseau's civil religion is useful because it allows us to address the "affect" that "was excluded from the contract" in which the state had to "found, authorize, and guarantee its own law by its own means," without recourse to a divine or transcendent ground (2006, 108). The republican religion produced in France following the 1789 Revolution is, perhaps, the most extreme expression of civil religion, but scholars such as Robert Bellah (1974 [1967]) have also charted its presence in the twentieth-century United States.[28] Civic religion, in contrast, gets at what the anthropologist of religion Michael Lambek describes as the "immanence" of religion, the way in which "religion is not simply a representation of the social, or a separate compartment within the social, but intrinsic to the social" (2013, 45). Civic religion, Boucheron argues, contains both ideology and dissent. Finally, the notion of secular religion arose following the Second World War as an account of the risks entailed in treating the nation-state as a religion.

Extending Boucheron's concept of civic religion to explore the context of colonial and postcolonial Canada, Pamela Klassen uses the term "civic secularism" to describe "local and national communities of debate, memory, and story that are born from acknowledging the diversity of peoples that make up the nation, as well as from selective forgetting of the nation's violent origins" (2015, 42). In France, however, Klassen's civic secularism does not quite hold. France's republican project has more often aimed at *overcoming* than at acknowledging the diversity of peoples that make up the nation.[29] Indeed, the manner in which laïcité is often described in France is as something more akin to "civil secularism," in which the state—rather than being itself the object of worship, as in secular religion—simply cannot be founded or reproduced without secularism.[30]

This is not to suggest that the secular in France does not contain debate. Dissenting views can certainly be found. But secularism in France tends to operate through what Mayanthi Fernando has described as a series of disruptions, tensions, disavowals, and deferrals. She suggests, for example, that certain components of the visibility of Islam, such as the headscarf, "index[] the relationship between authority and freedom that is central not only to the Islamic tradition but to republicanism as well" (2014, 179). Rather than confront the tension between authority and freedom within the republican tradition revealed by anxieties surrounding the headscarf, the French state responds to the exposure of these contradictions, Fernando argues, by disavowing them and deferring them onto the bodies of Muslim French. For example, when republican schools appear unable to produce idealized republican subjects, such failures could open a means to address the tension inherent within a republican tradition that presumes to inculcate individual liberty through the authoritative regime of the school. Instead, such tensions are deferred onto Muslim students' bodies that appear to refuse the liberty otherwise available to them in favor of submission to religious authorities. As my encounters with nuns' habits on the streets of Paris suggest, however, the appearance of Catholic materiality in the public sphere does not "unsettle" the republic in the way signs of Islam do. Secularism alone—whether civic, civil, or otherwise—proves insufficient in explaining how the banality of Catholic objects, images, and spaces allows them to move across divides in ways denied to others.

In a study of members of the Bible Society in England in the twenty-first century, Matthew Engelke (2013) uses the term "ambient faith" to explain how religious practices may bridge the supposed divide between the public and private, cultural and political, and religious and secular. Engelke describes how members of the Bible Society have developed a "strategic secularism" in order to make more space for Christianity—and for the Christian Bible in particular—in the public sphere. For Engelke, ambience provides an effective means of understanding public religion because it encourages attention to the sensory, material, and kinetic forms that distinguish spaces as public or private (Gal 2002), secular or religious. Ambience serves as both an analytic tool and an explicit strategy taken up by the members of the Bible Society in order to bring Christianity into the public sphere in ways that are not seen as evangelizing. In the context of Paris, I find Charb's use of the term "banal" productive because it implicitly points to how materiality might also be contentious. It allows us to address the inequalities that allow certain religious symbols to achieve the status of the ambient, while others are marked as religious and refused access to the background. In using the term "banal," I aim to chart this very uneven terrain of public religious life.

The privilege of banality contrasts to the lack of power associated with both invisibility and hypervisibility. Historically, invisibility has been a problem for minority groups in France, expressing their powerlessness as overlooked members of the national body.[31] Hannah Feldman's study of what she calls the colonial war (as opposed to the "post-War") period in France (1945–1962), for example, describes the aesthetic and political stakes of "achieving visibility" (2014, 15) for France's "subaltern" populations. She explores a variety of visual practices as "effort[s] to make room for an Algerian subjectivity within something other than the silent space otherwise allotted to them" (ibid., 14). It is, perhaps, the invisibility of these subjects in France in the 1940s to 1960s that can help to explain the present-day misperception that the presence of Muslims in France is a recent phenomenon. Fernando's study of Muslim French in the early twenty-first century speaks to the opposite problem: the problem of hypervisibility. Using the work of Frantz Fanon (1986 [1952]), Fernando points to the violence that comes with the hailing of an overdetermined subject: "Look, a Muslim!"[32] In contrast to the violence of both invisibility and hypervisibility, Catholicism's banality allows its symbols to move between the background and the foreground, the overlooked and the monumental (but never the hypervisible or the invisible) in the French public sphere.

IS THE SECULAR PROTESTANT?

What has become of Catholic materiality in a secular age?[33] What modes of subjectivity and agency does it authorize or deny? What relationships are forged between humans and this material inheritance? A number of anthropologists of Christianity have effectively turned to the concept of "affect" to address the ongoing power of Catholic material forms.[34] I am interested in how Catholic material forms and affective histories can serve to buttress myths central to Europe, including its equality and its secularity.[35] In so doing, I call into question the widespread assumption that, if the secular has a Christian bias, it is one that is informed by Protestant, rather than Catholic, Christianity.

Historical, sociological, and theological accounts tend to situate the Protestant Reformation as a key moment in the secularization and modernization of Europe. In the medieval Catholic past, according to these narratives, Europe was an "enchanted" world filled with "porous" humans easily moved by God's grace or by potentially dangerous spirits (Taylor 2007). Access to divine and demonic power was mediated by a variety of humans (priests, monks, mystics, saints, and popes), objects (altars, relics, and the Eucharist), images (painted on wood, canvas, and stone walls, carved into buildings and statues, or woven into tapestries and elaborate cassocks and gowns) and spaces (churches, monasteries, and sites of pilgrimage).

The Protestant Reformation indeed brought a powerful critique of these various media. Martin Luther insisted that all Christians were priests and argued for God's presence in the Word alone. The Swiss reformer Huldrych Zwingli mocked the doctrine of real presence (the claim that Christ's true body is present in the Eucharist) and called for the destruction of images and the building of simple spaces for Christians to gather so that they might stand in contrast to the ostentatious decor of monumental Catholic cathedrals. By transforming Catholic media into obstacles *to* rather than conduits *of* God's grace, reformers argued that their focus on the Word of God allowed for a more direct, unmediated encounter with God.[36] Numerous scholars, including David Morgan (2007, 2012), Webb Keane (2007), and Engelke (2007) have productively critiqued the supposed immediacy of Protestant Christianity, demonstrating how a host of images, objects, texts, words, and signs have served to mediate God in ways that are constrained and shaped by particular semiotic ideologies.

Teleological narratives of secularization, however, tend to take for granted the world of absence supposedly produced by the Protestant Reformation and argue that the ideal of absence had numerous unanticipated effects. It contributed to the creation of "buffered" selves, impervious to the work of objects, images, spaces, and spirits. It disenchanted the landscapes of Europe, laying the foundation for a rationalized space in which God's power receded and humans alone created and reproduced the social worlds they inhabited.[37] According to such narratives, this world of absence ultimately paved the way for the rise of capitalism. The work of Max Weber (2009 [1930]) offers one example of attempts to connect the rise of capitalism to experiences of absence and asceticism. Calvinists living in northern Europe in the century following the Protestant Reformation faced the potential of a bleak nihilism in light of the doctrine of predestination and Calvin's insistence upon God's distance in ways that could not be reduced by any media. They struggled with such problems by behaving as if they were saved, working tirelessly while maintaining a strict asceticism. The resulting wealth produced by their labors was then available for reinvestment in the means of production, providing the engine that fueled the rise of capitalism.

In a very different vein, Jane Schneider (1990) argued that abundant Catholic practices could serve as powerful means by which to demand the redistribution of resources in early modern Europe. She posited that spirits, the dead, objects, images, and spaces offered individuals and communities numerous actors with whom to negotiate and upon whom to place demands. They provided a plethora of paths not only to God but also through which the inequalities and indignities of the earthly realm could be protested and renegotiated. Religious materiality, in other words, provided various means through which humans could attenuate the disparities in privilege that marked social life.

These various pathways to God, however, could both reduce and reproduce inequality. While a day celebrating a patron saint could require a local lord to host a feast for his peasants, it could also help to legitimize his hold on wealth and power. The equivocal nature of Catholic materiality continues to be a relevant site of exploration under conditions of capitalism. Rather than a premodern relic, Catholicism's debated and contested abundance has played and continues to play a vital role in modern perceptions of individual human agency so "essential," in Asad's words "to our recognition of other people's humanity" (1996, 272).

In exploring the place of affective and sensuous encounters between humans and objects in France and Europe, and by asking how Catholic materiality may buttress power and inequality in the present, I also aim to unsettle Europe's presumed morality and universality. Despite the horrific violence wrought by European nations (within Europe's borders and beyond) since the rise of the Enlightenment, the myth of Europe as the truest expression of equality, liberalism, and modernity has proved remarkably resilient. In the words of theorist Dipesh Chakrabarty, "a certain version of 'Europe,' reified and celebrated in the phenomenal world of everyday relationships of power as the scene of the birth of the modern, continues to dominate the discourse of history" (2000, 28). The resilience of this myth, Chakrabarty argues, is due in no small part to European philosophers' tendency to theorize the human in abstract, universalizing terms, despite the highly "provincial" model of Europe upon which this vision is based. While recognizing that secularism has produced similar inequalities in diverse spaces and refusing the specificity of France's laïcité used to justify its unequal effects, I am interested in emphasizing the particularities of Catholic privilege in France in the present. By exploring elite Catholic practices, I highlight the contingencies and active strategies that go into their production, denying them the universal status they claim and rely upon.

Given that the archdiocese owns the Collège, and that the space foregrounds its medieval Catholic roots, visitors inevitably engage with it, at least in part, as Catholic. In order to understand the kinds of practices encouraged at the Collège, I analyze the strategic decisions made by those connected to the French Catholic hierarchy (as well as their unintended effects). This book, therefore, is both a study of the secular in France and of a particularly elite expression of Catholicism in what Brenna Moore has described as "its Parisian idiom" (2013, 107). The fluidity and flexibility of Catholic materiality speak to the privilege of Catholic banality that contributes to the difficulty of distinguishing between the Catholic and the secular, not only in this space but also in Paris more broadly. For this reason, this study cannot confine itself to either Catholicism or the secular. It instead works to reveal the power and privilege of those who are able to occupy and reproduce the space in between.

The Collège's contemporary arts program operates by what Donna Haraway (1985) describes as "politics by other means." Chandra Mukerji uses this concept to analyze elite practices at a different historical moment in France: the consolidation of power in the figure of the king by Louis XIV in the mid-seventeenth century. With little in the way of protest, the king was able to displace the power and authority of the nobility and the Catholic Church. He was able to do so, she argues, by establishing ancient Rome as a desirable model for French power, a model that would require a strong leader and a centralized government. It was in the gardens at Versailles, and the seemingly innocuous modes of play in which the nobility were encouraged to participate, that the ideal of Rome was made desirable, even for those whose relative position of power would be diminished. "Through rituals and parties at Louis XIV's domain, nobles were enrolled in a new dream of power, taking pleasure in the classical beauty surrounding them and learning to see themselves through the optics of imperial ambition and classical inheritance" (Mukerji 2012, 510). The gardens were so powerful, Mukerji insists, because they "were not discursive, but rather materially exemplary" (ibid., 511). At the Collège, the archdiocese similarly celebrates certain political claims by way of an exemplary material form. By building upon desires for the medieval past cultivated in France since at least the nineteenth century, the Collège is able to constrain visions of France in ways that secure its privilege.

IS CONTEMPORARY ART SECULAR?

At the time of the Renaissance, numerous Catholic material forms shifted from the status of what Hans Belting (1994) describes as "cult images" to the category of "art images." Belting argues that the long history of image creation prior to the Italian Renaissance can only be categorized as art if we overlook the nature of its production and reception. He contends that, when gazing upon cult images, Christians through the medieval period experienced awe at the presence of God they made available. In contrast, art images from the Renaissance onward tend to be admired as an expression of the skills and intentions of the artist.

Put another way, objects that have been proffered the status of art are generally understood to be secular. This association arises from two assumptions. First, art is generally taken to be that which artists produce, and present-day notions of the artist presume a particularly modern, secular conception of autonomous subjectivity and individual creativity. Karin Zitzewitz has highlighted how even theorists such as Foucault were "attracted to the possibilities art held for a truth independent of authority, whether political or religious" (2014, 6). Thus, even those who would critique the idea of unmediated human agency often hold up artists and the art they produce as a potential exception to the rule.

The second way in which modern art and contemporary art are presumed to be secular relates to the very particular way in which religious—and, in particular, Christian—motifs may be drawn upon and repurposed. Art historian James Elkins (2004) argues that while explicitly religious signs may still be found in contemporary art, in order to achieve the category of art these works must express a certain distance from or critique of this imagery. The art historian Alena Alexandrova similarly highlights how contemporary and modern artists borrow Christian motifs in order to modify them. Some artists, such as Francis Bacon (1909–1992), used Christian imagery in explicitly critical tones. Others, such as Andy Warhol (1928–1987) used Christian motifs including the cross in order to address "such issues as originality and authorship—issues not necessarily religious, but internal to the articulation of the regime of art itself" (Alexandrova 2017, 44–45).

In chapters 3 through 6, I explore how questions that appear "internal" to the regime of art are deeply embedded in political, social, and religious processes. For now, I want to highlight how artists who explore Christian motifs in explicitly religious terms generally have a hard time finding a place to exhibit their work in the contemporary art world. This was even true at the Collège. At times, when visitors expressed reticence about the contemporary and seemingly secular works they saw displayed under its medieval vaults, they would reveal that they, too, were artists. They would insist that their paintings of, for example, the Virgin Mary, would be far better suited to this space than the works before them. I would encourage them to submit a dossier to the arts coordinator, knowing full well that their chances of exhibiting were low. In Elkins's terms, only artworks that attempt to "burn away" religion's external trappings to find its universal or "sublime" core are able to occupy space in the modern and contemporary art canon. Artworks can only serve spiritual, rather than religious, purposes—thereby securing their secular status. And yet numerous scholars have argued that the boundary between spiritual and religious is difficult to maintain. Courtney Bender (2010) demonstrates how religious institutions continue to anchor and shape "spiritual" practices that people experience as highly individuated and, therefore, not "religious."

Responses to the contemporary art displayed at the Collège similarly cannot easily be categorized as either secular or religious. As I demonstrate in chapters 1 and 4, a great deal of overlap persists between these supposedly distinct modes of being. The decision to exhibit contemporary art at the Collège was highly contingent, but it was also the result of a series of strategic maneuvers aimed at emphasizing the project's catholaïcité.[38] Members of the French Catholic hierarchy are not aiming to secularize or modernize Catholicism. Rather, they are arguing that the elite practice of art viewing, while typically deemed secular is, in fact, Catholic.

As my guide's dismissal of the contemporary art installation suggests, employees at the Collège encountered extensive and intensive resistance to the exhibits they displayed. Rather than viewing anxieties surrounding contemporary art as those of religious viewers unsettled by seemingly secular art in the space of the Collège, I see them as an expression of the problem of legitimacy that haunts Catholic privilege in Paris today. The contemporary arts project at the Collège proved to be so controversial because, in aiming to aestheticize France's distinctions, it also made them visible, highlighting that this space was only available to some and not to all. Moreover, while those who operate the Collège are far more likely to account for the present through the framework of catholaïcité, the specter that what they have been producing is, in fact, a secularized Catholicism has hovered over many of their activities. In order to appear as self-evidently French—as banal— the practices that occur under these vaults cannot be too distinct from those found in other cultural spaces in France. And yet, as I explore in more detail in chapter 1, how to reproduce the privilege of Catholicism's banality without also making Catholicism too capacious has proved to be an ongoing challenge.

Art viewing is not the only elite practice available at the Collège. Conferences on topics ranging from "Reforming the Corporation" to "The Challenge of the Digital Age" feature highly regarded experts. A theology school—the École Cathédrale—operates in the basement. The Collège and the École Cathédrale are separate institutions, but they also contain considerable overlaps. The most significant distinction between them, however, is that the École Cathédrale is more explicitly advertised as a space in which Catholics may deepen their faith through knowledge. Numerous research initiatives link theologians at the Collège with scholars from France's secular universities to engage in rich and fascinating explorations of the paradoxes of the present. Many, however, such as a research group exploring how to reform corporations, encourage a set of limited changes, rather than radical alternatives to political, social, and economic processes in the present.

The contemporary art exhibitions proved to be the most controversial, contested, and visible of the activities occurring in this space during the two years I spent there. The sheer number and power of emotions I encountered surrounding contemporary art at the Collège speak to the high stakes involved in thinking about the Catholic in relation to the secular. It is not only the nature of Catholicism that is at stake but also—and perhaps more importantly—its privileged banality in French public life.

PRIVILEGE

The term "privilege" is often used in a very different setting: discussions of race in the United States, a context that many would insist has little to do with religion in France. Like the taken-for-granted decline of white supremacy following the Civil Rights movement in the United States, however, news of Catholicism's demise in France has been greatly exaggerated.[39] The very narrative of decline has, in both cases, allowed their ongoing presence in the public sphere to go overlooked. At those moments when Catholic materiality moves from the background to the foreground, it does so in ways that do not appear threatening and cannot be threatened. What is more, as in the United States, privilege comes with a whole host of benefits, including escaping a great deal of state violence. The expansion of the security state apparatus and police powers in recent decades in France has disproportionately affected young Muslims (see Susan Terrio 2009). While state authorities have closed numerous mosques deemed too "fundamentalist" since 2015 (Sheran 2016), St. Nicolas du Chardonnet, a Catholic church located around the corner from the Collège, has served as the headquarters for the radical far-right Catholics of Marcel Lefebvre's Society of St. Pius X for decades. This space has not been closed or recuperated by the state (although the municipality is, in fact, the owner of the site[40]), despite the society's antirepublican commitments and its excommunication from the Catholic Church by Pope John Paul II in 1988.[41] Privilege, both in France and in the United States, allows those who occupy the status of the banal to stand above reproach, while others are forced to endure the oppressive surveillance that shapes the experience of the marked.

Catholic materiality in Paris also tends to be intimately connected to class-based distinctions of wealth and inequality. As I explore further in chapter 6, the project underway at the Collège is aimed at precisely the elite kinds of actors that give Paris's Catholicism its "bon-chic-bon-genre" flair (Lavergnat 2007, 164). I take seriously the possibility that Catholic abundance may continue to buttress racial, religious, and class privilege. The objects and images that populate Paris's museums, and the apparent timelessness of the spaces that make the city the most visited in the world, are replete with Catholic motifs. In their banality they appear to demand little in the way of particular actions on the part of those who view, engage with, or inhabit them. Many Catholic and secular actors revel in the banality of Catholic materiality, enjoying the pleasure of viewing these forms without being called into relationships of exchange with them, or with other humans. As I demonstrate in chapters 5 and 6, visitors to the Collège during my time there were often made uncomfortable by any demands to laboriously submit to the art objects they encountered. Engaging with Catholic materiality in its banality allows actors to overlook the wide array of social debts upon which its privilege stands. By receding into the background in ways that reproduce—rather than question—the privilege and inequalities of Paris and France today, this inert matter offers aesthetic authorization of such privilege. And yet, privilege, as Weber (1946) has argued, is haunted by its illegitimacy. At the Collège, this haunting was often expressed both through desires for sensuous engagements with objects that modern subjects are supposed to abhor and in anxieties surrounding how artistic, cultural, and economic value at the Collège is produced and secured.

As an ethnographic study of privilege, this project posed particular challenges. The inequalities that structure the majority of ethnographic research tend to produce a situation in which the ethnographer has more wealth and power than those he or she is studying. This inequality can, at times, serve to facilitate ethnographers' entry into the lived experiences of those they research. In such relations of inequality, ethnographers are often able to access private spaces, such as homes. This was not the case for my ethnographic research among Paris's upper classes. I was raised in a lower-middle-class Protestant family in Canada; I did not easily fit into the privileged classes I encountered at the Collège. Wealthy patrons of the Collège saw through me. I did not hold the connections and cultural capital required for entrance into their milieus, and they did not go out of their way to make space or time for me. Only on a few occasions was I invited into the homes of my interlocutors. Most often we met at the Collège, or out at a café or restaurant.

I quickly realized that if I wanted to focus on the elite public the Collège attracts, I would have to let go of certain ideals of ethnographic study, in which researchers are able to access a variety of spaces and moments in the lives of their interlocutors. Focusing my research on a place in which this class circulated offered a solution to the problem of access. Rather than depth, I would access breadth, speaking with dozens of visitors each day in my work as a mediator. Managers and employees at the Collège had full knowledge that I was there conducting research, and many of them (including fifteen permanent employees, one of the two directors, six temporary staff, and three volunteers) agreed to sit down for formal interviews with me. Beyond the exhibitions, I also attended forty-eight conferences and lectures held at the Collège. At home in the evenings I analyzed the Collège's publications, website, brochures, and promotional material. Before leaving Paris, I spent two months conducting archival research on the history of the Collège at the National Library, the Archives of Paris, and the Lustiger Institute.

Beyond the Collège, I visited approximately half (sixty) of the city's Catholic churches, interviewing priests and parishioners, touring the buildings' artistic treasures, and gathering the printed material that described the activities and objects found within. I engaged in the cultural activities available at some of these churches, in particular at St. Merri, located near the Centre Pompidou, and at St. Roch, near the Louvre. Both of these churches capitalize on their proximity to the city's most famous museums by emphasizing their arts programming. As with my encounter with Notre-Dame de la Sagesse, however, I generally found attendance at these programs to be relatively sparse compared to the Collège. Cultural projects are not the only activities of parish and diocesan associations in Paris today. Many devote their time to the sacraments and charitable work. I also met with diocesan staff and parishioners engaged in some of these more traditional Catholic projects, such as marriage preparation classes. The Collège, however, receives a disproportionate amount of the ambitions of the archdiocese and occupied the majority of my attention while in Paris. Friends I made while living in Paris often teased me that I spoke of little else.

Finally, to better understand the context of art viewing in Paris, I regularly attended exhibits at many of Paris's museums, including the Louvre, the Musée d'Orsay, the Musée de l'Orangerie, the Musée Rodin, the Musée des Arts et Métiers (a museum also constructed in a former monastery), the Centre Pompidou, the Jeu de Paume, the Musée des Invalides, the Grand Palais, and the Palais Tokyo. These sites were vital to expanding my understanding of mediation, museum practices, and modern and contemporary art.

In my work as a mediator, some of the conversations in which I engaged were far too brief to allow me to explain, or engage my interlocutors in, my broader research. Others, however, would continue for long stretches in which visitors would eagerly offer up their thoughts on the current state of Catholicism and secularity in France. At times, because of the antagonism many expressed toward the exhibits, I ended up on the receiving end of their rage. In response, I often found myself abandoning the supposed neutrality of the ethnographer in order to defend the exhibits against the critiques of visitors. I spent many hours deeply engrossed in each of these exhibits, whether alone or with my fellow mediators. This intimacy brought a certain degree of partiality that I had difficulty suppressing. Despite the light touch that mediators are supposed to bring to their work, my attempts to offer ways of engaging with the artworks often produced significant and unanticipated results, as I demonstrate in chapter 5.

As with any narrative, the account I offer here of the first two years of contemporary art exhibits at the Collège is partial. Due to the low level at which I worked at the Collège, there were certain decision-making processes to which I did not have access. I never, for example, was able to view a budget laying out the costs associated with the exhibits. Moreover, while I attended numerous lectures and debates at the Collège and have read some of the publications produced by the research department, by no means does this book offer a full assessment of the intellectual program underway there.

What my particular vantage point—a low-level employee in a site devoted to elite publics—offered was a capacity to recognize patterns over time. I engaged in similar conversations in similar contexts day after day over nearly two years. Having done so, I can represent with confidence the kinds of interactions that were typical and those that were exceptional. I can speak to the expectations people brought to this space at the interstices of French secularism and Parisian Catholicism. I can identify the means by which they rejected or embraced the project they saw. By complementing my time at the Collège with visits to museums, galleries, parish organizations, and churches, I have been able to discern the characteristics the Collège shares with other institutions and those that make it unique. Ethnography does not allow the researcher to inhabit another's point of view in any straightforward way. Instead, I understand ethnography to be a certain way of paying attention in a particular place and time, allowing the anthropologist to identify the continuities, shifts, and contradictions in the social worlds they encounter.

CHAPTER OUTLINE

The text is divided into three parts. The first, entitled "Curating Catholic Privilege" and containing chapters 1 and 2, explores the careful but also unwieldy work of "curation." I use this term to describe the forging of particular relationships between elements otherwise presumed to be separate. In chapter 1, I describe how maintaining Catholicism's privilege requires two distinct processes—those of evangelization and those of normalization—both of which are found at the Collège. They differ significantly on the most effective means of maintaining Catholicism's privilege and at times they came into significant tension. Normalizing voices aimed to highlight France's catholaïcité. In response, evangelizing voices often worried about the Collège's capaciousness and the risk that, rather than catholaïcité, it was producing a secularized Catholicism. This concern was partly addressed by the selective incorporation of some modes of difference—in particular, the incorporation of strands of French feminism that explore gender in ways recognizable to evangelizing desires—and the exclusion of others, in particular practices associated with Islam.

Chapter 2 explores how the privilege of Catholicism necessitates claims of continuity, articulated in terms such as "renaissance" and "crystallization." I show how, in the face of contingency, claims of renaissance and crystallization require the careful work of curating in order to efface and downplay equally significant moments of rupture. Through an exploration of the Collège's archives and the biography of its founder, Cardinal Jean-Marie Aaron Lustiger, I highlight the contingent nature of the formation of the Collège in the first decade of the twenty-first century. Born Jewish, Lustiger converted to Catholicism at the age of fourteen while living with a Catholic family during World War II. Rejecting evidence of proselytism, and despite protests from Catholic and Jewish groups, Lustiger maintained that his conversion allowed him to be both Catholic and Jewish. Here, again, we see how the Collège selectively incorporates particularly limited forms of difference, such as a Judaism that remains open to Catholicism.

Part II, "Mediating Catholic Privilege," addresses how the Collège's contemporary arts programming forges connections to the past through a variety of means, emphasizing in particular those I describe as "enlivening" and "aestheticizing." In chapter 3, I analyze how discourses and practices at the Collège and engaged in by the artist responsible for its inaugural exhibit mediated the relationship between the past and the present by enlivening the materiality of the space of the Collège. The artist's emphasis on the agency of objects, rather than the effects of human-material encounters, produced a context ripe for the exclusionary ideas expressed by visitors in response to the installation. For their part, visitors misunderstood how their own perspectives overlapped with those of the artist. They dismissed him by connecting his work to that which they understood to be irretrievably other: the actions of Muslim youth from the banlieues.[42]

In chapter 4, I describe the most popular early exhibit at the Collège in order to explore how art-viewing publics were encouraged to see the religious motifs repurposed in the artwork as aesthetic, rather than religious, images. I address how the mediators often unwittingly participated in the subtle work of encouraging visitors to view the work in aesthetic terms, while discouraging a more visceral, sensuous, or reciprocal encounter with objects. In so doing, the artist and the mediators ultimately reinforced the powerful place of Catholicism in the European art canon, thereby reproducing claims of catholaïcité. They also helped to emphasize the elite nature of the desired public and the exclusion of those with less cultural capital.

Part III, "Reproducing Catholic Privilege," uses the final two exhibitions on which I worked to address the ongoing power of Catholic materiality in securing Catholic privilege. Chapter 5 describes how an installation piece at the Collège encouraged viewers to inhabit the radical contingency of the Collège and denaturalize the visceral access to the medieval past so often promoted in narratives surrounding the space. By pointing to the contingency of the Collège, rather than to its timelessness, the installation denied visitors the visceral and immediate encounter with the medieval past they desired. Refused this opportunity, visitors violently rejected the exhibit. In another articulation of the privilege of banality, many of the same voices who, during the first exhibit, insisted that the violence of Muslim vandals ought to exclude them from spaces such as the Collège subsequently violated this installation for the ways it appeared to mar their visceral access to the medieval past.

While much of this book focuses on the privilege of banality, the final chapter explores the banality of privilege through the lens of an exhibition of works of abstraction. The exhibit asked visitors to see the simple material surfaces as a means of training the attention, transforming art viewing from a mode of modern leisure into one of monastic or mystical labor. Visitors' refusal to take up this challenge highlights how capitalist perceptions of value permeate the space of the Collège, making the take-up of medieval expressions of labor and time challenging if not impossible in this space. I turn to the writings of Simone Weil and Hannah Arendt in order to underscore the limits of the Catholic privilege the Collège reproduces. Here, again, we see the selective incorporation of certain forms of difference, all the while refusing the possibility of broader expressions of empathy and inclusion. This partial incorporation ultimately underscores the banality of the privileged practices the Collège encourages. The book ends with a brief epilogue that addresses the broader privilege of banality and banality of privilege of Catholicism in the French public sphere.

I
CURATING
CATHOLIC
PRIVILEGE

EVANGELIZATION AND NORMALIZATION

EACH SPRING THE COLLÈGE HOLDS "Bernardins Day" to celebrate the accomplishments of the prior year and provide a preview of the courses, conferences, and exhibitions of the year to come. In the nave (*la nef*)—a large vaulted open space on the ground floor that is freely accessible to visitors—pamphlets, course catalogs, and books for sale are displayed on tables manned by volunteers and employees. In the auditorium on the third floor, a series of invited speakers are given fifteen minutes to reflect on a chosen theme.

The most discussed talk of Bernardins Day 2010 was by a comedian named Frigide Barjot. Her stage name is a play on the French actress Brigitte Bardot, who appeared in many of Jean-Luc Godard's films. Dressed casually in a t-shirt, with rosary beads dangling like a necklace on her chest and her hair piled loosely atop her head, Barjot engaged easily with the packed auditorium before her. "My first thought," she began, "goes to Monsignor Lustiger. Because it's magnificent what has happened, what he could do in this place and also in all of France for the Catholic Church. . . . So, that, that is the first thing. Bravo for Monsignor Lustiger. Next . . . uh," she paused, appearing uncertain as to whether the crowd had fully understood her meaning. "No, but it's true!" she insisted. "Do you realize that it's a miracle that we have this place? This place to promote *Christian* culture? Fine, fine, I know, there are many cultures, fine. But *Christian* culture? We understand each other, right? We are in agreement? I'm not unveiling any secrets, am I? I didn't think so!" The audience laughed and clapped appreciatively.

Barjot pointed directly at an important purpose of the Collège, while simultaneously acknowledging that such an explicit account might be better left unsaid. A few months later, when I explained to a businesswoman

involved in fundraising for the Collège that I had not seen the talk in person
(I was working one of the tables in the nave at the time) but that it was readily available now for anyone who wished to see it on the Collège's website,
she shook her head in embarrassment and suggested that someone should
remove the video from the site.[1] Barjot's talk that day quickly devolved from
a celebration of "Christian culture" to a denigration of other "cultures." "The
world today," she lamented at one point, "is in the process of dying. I'm sorry,
but that's how I see it—it's dying." She then enlightened the crowd to various
"materialist ideologies" such as "*les études de genre*—gender studies," she
clarified in heavily accented English—that compete with Catholicism in the
public sphere. "According to gender studies, you are not biologically determined, but you choose your biology. . . . And God has nothing to do with it!
Voilà! You ought to know, you ought to know what they are saying!" Worse
yet, she continued, "gender studies are now obligatory at Sciences Po!"[2] It is
this kind of language for which Barjot would become famous as she helped
to lead large public demonstrations against same-sex marriage and same-
sex couples' access to reproductive technology in the winter of 2014.[3] Such
language is what I will describe as "evangelizing." It calls for the rectification
of a misguided social world by reorienting it toward (a particular version
of) Christianity.

Many in the auditorium that day clearly agreed with Barjot's evangelizing bent, taking delight in her celebration of this space of "Christian culture." For many, her claims—such as her critique of "materialist ideologies"
and "gender studies"—would have been quite familiar. While seemingly
free-flowing, her rant was well informed and structured by conservative
Catholic arguments that equate critical accounts of power and inequality
that foreground materiality—such as feminism and Marxism—with the
materialistic and hedonistic practices of modernity. What Barjot referred
to as "gender studies" has come to play a particularly powerful role in this
mode of Catholic critique. In 2003, the Pontifical Council for the Family
produced a text entitled *Lexicon: Ambiguous and Debatable Terms Regarding Family Life and Ethical Questions*, a significant portion of which was
devoted to fears regarding apparent "threats" to "natural sexuality" posed
by the distinction between sex and gender (Fassin 2016, 176). But Barjot
also relied on other tropes that are more widely accepted in France, such
as her use of the term "dying" to describe the present. A journalist and
right-wing public intellectual, Éric Zemmour, published a book entitled *Le
suicide français* (French Suicide) in 2014; Michel Houellebecq's best-selling
2015 novel *Soumission* (Submission) describes a France in which the coun-

try elects the Muslim Brotherhood to form the federal government as a sign of its self-vanquishing. Barjot's response to the supposed threat of self-destruction was that of evangelization: the revival of a loud Christian voice in public life. Her talk that day—entitled "Un Média Pentecôte," (A Media Pentecost)—demanded that Catholics do more to be heard and seen in the public sphere.

Despite the presence of many evangelizing voices at the Collège, Barjot's talk was clearly out of place in this space. Part of the problem was that she did not conform to the elite modes of self-presentation typical of the Collège. Her clothing and hairstyle did not fit in with the elegant modes of comportment I most frequently noted in this space. Her words stuck out in part for the way they more closely aligned with "popular" than elite modes of spoken French. Her talk clearly betrayed her concern with the supposed risks of flexible modes of gender and sex identification, yet her own dress and gestures did not hew particularly close to the rather rigid modes of hetero-feminine self-presentation I often observed in Paris. Her stage name, Frigide (frigid), suggested a playful critique of these same norms. Her clothing fit loosely in contrast to the structured garments many middle- and upper-class women at the Collège wore that, in the words of the feminist historian of France Joan Scott, "conform[s] to prevailing norms that define femininity in terms of male desire" (2018, 158).[4] Similarly, her tone was far less demure than that I typically noted among women who visited the Collège.

Barjot's paradoxical self-presentation has been described by French sociologist Éric Fassin as one of many examples of the use of "drag" in protests against same-sex marriage and "gender studies" in France. Explicit homophobia has long been rejected as a legitimate political position in France, and so those who engage in arguments against the expansion of gay rights must do so in ways that mask their intentions and social status. During the 2014 demonstrations, "Barjot even warned demonstrators that they should not look like . . . what they were: they had to avoid headbands, Hermès scarves, and other telltale signs of their conservative bourgeois life-style" (Fassin 2016, 175). Barjot knew all too well how those the Collège tends to attract appear to others: elite, privileged, bourgeois, and out of touch. Dressing and behaving in ways that contradicted these stereotypes could increase the legitimacy of the positions they held by making them appear more broadly palatable.

Evangelization is not unusual in France. Indeed, in response to the global Catholic push for a "New Evangelization," in recent decades the archdiocese has taken it up as an explicit strategy in response to the supposed de-

Christianization of France. In 1996, Bishop Dagens of Augoulême penned a "Letter to the Catholics of France" (Dagens 1996). The letter, according to historian Stephen Englund, "is a resolute call to live the faith, 'not as some sort of pastoral strategy adapted to present-day needs but as a spiritual experience'" (Englund 2008, 16). While this evangelization is generally described as aimed at the interiority of French Catholics, it has also contributed to the "renewal that has been building in French Catholicism for at least a quarter of a century" (ibid., 17). Since the late 1990s, a marked increased flourishing of Catholicism has occurred, particularly in Paris. One Irish Catholic priest, Father Noel O'Sullivan, remarked upon his amazement during a visit to Paris in 1999 at "the transformation in the ecclesial landscape. Churches were full with animated liturgies and young congregants. A perceptible presence in the streets of young priests in Roman collars and young women in religious garb gave a sense that something had changed'" (O'Sullivan 2008).

At the Collège, it was not always clear who among the fundraisers, communications strategists, curators, and public relations specialists would describe themselves as committed Catholics. But when I would speak about my interest in the nature of Catholicism in Paris today, those further from the Church would tend to direct me to those they understood to be more committed. In our conversations, these committed Catholics would make remarks similar to that of the Irish Catholic visitor; in their eyes, Catholicism had recently taken on a renewed vibrancy in the city. They would insist that the pews in many churches in Paris were full (an observation I confirmed on my visits to Sunday morning masses) and speak with admiration about the "cultivated" priests who led these parishes. The decline in Catholicism, they insisted, was much more of a problem in the countryside, in part because the intellectually engaged priests all wanted to be in Paris.

And yet, evangelization was not the strategy these same employees took up at the Collège. What makes Barjot's evangelizing voice at the Collège particularly surprising—and, for the fundraiser, a source of some embarrassment—is the contrast it presents to the approach more often taken at the Collège: that of "normalizing." For many elite actors in this space, evangelizing is a less than productive way to accomplish the work of the Collège. Given the high stakes, serious tensions accompany debates regarding the best way to secure the privilege of Catholicism's banality. As Barjot betrayed in her dismissal of "other cultures," evangelizing voices can, at times, risk presenting Catholicism as one religious culture among many. According to the logics that undergird normalization, Catholicism cannot simply be one particularly downtrodden culture or religion among others. In order to best maintain its privilege, in the eyes of normalizers, Catholicism has to occupy a foundational space in French culture and, indeed, in the "West."

Normalization is an effective strategy for those who, in contrast to Barjot, prefer not to shed their elite demeanor yet need to legitimate their privilege through something less explicit than evangelization. My interviews and interactions with dozens of employees revealed that, for many, the work of producing the Collège is the work of demonstrating that French culture (particularly "high" culture) is *always already* Catholic. If evangelization requires the transformation of an excessively secular or immoral public sphere, the practices I describe as normalizing presume that the elite practices of art viewing and intellectual debate are, in fact, Catholic, even if they are not typically perceived this way.

Many employees at the Collège did not aim to create particularly Catholic events. Rather, through advertising, branding, and shaping the Collège's programming, they worked to produce practices, images, and signs that blended into elite Parisian cultural life. At the Collège, visitors—rather than needing to transform or alter their behavior—ideally should engage in activities, such as attending intellectual debates or viewing contemporary art exhibits, as they would elsewhere. By doing so under the medieval vaults of the Collège, however, they could be prodded to see seemingly secular practices as Catholic.

Under the auspices of democracy, the reproduction of privilege must appear to benefit a diverse public. As such, processes of normalization tend to make space for some forms of difference. In this chapter and the next, I demonstrate how discourses and practices found at the Collège allowed for the inclusion of certain kinds of feminism and Judaism. I do not mean to suggest that the privileges extended to the bearers of these modes of difference were the same as those enjoyed by the elite actors with whom I interacted. This incorporation was only partial as there are always limits to privilege's opening. As I will demonstrate, catholaïcité cannot appear so capacious as to potentially include all differences; this would drastically undercut the benefits of privilege. Thus, in addition to highlighting the partial incorporation of certain forms of difference, I will also demonstrate how others—in particular those associated with Islam—were unequivocally maligned and excluded.

To be clear, I use the terms "evangelization" and "normalization" as a means of analyzing the debates and tensions I encountered at the Collège. None of the employees described their work in this way. Yet while they would not have used these terms, it became clear that a debate of sorts

existed between those desiring to use the Collège as a space for transforming the present to conform more closely to a certain vision of Catholicism
and those whose efforts were geared toward insisting upon Catholicism's
unmarked, self-evident place in the Parisian cultural landscape. Beyond the
distinct narratives shaping the work of evangelization and normalization,
they also differ in terms of the kinds of labor they require. While the work
of evangelizing tends to be explicit, the work of normalizing is most effective when it is effaced. To claim that the place of Catholicism in the French
public sphere is self-evident, after all, implies that it requires little in the way
of effort or attention. It is for this reason that I highlight such efforts here.
Attention to the Collège's identity required the careful selection of speakers and artists, precise attention to all aspects of its visual display, and the
production of repeatable narratives surrounding the project. My interlocutors' efforts shared much in common with corporate practices under late
capitalism.

The Collège is far from the first space in which connections between
religion and capitalism have been forged or imagined. In his early study of
advertising, Michael Shudson compared the work of advertising to that of
praying: "'[Corporate] executives go on the assumption that advertising is
doing something, just like praying or going to church is doing something'"
(quoted in Mazzarella 2003, 27). Kathryn Lofton has made a similar comparison in far more nuanced terms in her efforts "to describe how much of
consumer life is itself a religious enterprise, religious in the sense of enshrin-
ing certain commitments stronger than almost any other acts of social participation" (2017, 6). I want to highlight here the high stakes involved in
evangelization and normalization. They both aim to "enshrine" Catholic
"commitments" in a broad public but differ in terms of the strategies they
see as the most productive means of achieving this end.[5]

The narratives and labors of many of the employees with whom I engaged
contrasted sharply with Barjot's words. And yet, Barjot's views were widely
known at the time she was invited to the Collège. The decision to invite
an explicitly evangelizing voice such as Barjot's is best understood as part
of an ongoing oscillation between practices of evangelization and those of
normalization. In the eyes of evangelizers, the work of normalizing can risk
making Catholicism too capacious. When confronted with the suggestion
that Catholicism is simply that which elite Parisians already do, many I met
at the Collège worried about the diminishment of Catholicism's power and
distinctiveness. They worried that practices of what I am calling normalization could contribute to the secularization of Catholicism in France, rather

than emphasize its catholaïcité. If evangelizing voices could appear too abra-
sive and thus reduce Catholicism to another "ostentatious" religion whose
power in the French secular public sphere must be contained, normalizing
voices could potentially open Catholicism up too widely, making it into the
broadly generic culture of France that needed no correction. It could reduce
Catholicism's ethical edge by secularizing it. The decision to invite someone
like Barjot was intended to make space at the Collège for just such an ethical
Catholic voice. Welcoming this voice, however, appeared to the fundraiser
as an action that veered too far toward evangelizing.

I will use the term "curating" to describe employees' efforts to engage in
practices of normalization while simultaneously placing certain limits on
this space of "Catholic culture." While insisting upon the self-evident place
of Catholic ideas and materiality in French culture, these employees also
work hard to maintain Catholicism's distinctiveness. The term "curating" is
used in museums to describe the display of disparate objects alongside one
another in order to make arguments about the connections or disjunctures
between them. Here, I focus on employees' attempts to bring together that
which many take to be separate in France: Catholicism and certain visions of
French history and culture. At numerous points, however, they also placed
Catholic materiality alongside elements whose distinctiveness and lack of
belonging were emphasized, rather than downplayed, in particular those
associated with Islam.

When I asked employees at the Collège to describe the complex project
in which they were engaged, three terms came up most frequently: *renaissance* (rebirth), *rencontre* (encounter), and *ouverture* (opening). In distinct
ways, each of these terms contributed to the curatorial work of normalization, aiming to attract both a committed and a tacit Catholic public without
demanding the transformation of either. Whether Collège employees succeeded in this goal, however, remains decidedly unclear.

RENAISSANCE

In the spring of 2010, when I asked an employee what the Collège was for
him, he pointed almost immediately to the space in which we sat and its
significance for the project more broadly. "In choosing this place and not a
modern building, or an anonymous building . . . we are saying something
about what we want to be. We are charged here with the *renaissance* of a

project." Renaissance was one of the most effective tactics of normalization for two reasons. First, with this term, employees at the Collège were able to downplay the strategic nature of their efforts, suggesting that they were merely taking up a project implicit in the very space itself. In so doing, my interlocutors implied that not only the thirteenth-century building but also the intentions of its Cistercian occupants had lain quietly buried beneath layers of the city's history, awaiting resurrection. How, precisely, the opening of the Collège in 2008 constituted a rebirth or renaissance of a medieval space and a Cistercian monastic project can be hard to pin down. While there continue to be active Cistercian monasteries around the world, no Cistercian monks or nuns sit on the boards of directors of the Collège.[6] What employees at the Collège aim to rebirth is not a project of monasticism but rather an ambiguous sense of a medieval past. Or, more precisely, they make the audacious claim that it is possible and desirable for the medieval past to be brought back to life in Paris in the present.

Second, the term "renaissance" allowed a variety of voices to claim that the seemingly secular present was, in fact, the result of particular practices in the medieval past. Like the revival of classical aesthetics during the Italian Renaissance and French Enlightenment, a particular image of the past could serve as a model for all that was desirable in the present. In this case, the past selected for an unproblematic rebirth in the present was medieval Catholicism. Thus, the use of the term "renaissance" served to celebrate France's catholaïcité.

The idea of turning to Catholicism's past—and particularly to its medieval past—in order to motivate and inspire actions in the present is hardly novel in France. The interwar period, for example, saw a widespread cultural and intellectual movement aimed at what has come to be known as the *Renouveau Catholique* (Catholic Renewal) in France.[7] This movement centered on a group of writers and artists in Paris, including Jacques and Raïssa Maritain, Léon Bloy, Charles Péguy, and Emmanuel Mounier. In contrast to the project at the Collège, however, those involved in the Catholic Renewal hoped that their turn to medieval Catholic writings and concepts would be powerfully transformative. According to Stephen Schloesser, participants proclaimed that Catholicism "constitute[ed] the truest expression of 'modernity'" and "sought to move Catholicism from the margins of culture to its very center" (2005, 5). He argues further that members of the Catholic Renewal turned to long-standing Catholic theologies of materiality and presence—hylomorphism, sacramentalism, and transubstantiation—in order to argue for a renewed place for Catholicism in French culture in the present. In Schloesser's words, these concepts

> all exemplify a vision of the world as a dialectical composite of two inter-
> penetrating planes of reality: seen and unseen, created and uncreated,
> natural and supernatural. As such, they offer an alternative way of imag-
> ining relationships. Two entities—God and world, divinity and human-
> ity . . . Catholicism and culture—need not be seen as two extended bodies
> in competition with one another, jealously fighting over a small amount
> of space. Dialectical images suggest other possible modes of interrela-
> tion: one thing can point to, participate in, bear within, carry, actualize,
> perfect, translate, transpose, transform—or even become—something
> else. [ibid., 6–7]

The goals of the renaissance underway at the Collège are decidedly less uto-pian or transformative. "Actualize," "perfect," and "translate" point to a desire and willingness to become something new. "Renaissance," by contrast, does not require the alteration of those it engages. It forgoes the transformative in favor of the self-evident.

By pointing to the building itself as that which most clearly conveyed the project underway, the employee highlighted just how much weight the space of the Collège carries in the work of normalization by way of renais-sance. However impossible the claim of renaissance may be, the stunning beauty of the building serves as a powerful means of making the impossible appear tangible. The soaring vaults, arches, and columns of the central nave and former sacristy allow visitors to feel as though they have arrived in the cultural apex of the Middle Ages. In describing the significance of the space of the Collège, one employee explained to me how the building is "a *lieu de mémoire* [place of memory] of medieval monasticism . . . that evokes some-thing, and something positive—a space of study and a space of prayer. . . . Study and prayer are the two most interesting dimensions of the Christian religion for our contemporaries."

The employee's use of lieu de mémoire references the work of the French historian Pierre Nora. For Nora, France is left with mere lieux de mémoires because it lacks milieux de mémoire, or environments of memory. "If we were able to live within memory," Nora argued, "we would not have needed to consecrate lieux de mémoire. . . . Each gesture, down to the most every-day would be experienced as the ritual repetition of a timeless practice in a primordial identification of act and meaning. With the appearance of the trace, of mediation, of distance, we are not in the realm of true memory but of history" (1989, 8).

The employee likely knew the source of her term, but I wonder if she had followed through the logic of describing the Collège as a lieu de mémoire. It seems to me to offer a very different sort of framing than that of renaissance. To evoke the concept of a lieu de mémoire is to acknowledge a gap between the past and the present. Lieux de mémoire are often established by the state, says Nora, "in a historical age that calls out for memory because it has abandoned it. They make their appearance by virtue of the deritualization of our world—producing, manifesting, establishing, constructing, decreeing, and maintaining by artifice and by will a society deeply absorbed in its own transformation and renewal, one that inherently values the new over the ancient, the young over the old, the future over the past" (1989, 12). In other words, a lieu de mémoire is an artifice made necessary by modernity's attempt to demarcate the past as irretrievable in a trajectory now permanently oriented toward the future.

I am unconvinced by Nora's historical argument and do not see the difference between the medieval past and modern present in such stark nostalgic or romantic terms. Instead, I see his comparison as a telling ideological account of France as tragically marred by a secularized Catholicism, in which meaningful ritual practices can no longer be experienced. Nora's perspective in this regard offers a further contrast to the kind of narrative the employee was hoping to reproduce, one that would make more space for catholaïcité, in which Catholic ritual forms may persist in practices such as contemporary art display.

As a lieu de mémoire, the Collège would be an artificial and strategic project. But the Collège is framed as something quite different. As a renaissance, it is framed precisely as an expression of a milieu de mémoire that Parisians can still inhabit in the present if only they look at their city and their practices in a particular way. This argument is written into the redesign of the space. One of the characteristics many admire about the Collège is its austere emptiness. The renovation of the Collège emphasized the simplicity of the Cistercian architecture, while also incorporating a number of features of modernist design. In so doing, the space itself implicitly argued for a connection between medieval Cistercian and modernist aesthetics.[8] The sleek lines of its exterior and interior, the furnishing choices made by the architects, and the manner in which it was renovated to emphasize the vastness of the space demonstrate careful attempts to forge a connection between modernist minimalism and medieval Cistercian monasticism.

One point of contention in this design was the decision to include a bookstore, widely disparaged by many visitors. In their critiques, I understood them to express concerns about the risks of Catholic capaciousness—and of a secularized Catholicism—as they lamented how such additions could make the Collège indistinguishable from other commercial cultural sites in the city. Indeed, most museums and theaters in Paris include carefully curated bookstores. The design of the store may well have contributed to their concerns. Describing it as *moche* (ugly), many saw its modernist shape as an inappropriate intrusion upon the medieval space. The renovation architects had, in fact, allowed the sightline of the vaults to go unimpeded, reducing the bookstore to a small white box. In so doing, however, they also referenced modernist preferences for open, continuous spaces that make visible buildings' skeletons. A sleek white desk and wall immediately opposite the entrance provide a space for volunteers to sit with visitors and go over the various offerings at the Collège. The café is even more discreet: a single counter tucked behind the bookstore with a small chalkboard displaying the choice of entrée/plat/dessert or quiche and salad for the day. During the years I spent at the Collège, the tables of the café, as well as a few dozen Eames designer chairs, lined the wall to the right of the bookstore. The southern side of the nave was almost always entirely empty—except, as I describe in chapters 3 through 6, during contemporary art exhibitions. The only "figure" in the Collège is a statue elevated on the back wall. It was discovered unexpectedly during the renovation but is too damaged for even experts to know with certainty whom it represents.

Medieval Cistercians often practiced an aesthetics of austerity. In contrast to many of the highly decorative designs of Gothic architecture, early Cistercian reformers such as St. Bernard of Clairvaux (1090–1153), for whom the Collège is named, were deeply concerned about the inappropriateness of "excessive art" in the space of the monastery. While Bernard did not refuse the possibility of Christian art and opulence as such, he desired for the monastery to be a space apart, in which those committed to what Giorgio Agamben has described as "the attempt to make habit and form of life coincide in an absolute and total habitus" (2011, 16) would be liberated from the distractions that could lead them away from the monastic rule.[9] The design of the Collège argues for a connection between Cistercian austerity and the sleek, boxy, white aesthetics of European modernism.[10] The architects forged a connection between Cistercian medieval monasticism and the project at the Collège through the design of the space itself, and in so doing, bolstered employees' claims of renaissance. Making the argument implicit in the space reduced the need for explicit, discursive framing of the project underway.

Descriptions of the Collège as a site of renaissance can be found in numerous publications and advertisements. According to its website, for example, "after four years of renovations, the Collège des Bernardins renewed its initial vocation in 2008 by becoming a space of research and debate for the Church and society, focused on the question of mankind and his future" ("Huit siècles d'histoire"). The broadly cultural and potentially catholaïc goals of this renaissance could be seen in the list of attendees at the two events that inaugurated the space. The first was held on September 8, 2008, and was attended by a number of politicians, including the minister of culture and communication, the mayor of Paris, and the president of the regional council of the Ile-de-France. The "second" inauguration, which occurred on September 12, was in many ways the more significant. Pope Benedict XVI addressed a packed assembly of seven hundred members of Paris's artistic and cultural elite at the Collège, including many of the same politicians who had attended the event days earlier, as well as a few more, such as the former president of France, Jacques Chirac.

The pope began his speech by explaining that he intended to speak about "the origins of western theology and the roots of European culture." He gestured to the massive nave in which they were seated. "The place in which we are gathered is in a certain way emblematic" of these roots of European culture, he explained, which are "monastic." The Collège, he said, is a space where, in its original form, "the treasures of ancient culture survived, and where at the same time a new culture slowly took shape out of the old." It was not, he continued, the "intention" of the monks at the Collège to "create a culture nor even to preserve a culture from the past. Their motivation was much more basic. Their goal was: *quaerere Deum* [to seek God]" (Benedict XVI 2008). This journey of monasticism—the search for God—meant the study of the Word: "Because in the biblical word God comes towards us and we towards him, we must learn to penetrate the secret of language, to understand it in its construction and in the manner of its expression. Thus it is through the search for God that the secular sciences take on their importance, sciences which show us the path towards language" (ibid.). In a country with a history of anticlericalism as virulent as that known in France during the nineteenth century, the pope's assertion that monks and social scientists, instead of being antagonistic foes, have actually been working at the same project was surprisingly well received by the assembled crowd. Moreover, his words insist that the project that originally occurred in the space was, like the present-day renaissance, not a *strategic* project. It was simply the natural outcome of the work with which the monks had been charged: the search for God.

Like other Catholic thinkers of the nineteenth and twentieth centuries, Benedict XVI sees the origins of Christianity in the "'Hellenization' of Judaism," an "event" which he understands as part of the inaccurate trajectory of the *logos* that has subsequently shaped European history (Smith 2011, 259). Today, however, as the philosopher John H. Smith describes Ratzinger's thought, Europe is undergoing a "'de-hellenization' . . . through the reduction of reason/*logos* to a purely secular concept, divorced from its theological connection to faith" (ibid.). To understand Europe's crisis as induced by a move away from its universal, Christian origins, however, requires a very selective understanding of late antiquity Judaism and Hellenism—and certainly of European history. This understanding of Europe's "crisis" also buttresses perceptions that its causes are due to recent transformations, most often expressed in popular discourse as the rise of "multiculturalism," and of Islam in particular.

Benedict's speech—in addition to inaugurating the Collège—was the second of five speeches known as the "September Speeches," all of which, in various ways, argued for Christianity and Europe's essential identities being forged by the merging of reason and Christian faith (de Souza 2018). The first speech in the series (Benedict XVI 2006)—given in September 2006 at the University of Regensberg—was revealing of the ways in which this political theology is both built upon and feeds into Islamophobia and exclusionary visions of Europe. Entitled "Faith, Reason and the University," the talk laid out a contrast between Christianity, as "a religious project" in which "faith and reason are not mutually exclusive but instead are dependent upon one another," and Islam, in which "faith and reason . . . are mutually exclusive" (Emon 2006, 304–5).[11] The pope's contrast sparked public protests in countries throughout the Middle East. As the legal scholar Anver M. Emon points out in his critique of the speech, while Benedict XVI acknowledged (obliquely in a footnote) that medieval Christians had debated the extent to which God's will could be arrived at through reason, he made no mention of the fact that the relationship between faith and reason was similarly a topic of debate—rather than an impossibility—among Islamic scholars of the same period and beyond.[12]

At the Collège in September 2008, the pope similarly buttressed his vision of Europe through a selective account of its medieval history. He expanded upon the connection between faith and reason in Christianity by pointing to the medieval monastery as a site in which the search for God was made possible through reason and study, particularly through the recovery of the texts of Aristotle in Europe in the twelfth century. What Pope Benedict XVI failed to mention, however, was the source of the revival of Aristotle in Europe and the subsequent intellectual "flourishing" of Europe's universities and monasteries: texts and translations produced by Muslim scholars (Rouche 2008, 37; Graeber 2014 [2011]). In his attempt to reduce Europe to a singular, universal Christian project, the now-retired pope engaged in discursive practices that could also serve to support anti-Islamic sentiments through selective accounts of Islamic history or else by failing to identify Islam's integral role in European history. For its part, the Collège's website makes no mention of the link between the pope's speech at the Collège and the Regensberg address. Instead, his words are described as the first in a series on the relationship between faith and contemporary culture.

By collapsing the roots of monasticism, Western culture, civilization, and social science into a singular narrative, the pope also offered a powerful account of renaissance and catholaïcité. In so doing, he supported the project of normalization underway at the Collège: the creation of a space in which "true" culture can flourish. In one of the most celebrated colloquia of the inaugural year at the Collège, the novelist, essayist, art critic, and one of the founding editors of the postmodern literary review *Tel Quel* (As It Is) Philippe Sollers spoke on the works of Dante. The director of research at the Collège introduced him with the following words: "I don't know if you have already entered [the Collège], but the Collège has entered into your writing." He then proceeded to quote from Sollers's latest novel, published only a few months prior.

> The people whom the popes annoy make me laugh . . . . I listen, distraught, to the speech of the current Pope. . . . In a former medieval college, superbly renovated, and which has seen the passing of many excellent spirits, he addresses those "responsible for culture," the motley well-paid deaf. . . . I listen, however, to his words, pronounced with a light but undeniable German accent: "The desire to understand God through the love of letter, the love of the word, its exploration in all of its dimensions." This is what I never stop doing. And also (I am not dreaming): "He is thus truly here, in reality, the *Logos* [Word, Greek] is here, the Logos is present among us." [2009, 238–39]

While the director of research feigned ignorance regarding the author's presence at the pope's speech, the words from his novel can leave one in little doubt. Found in the concluding pages of a story about a Parisian time traveler, the paragraph is astounding in its powerful affirmation of the project of the Collège (and of the political theology of the pope). Sollers took up the pope's call and recognized that, as a writer, he has in fact been doing the work of the logos—or, perhaps, engaging in the renaissance of medieval Catholicism—all along.

In a 2013 debate held at the Collège among philosophers and theologians discussing the significance of the pope's speech, one participant reminded the audience that "monks don't only pray. Monks are men of culture; monks have libraries; monks sing; monks do manual labor."[13] He described these activities as "not pious, but intellectual." The copresident of the Collège at the time, Monsignor Beau, furthered these insights by remembering how much the pope "had wanted to give this speech to the world of culture." For those gathered at the inauguration, the discussion of the relationship between reason and faith, and between religion and culture, "came as a surprise," Beau explained, because

> I think it was not the immediate or first question that was expected. We can see that the world of culture in September 2008 . . . did not anticipate a speech like the one he gave. They were still in a problematic of a church that is going to criticize the world. . . . Instead, the pope . . . described the figure of the true man as the figure of the monk. . . . He wanted . . . to show . . . not the monk as monk, but as man, open to transcendence, open to the encounter with God, reason open to faith. . . . He bypassed the polemic that was expected, that the journalists expected at this moment, a polemic between a culture and an anti-culture; he bypassed it by showing another path. ["Foi et culture chez Benoît XVI" 2013]

Here we see the auxiliary bishop of Paris, who, along with a nonpriest, directed the Collège for a number of years, engaging powerfully in the work of curating. He laid two seemingly disparate elements next to one another—man and monk, culture and Church—in order to demonstrate how they are not so distant as it may appear. Just as the pope had curated a different relationship between faith and reason than that anticipated by many in the audience, the auxiliary bishop at the Collège furthered the pope's curatorial efforts by emphasizing how he had made an argument for monks as "intellectuals." Beau took delight in the way Benedict XVI had eschewed the expectations of the world of culture to argue that, while engaging in activities the artists, writers, and intellectuals gathered understood to be outside of the Church, they have in fact been doing the same work as the medieval monks who once occupied the space in which they now sat. In other words, at the moment when members of the world of culture may have anticipated an evangelizing voice from the pope, he offered them a path toward normalizing by way of renaissance. He insisted that practices one thinks are no longer coherent in the modern world are, in fact, integral to that very modernity. As I have argued, normalization is most effective when its efforts are effaced. When claims of renaissance succeeded, they provided evidence that visitors only needed to engage in those practices that already undergirded their (elite and cultured) lives in order to access the medieval milieu de mémoire that the Collège seeks to rebirth.

ENCOUNTER

In the late summer of 2010, I found myself debating issues of translation with an employee of the fundraising arm of the Collège, the Fondation des Bernardins. She had asked my opinion of her English translation of one of the Collège's fundraising brochures. While she had initially been enthusiastic about working with me, we quickly ran into disagreements on the best way to translate a variety of phrases. I suggested, for example, that her formulation "whither goes mankind?" was too formal, and I offered instead "where is mankind headed?" "Really?" she asked, raising her brows. "Isn't that too colloquial?" Our next stumbling block came when she laughed at my use of "encounter" as a translation of *rencontre*. I asked what she found amusing and she suggested that "encounter" was the English word used to describe gay men's sexual liaisons in airport bathrooms. Chuckling, I did my best to reassure her that this was far from the only meaning the term brought to mind. The employee still hesitated in taking it up, however, worrying that this potential connotation created too great a risk in the final formatting of expensive publications aimed at potential donors.[14]

Our debate about the meaning of encounter arose in part because it appears so frequently in the literature about the Collège. The Collège's website describes the project as "a space of encounters, culture, and research" (lieu de rencontres, de culture, de recherche). The Fondation employee was not just testing me nor purposely giving me a hard time that afternoon.

She took her work seriously, and she knew that our work of translation was twofold that day: translating a French text into English, and also, as with all work at the Collège, engaging in the preemptive work of encounter. As Monsignor Beau had described, when the "world of culture" was invited to hear Pope Benedict XVI speak at the Collège, attendees were not expecting the address he gave. They were anticipating a far more confrontational encounter between the Church and the "secular" world. Employees repeated this challenge most days—addressing visitors and potential donors' presumptions that the Collège was primarily a religious or Catholic project and, therefore, not one in which they could (or would) participate.

In the eyes of many employees, one of the primary risks of allowing too much space for evangelization at the Collège was that it could turn away these kinds of visitors before they set foot in the door. While certain they could count on the arrival of a number of committed Catholic visitors, the challenge was how to attract a broader public. At a seminar on the strategic vision of the Collège held five years prior to its opening, the founders recognized that the École Cathédrale would provide a reliable stream of committed Catholics.[15] "Young and old, they are already constituted and offer a convinced and motivated public that is increasing year by year. This public will invest enthusiastically in the creation of the Bernardins," Cardinal Lustiger, the archbishop so celebrated by Barjot, announced confidently at the seminar. After the cardinal had offered his opening thoughts, those gathered broke into small groups to strategize how to best sketch out a vision for the Collège. In one breakout session, the seminar leader spoke to the struggle of attracting a wider public in the following way: "How will we attract those other than us?" The goal of these breakout sessions was not to imagine how to attract a multicultural or multifaith crowd. Rather, those they hoped to reach would likely identify with a Catholic culture or heritage but not engage in Catholic practices on a regular basis.[16] Answering this question was important not only as part of a desire to attract crowds to the new and rather costly space; allowing for an encounter between committed and tacit Catholics was central to the very project itself.

The idea of encounter supported the work of normalization in two ways. First, it pointed to the need to address two disparate audiences: committed and tacit Catholics. The distinction between committed and tacit Catholic actors is often seen as one of "belief"—the decision to assent or not to assent to a series of assertions about the world and God. In contrast, I want to highlight the complex affective, aesthetic, and cultural practices required in order for Catholicism to resonate both with those committed to Catholic practice and those who only rarely engage in it. Second, through the careful work of curation, the term downplayed the potentially fraught nature of this encounter. In their efforts, employees implicitly argued that these two potential publics were not as distinct as they might appear. Work at the Collège was often aimed in this bidirectional manner—drawing in an audience not likely to associate with the Catholic Church, while not turning away those who did so with pride. This required the careful translation of terms that carried religious connotations into those that also held potentially secular ones, without negating the religious reading entirely (as, presumably, a word used to refer to illicit nonnormative sexual encounters would). The abundance of caution the fundraising employee demonstrated that afternoon points to the challenges of curating encounter. Not wanting to risk allowing Catholicism to occupy a space so capacious it could include nonnormative sexual encounters, the employee allowed words to become overdetermined and carry weight well beyond the vagaries of their use.

In our interview, the same employee who insisted that, at the Collège, they are "charged with the renaissance" of a medieval project described that project as one of "encounter in which the Church is the servant of the encounter . . . between the society of today, of which we are all a part, and Christian wisdom, Christian tradition, the Word of God."[17] I was often struck by the effectiveness of the ambiguities in this employee's carefully selected words. His vagueness allowed him to speak to more than one audience simultaneously, to engage in what Mikhail Bakhtin (1981) has described as double-voicing.[18] The employee engaged in effective double-voicing in a variety of ways. When describing an encounter between the Church and society, he was quick to overcome the gap that this project of encounter might imply by insisting that the Church cannot be separated from the society of today, as it is that "of which we are all a part."

The ambiguity of the employee's claim was furthered by his use of three very different terms to describe the Catholic side of the encounter underway at the Collège: Christian wisdom, Christian tradition, and the Word of God. Christian wisdom (*la sagesse chrétienne*) is a broad enough term to encompass those desiring to take something from Catholicism without necessarily engaging in all of its political and ethical positions. It effectively speaks to those desiring something "spiritual" rather than "religious." Wisdom is a term that allows for a tacit engagement with those ideas and concepts that individuals find most relevant. The Christian tradition (*la tradition chrétienne*), on the other hand, implies a particularly Catholic argument about the sources available for revealing Christian wisdom. Rather than Scripture alone (as Protestant reformers of the sixteenth century argued), a variety of media and texts might be looked to for amplifying and nuancing Catholic knowledge. These might include the writings of the Church fathers, apocryphal legends surrounding the Christ family, the lives of the saints, images, and papal decrees. As the pope's speech and Sollers's novel suggest, these sources might be further expanded to include philosophical and artistic traditions deemed sufficiently "cultured," "Hellenist," or "European." Finally, the Word of God (*la parole de Dieu*) is familiar to anyone who attends mass regularly, as the priest reading from the Gospel proclaims it to those gathered upon completion of the selected verses. As such, the term would likely be most relevant to committed Catholics.

By listing all three terms as if they were equivalent, the employee demonstrated his capacity to speak to tacit and committed Catholics simultaneously—to address those who desired access to the Word of God or the Christian tradition, as well as those seeking something more tacit, like Christian wisdom. While his work was primarily aimed at attracting the latter group, he was savvy enough to know that, in order to be successful, the Collège would have to make space for a variety of voices and desires. Engaging in double-voicing while disguising its heteroglossic nature is far from straightforward in part because "religious observance tends to demand highly marked and self-conscious uses of linguistic resources" (Keane 1997, 48). Religious language, according to Keane, is often highly marked as such. And so, the work of normalization by way of encounter requires addressing those seeking out particular words and frames that would distinguish the space and the project as "Catholic," without going so far as evangelization.

These efforts were evident right from the Collège's inauguration. The language used by the archbishop and the politicians alike at the opening ceremony convincingly engaged in double-voicing and, in so doing, participated in the work of normalization. Cardinal Vingt-Trois, the archbishop of Paris at the time of the Collège's opening, described its vocation as "a space of encounter and dialogue open to all." According to the president of the regional council of the Ile-de-France, the site was "a symbol of opening and the intelligence of the heart." Paris's mayor admired "the art of putting together our competencies, our means, our convictions, and a certain idea of civilization as that which is bigger than us" ("Inauguration du Collège des Bernardins" 2008). With such terms, the mayor described the encounters at the Collège as propelling powerfully modernist visions, such as capitalist ideas of entrepreneurship ("the putting together of our competencies and means"), and the obfuscation of religion into "civilization" so frequent in modern colonial rule around the world. By including the term "convictions," moreover, he offered a secularized account of religion as merely one of a variety of beliefs firmly held.

In my time at the Collège, I observed employees working to bridge the encounter between committed and tacit Catholics through the curatorial work of branding. Like much corporate advertising, branding at the Collège has aimed at the subversion of expectations. As evidenced in my translation debates, the language that employees chose was intellectual but also accessible and informal, though not colloquial. The work of branding, moreover, could never go so far as to potentially offend more-committed Catholics. The everyday curatorial labor of branding also became evident in my work as a mediator for the contemporary art exhibitions at the Collège. While we were given very little in the way of explicit instructions on how to interpret the contemporary artworks for visitors, we were cautioned to always use the word Collège rather than monastery to describe the site, both in its thirteenth- and twenty-first-century instantiations.

The Cistercian monks who had built the thirteenth-century site had indeed intended to provide a space for monks to come to Paris in order to gain access to a broader curriculum of education than that found in many countryside monasteries. Through interactions with students and professors at the University of Paris, the Cistercian monks would open themselves to a wider world of ideas and debates. Whether or not this meant that the site was not also a monastery, however, is far from clear (Sternberg 2013, 240-259). For employees, it was the broadly educational and cultural mission that they were bringing back to life, and the term they chose to use for the project, Collège, is decidedly secular in comparison to its alternatives.[19]

In 2017, one of the key players in the restoration of the Collège, Bertrand de Feydeau, published a book detailing many of his efforts. He explained that the decision to name the space the "Collège des Bernardins" was arrived at "methodically and meticulously, as would be suitable for the branding of a large corporation" (de Feydeau 2017, 107). Ideas such as the "Catholic Academy" and "Catholic Cultural Center of Paris" had been rejected, as had the terms "convent" and "Cistercian." Here, too, one can see debates between normalizers and evangelizers at play.

Describing the space as a Collège rather than a monastery in the past and the present, however, required a great deal of effort and discipline. Committed Catholic visitors often bristled when we corrected their language. The offense they took suggests that we had veered too far toward normalization. Even the founder of the Collège, Cardinal Lustiger, had to learn to use the right terminology. An article published in the daily newspaper *Le Journal de Paris* when the restoration project was announced on December 19, 2000, opens with the following quote from Lustiger: "In the 1960s, when I was the chaplain of students, I saw the Bernardins monastery occupied by a fire station. I imagined that it could rediscover its original thirteenth-century vocation and be a space of culture and exchange" (Le Mitouard 2000, 1).

A review of other articles published at the time demonstrates that terminology for the space was still very much in flux. An article published in the right-of-center newspaper *Le Figaro* on December 17, 2000, describes the site as a *collège-couvent* (a college-convent). Recounting the unanimous decision by the Council of Paris to sell the site to the archdiocese, the article cites the presentation by the mayor of Paris of "'the restoration project of the Bernardins convent'" in which the archbishop of Paris wants "to give back to this space of reflection its tradition of opening to culture in a broad sense—history, philosophy, music—in order to welcome believers and non-believers" (Maréchal 2000, 13).[20] The multiple terms used to describe the project in its early years hint at the difficulty of defining the historical site in any singular way. The fact that employees have now largely succeeded in disciplining commentators and the media to use the term "Collège" rather than monastery or convent speaks to the success of their efforts at branding the space. In an interesting reversal of this strategy with remarkably similar effects, the terminology used to refer to various spaces within the Collège—such as crypt, nave, and sacristy—borrow from explicitly Christian architectural terms. Letters that circulated between the archdiocese and the City of Paris when the purchase of the space and its renovation were first being explored demonstrate how, like "Collège," these terms were not always so carefully applied. In one letter from the archdiocese to the mayor's office, for example, the space now referred to as the nave is described as "the longest Gothic room in Paris." The power of terms such as nave and sacristy, which are typically used to describe particular spaces in churches, comes from their location inside a potentially secular space such as a Collège. That these spaces play host to nonsacramental and non-Christian practices further emphasizes the overlap between Catholicism and culture underlined in the Collège's project of encounter.

In addition to careful attention to terminology, branding also required the production of a visual identity that, as one communications staff described to me, people would come to easily connect with the Collège. She offered the example of seeing advertisements for museum exhibits. "Even if you barely catch a glimpse, you know immediately which museum the exhibition is happening at because of the visual display. This is what we want to do for the Collège," she explained. Her next statement was even more specific. "We really want to install ourselves in a landscape, the Parisian cultural landscape." Her efforts, and those of her colleagues, have seen remarkable successes. In February 2009, the Collège received a national web design award from the Parisian business community for its logo and the visual design of its website. *Le Figaro* celebrated this coup, noting in a short article that although

> only inaugurated six months ago, the Collège des Bernardins, imagined by Cardinal Lustiger as a space of cultural, artistic, and intellectual exchange for the Church and society has known a true success. Not only is it never empty (1,500 visitors a day), its operating budget . . . balanced, but it is also going to be crowned by the top dot com prize in 2009 for the creation of its logo and visual identity, a prize given every year by the professionals of business communication. ["Médaille d'or pour le Collège des Bernardins" 2009]

A few months later, the *Design Observer* gave the Collège a "design star" for its "visual identity." This visual identity is everywhere: on its publications, its advertisements, its posters, and its programs. It is printed on the plastic bags given with purchases at the bookstore, on pencils, notebooks, and its website. The logo mimics the Gothic arches that define the ground floor of the building but turned on their side to create the shape of the letter B. The introductions to videos of events at the Collège make this connection all the more clear by animating the image, turning it from a B into the arches associated with the space. In an interview, a member of the communications' staff explained that outside consultants had been brought in to create the visual identity and that the communications' department was, at the time, working to ensure that it appeared in logical, coherent, and regular ways.

The visual identity—as a symbol signifying an institution associated with the Catholic Church—is striking in its refusal of the host of images, icons, and symbols available within a variety of Catholic traditions (including the cross, Christ, the sacred heart, the Eucharist, and the saints, just to name a few). Instead, the name Bernard (B), and not his sainthood, is invoked along with the site's medieval architectural forms. With this brand, employees defy expectations that the Collège is a purely Catholic space. The use of design consultants and the desire to regularize a visual identity in order to make it legible within a broader cultural and tourist landscape demonstrate the extensive curatorial work required to reduce the significance of the encounter employees aimed to make possible.

There are many temporal and material practices in France that undergird the assumption that those whom I have been calling "tacit" Catholics may have a great deal in common with those more committed.[21] In an example of what Pamela Klassen and Monique Scheer have called "Christian affordances" (2018, 8–9), various moments of Catholic liturgy, both old and new, mark the national calendar and more intimate yearly cycles in France.[22] Much of the city is closed not only for Christmas Day, New Year's Day, Good Friday, Easter Sunday, and Easter Monday but also for the Day of Ascension, the Assumption of the Virgin Mary, and All Saints' Day. Klassen and Scheer see Christian affordances, such as legally enforced national holidays and extensive support for Christian heritage spaces, as materializing an infrastructure of Christian public memory. These Christian affordances, in other words, point to the role of the state in the curatorial efforts necessary to maintain Christian privilege.

[margin note: Christian afford-ances]

Christian affordances highlight how the Collège is not alone in reducing the gap between these groups. The effects of such affordances are numerous, but I want to focus here on the highly flexible modes of engaging with Catholicism available to French citizens, thereby reducing the profound distinctions that many presume distinguish tacit from committed Catholics. A woman whom I will call Céline—and whom I met through connections outside of the Collège—offers an example of such flexible modes of attachment. An attractive, slim, middle-class woman in her early fifties, Céline was the kind of French woman presumed in the popular slate of American self-help books published in the early 2000s (such as *French Women Don't Get Fat* [Guiliano 2004] and *Bringing Up Bébé* [Druckerman 2012]), which claimed that all American women needed to do to achieve marital bliss, bodily perfection, and orderly children was to follow the model of (white) French women. She quickly took me under her wing, correcting me when I neglected to use the subjunctive or erred in my choice between the imperfect and the compound past. She also offered the kinds of summaries of life in Paris that the mere presence of an anthropologist in a room can provoke.

At a dinner party at Céline's house one evening, the assembled guests discussed the private school her son attends. "Is it Catholic?" I asked. "Of course it's Catholic," she replied. "Most of the private schools in France are Catholic. But it is not Catholic Catholic." I furrowed my brow to show that I did not understand the distinction. "It still operates under the auspices of the state and receives state funding. So, they always have to ask permission ahead of any religious teachings." She explained that most of the religious teaching is "harmless," such as religion in art—they took a trip to the Louvre to explore iconography and representation in art history—but she was similarly unconcerned when her son heard lectures by priests, engaged in catechism classes, or participated in mass. "In order to understand history and art in France, one must understand the history of the Church, the Bible, the traditions. In order to understand the secular, one must understand the religious!" she explained. A friend of Céline's—a younger woman—vigorously nodded her head in agreement.

I encountered such pronouncements frequently, such as during one summer afternoon in 2009 while working at the Collège. Two women who described themselves as not religious expressed regret at having denied their children access to the Church, because this decision had diminished their cultural knowledge. Like Céline, they insisted that there are many things—such as art and architecture—that one cannot understand if one does not know Catholic liturgy or stories. In many respects, they were not wrong—Catholic objects and images take up prime real estate in many of Paris's museums, such as the Louvre.

Céline had not baptized her son, but she acknowledged that "there are certain Catholic values that I am perfectly fine with him learning—respect, respect for others."[23] She repeated these words several times as she searched for other examples. She took him to mass a few times, she explained, because he was curious, but that was all. Céline's arguments justifying her decision to send her son to a Catholic school, despite being neither a believer nor a practicing Catholic, are remarkable for the way in which the supposedly profound gap between the secular and religious in France fades away. To suggest that an understanding of the secular requires prior knowledge of Catholicism betrays how, for Céline and many others, Catholicism stands as both the standard-bearer of religion and the foundation of the secular in France.

Secular and Catholic schools alike close early on Wednesday afternoons, precisely the same time of the week when the city's churches offer catechism classes. Pierre, a father of three children and a partner in a small urban planning firm in central Paris, told me with some pride that he attends church only for "weddings and funerals." Why then, I asked him, did he decide to send his twelve-year-old son and thirteen-year-old daughter to catechism classes at the church located near his home? In response, he explained that as members of a Judeo-Christian society they needed to learn the morals and culture at its core. He invited me to the celebration following their confirmation held at a nearby restaurant. Wearing a shiny, metallic-colored suit, he laughed at what he presumed was his unusual dress and behavior in the church but was clearly touched by the moment of transition the ceremony marked in his children's lives. Pierre and his partner, Cécile, had never married. For Pierre and Cécile, there was no contradiction in living so far outside of the Church's sacramental structure and sending their children to learn its doctrinal and liturgical forms.

Many in France celebrate a second birthday, or Saint's Day (*fête des saints*): the day marking an event in the life of the saint whose name one bears. The announcement of which saint is being celebrated on any given day concludes the weather report on most morning television news shows. From 1803 until 1966, it was illegal in France to give a child a name other than one of those found in the yearly calendar of the saints. Clearly, however, not everyone born in France today bears the names Jean, Marie, Laurent, Sébastien, or Geneviève. So, a project entitled "Nominis," run by the Conference of Catholic Bishops of France, works to attribute a variety of names to their closest saintly equivalent (at least phonetically).[24] January 21, for example, is the day of Saint Agnès and those named Aina, Aïssa, Ania, Nessie, and Oanell are also welcome to join in the celebration.

In many of the conversations I had with young couples recounting why they wanted to marry in a Catholic church (often for "aesthetic" reasons), they made the effort to discount their own relationship to the institution.[25] In France, only marriages performed by civil authorities are recognized by the state. Thus, a marriage in a church must occur in addition to the legally binding vows uttered in the office of the mayor of the arrondissement in which one resides. Some of my interlocutors explained that civil ceremonies were simply too perfunctory and lacked any real sense of ceremony. One woman I met at the Collège insisted that civil ceremonies are far too short and that generally the settings are less than inspiring. Many described with bemusement their participation in the marriage preparation classes required by the Church, which they saw as an unfortunate hurdle on their way to realizing their desired image of a wedding in the inspiring setting of a church. Many couples I met recounted variations on this story. On one occasion, however, I was struck when another woman I met outside of the Collège made a very similar remark from the opposite position. That is, in choosing to have only one marriage in the mayor's office in her small provincial city, she declared, "but don't get me wrong, I am Catholic!"

It is the remarkable flexibility of the mark of Catholicism that struck me again and again. One could have a secular ceremony in a church or a Catholic marriage at a mayor's office—just as one could attend a contemporary art exhibit in the nave of the Collège or witness the procession to open mass in the nave of a church—without worrying too much about the stark divisions that supposedly separate these spaces. In this context, the Collège serves not as a site to facilitate an encounter that might not otherwise occur, but as a space in which to demonstrate that the two parties to the encounter are not so distant as they may appear.

OPENING

I asked all employees who agreed to sit down for an interview with me what, in their words, was the Collège. One woman I spoke with replied,

> First of all, a space of opening, and a space for thinking together. But what is very important is that in order to be able to . . . arrive at thinking together, it is necessary to have different opinions. So, if this reflection is just between Catholics, that is not going to advance anything. So, the idea is precisely to work on this opening, to open to people who don't have the same ideas, who may not even have the same values and who want to reflect, by listening, by respecting, by advancing together.

Here, in addition to describing the experience of encounter, the employee articulated the third term deployed to describe the project at the Collège: opening. The term was partly necessary to justify the government's financial support for the space, which, as I describe in chapter 2, included approximately €14.5 million in municipal, regional, and federal funds. In order to access government funding, the project could not appear to be for Catholics alone.[26] What became evident early on in the Collège's operation, however, was the very limited nature of the opening available in this space. During the 2003 seminar in which the purpose of the Collège was first imagined and debated, some voices pointed to the risk of tapping primarily into an "elite world." Others, however, suggested that such exclusivity might not be a problem. "Can we accept being elitist?" those in one breakout session asked. "Excellence . . . might be a factor of attraction." Years later, however, when I happened upon a fundraising brochure for the Collège at a wealthy church in Paris's sixth arrondissement, I found implicit reference to the problem of the limits of the Collège's opening. "Contrary to what you may have heard," the brochure proclaimed, "the Collège des Bernardins is open to all."

What precisely is meant by "opening" in this space is far from clear. The Collège is not advertised or understood as an interreligious space. The "other" values and opinions described by the employee are generally those of an imagined secular, elite public. What is more, the goal of this opening is not the transformative vision of the Catholic Renewal in France in the 1920s and 1930s; the goal is that of "advancing together." While the idea of advancing suggests a teleology of sorts, it also implies that both sides are already on the right track and that, rather than transforming one another, they can continue to move along the path forward together.[27]

The limited nature of this opening became most evident in those moments when the Collège engaged with publics beyond those of the elite tacit Catholic publics it sought. In the fall of 2010, the Collège hosted a roundtable discussion entitled "L'habit, fait-il toujours le moine?" The phrase is a somewhat uncomfortable reversal of the saying L'habit ne fait pas le moine, best translated into English as "The clothing doesn't make the man" or, maintaining the religious connotations of the French rendering, "The habit doesn't make the nun" (in the French version, however, it is the monk, not the nun, who is the subject). The title of the roundtable discussion altered this common phrase, asking instead "Does the habit always make the monk?" The roundtable was part of the weekly series, Bernardins Tuesdays, which brings together a group of experts to discuss current events. The first hour was televised live on the Catholic television station, KTO, and then, once the cameras were turned off, the audience was given the opportunity to ask questions.[28]

I want to describe this debate in some detail because it shows how the claim of opening was belied by the powerful ways in which some groups were "encouraged"—implicitly and explicitly—while others were "discouraged" (Asad 2006). In public life, theorists such as Michael Warner (2002) have noted, one is rewarded for blending in, or at least for not shocking through displays, gestures, or expressions of distinctiveness. Warner's important argument hinges on the fact that structures of power allow certain subjects to blend in more easily than others. Those who move freely in the public sphere of the modern West, generally, are "implicitly, even explicitly, white, male, literate, and propertied. These traits could go unmarked, even grammatically, while other features of bodies could only be acknowledged in discourse as the humiliating positivity of the particular" (2002, 165–66). The debate on religious clothing proved fascinating precisely because it displayed how—through normalizing practices of limited opening—the Collège allows Catholicism to contain the secular, while relegating Islam to that which is irremediably religious.

To the immediate left of the moderator sat Mehrezia Labidi-Maïza, a French and Tunisian citizen, renowned scholar on reason and women in Islam, and, at the time, the vice president of the European branch of the "World Organization of Religions for Peace."[29] Next to her sat Jean Baubérot, a professor emeritus at the École Politique des Hautes Études and the research chair of the History and Sociology of Secularism project there. Finally, seated facing the moderator was Aude Roy, a former director of two fashion houses in France and currently a "life coach in professional images." Labidi-Maïza wore a headscarf in the form of a white scarf wrapped around her head, pulled back far under her chin, descending down her neck, and tucked into a loose-fitting red sweater over which she wore a black suit jacket. Baubérot, a small, older white man, wore a gray suit that was slightly too large for him and an equally large red-and-white-striped tie, not quite fastened around his neck. Labidi-Maïza and Baubérot's self-presentation was academic—professional but in a way that aimed to convey that they do not worry too much about their dress and comportment. Roy, a tall and slender white woman, wore a jacket that was cropped at the waist and made of a combination of black leather and red tweed. Her dark brunette hair was cut evenly just below her ears, and the low cut of her jacket and her shirt revealed her neck and chest (but not her cleavage). In contrast to Labidi-Maïza and Baubérot—and to Barjot—Roy carefully demonstrated her elite status through a variety of cues. These included her expensive-looking clothing, her posture (she sat upright, with her shoulders pulled back and her chin slightly raised), her language, which was carefully annunciated, and her gestures (her lilting voice, rising ever so slightly at the end of each of her sentences, was punctuated by the gently flowing movement of her hands).

After allowing Labidi-Maïza and Baubérot a brief moment to introduce themselves, the host of the program then turned to Roy. "You are a woman," he said with a grin, "for whom clothes play an important role . . . at least professionally speaking." He then asked her to account for her career shift from consultant in the fashion world to life coach. "Indeed, I spent many absolutely divine years surrounded by the most beautiful women in the world—that ought to make you dream, Monsieur," she said with a smile and arched brow to Baubérot—"and the most magnificent artisans who are the treasures of France, of course . . . who make marvels for women around the world." Roy went on to describe how she had been working the long, strenuous hours required in the world of fashion and then, she shrugged,

> I found myself married, and with a son . . . and I wanted, of course, to be more present both for my son, of course, and for my husband as well, to be his wife. . . . So, I decided to bring all that I had learned during these twenty years about beauty in all its forms to those people who either wanted or needed it. Now I am a coach in visual communication, which means that I can both take advantage of my knowledge in terms of cloth-ing, color, and form and also give to people all the secrets that concern gestures. Because our image is not only what we wear but also the way in which we move. It is everything that we present to be seen.

At this point, Baubérot and Labidi-Maïza appeared somewhat startled and confused. Although they had likely anticipated an academic-style roundtable discussion, Roy's words indicated that a very different sort of conversation would take place. With her introductory remarks, Roy gave a powerful demonstration of the work of encouraging normative standards in France. The ease of her speech showed how generalizable she took her experience of the world to be. Her encounters with beautiful women, she presumed, would necessarily pique the interest of the man to her left; the artisans she worked with were capable of designing clothing that are objects of beauty around the world; her desire to be a wife and mother would "of course" require her to be more present in the home and to shift careers accordingly. A broad-based public, she presumed, would benefit from the knowledge she had gained in the fashion world (both those who "wanted" it, as well as those who "needed" it). Statements such as these gesture to a pre-sumed openness while in fact doing the work of closure: normalizing certain kinds of signs, actions, and experiences to the implicit detriment of others. Such statements powerfully exclude women whose dress does not conform to the norms of French fashion or who do not ended their careers when they have children, as well as men who do not dream of beautiful women. Thus, the encouraging or opening work of normalization implicitly relegates those who do not display declared norms to outsider status.

In making such an argument, Roy was also aligning herself with certain expressions of French feminism that have been partially integrated into con-servative Catholic accounts of the family. Throughout this chapter, I have argued that the Collège offers an example of the Roman Catholic Church working to move toward a secular public, broadly conceived, while operating under the pretense that no such move is occurring; the connection is always already present in France's catholaïcité. Numerous secular actors—such as Philippe Sollers, in his novel I described above—contribute to the plausibility of such claims through their own movements toward Catholic figures, ideas, and practices. The flurry of scholarly interest in Paul of Tarsus around the turn of the century as a potential model for radical politics (see, for example, Agamben 2005, Badiou 2003, and Zizek 2003) offers one clear example of this movement and, as Klassen and Marshall (2012) have demonstrated, its mixed political effects.

In France, numerous feminist voices have also participated in such projects. Most famous among them, perhaps, is the philosopher Julia Kristeva (married to Sollers, she was invited to respond to the address Pope Benedict XVI gave at the Collège in an edited volume published along with his speech [Kristeva 2008]). Kristeva's feminist engagement with Catholicism is most widely known because of her essay "Stabat Mater," originally published in French in 1977. In the essay, she argues that the model of virgin motherhood addresses key paradoxes essential to the human experience. She insists upon the universality of these paradoxes by pointing to the "irreducible differences between the sexes and . . . the irreconcilable interests of both—and hence of women—in asserting those differences and seeking appropriate forms of fulfillment" (1985 [1977], 151). Roy articulated these visions of essential difference throughout her introductory statement, from Baubérot's obvious interest in the beautiful women she worked with to her desire, "of course," to be a true "wife" to her husband.

The host seemed to quite enjoy Roy's remarks and responded that he liked a certain phrase she has been known to use: L'habit ne fait pas le moine mais il le laisse d'entrer dans le monastaire (The clothing does not make the monk but it allows him to enter into the monastery). "What does this mean?" he asked with a bemused smile. "Well," she replied, "I find that the monk and the monastery provide an excellent metaphor for me because I can explain to people that, in order to facilitate their professional integration, and this is very French," she lifted her eyebrows suggestively as she paused for a brief laugh, "they need to dress according to the monastery [at which they desire to work]." Given the violence of the responses to signs of Islamic dress in France, the seemingly unproblematic way in which the monastery could stand in for—or contain—the secular French public or professional sphere in Roy's metaphor is remarkable. Her presumed authority in being able to describe that which is "very French" further amplified the normalizing effects of her words.

Next, the host turned to Labidi-Maïza to ask how, as a specialist on the role of women in Islam, she could help the audience understand a question currently at the heart of French society. "Because one of the most visible elements of women's Islamic identity, which you are wearing, and I was wondering if you could say, personally, for you, what place you give to the veil and do you think there is an important element of your identity that you would like to express, transmit to your colleagues, to those in the street, to those close to you?" Coming on the heels of the host's friendly and very lengthy conversation about monasteries with Roy, his question to Labidi-Maïza was abrupt and revealed the true inspiration behind the evening's debate. Labidi-Maïza is not the only woman in hijab to occupy a central role in an orchestrated event in France. Selby (2012) describes a community event in Petit Nanterre, a suburb of Paris, in which a young playwright had received a grant to bring Muslim women and children into a work of theater that would require the women to remove their headscarves in favor of a crown as they took their place as queens and rulers in their own right. Selby highlights the multiple ways in which women refused the roles assigned to them, not only by the playwright but by discourses of their "oppression" found more widely in the French public sphere.

Like these women, Labidi-Maïza refused the premise of the question. Folding her hands and leaning forward, Labidi-Maïza repeated his phrase, "An important place? Not really," she said. "That is to say, it is part of an entire manner of living and it is not the essential. . . . In the Qur'ān there are two verses that speak about women's clothing. . . . It is a question of covering oneself, and above all covering one's breasts. . . . The most common reading is to place a scarf over one's hair and to cover oneself." She went on to explain that these readings have held various levels of importance over time and that a woman wearing a headscarf "does not have to justify herself, just as she would not have to justify praying."

Baubérot then offered a complex history of laïcité in France, including reference to a moment in the early twentieth century when elected representatives worried about the effect the sight of nuns in their habits in hospitals would have on the republic. The host offered no follow-up questions to either Baubérot or Labidi-Maïza and instead turned with a leading question to Roy: could she understand why there might be some concerns about the sight of religious signs, such as the headscarf, in France today? With such an opening, Roy was able to shift her approach from that of encouragement to that of discouragement. She acknowledged that she found Labidi-Maïza's accounts of the two verses in the Qur'ān to be very interesting. She always made clear to her clients that "no intimate articles of clothing and no intimate parts of the body should be shown in spaces of business. . . . Once these are visible, the nature of the conversation changes. The conversation is no longer a professional conversation but an intimate conversation—that is, a seduction." After lamenting the display of intimate articles of clothing by young people today, she made a surprising shift. "And religion is part of intimacy, of the intimate convictions of each of us within ourselves. And so it seems completely logical that this intimacy does not have a place in the professional world either. This intimacy—that which I believe, my religion—is of the order of my intimate convictions."

Labidi-Maïza countered Roy's claim and argued that "there is a difference between the intimacy of the body and the intimacy of religion, of ideas, of philosophy. . . . I could, without shocking others, speak about my religion, about my philosophy. I could do this without entering into contact with the intimate space of others. I would not use the word 'intimate' to describe that which concerns people's ideas, religious or philosophical."

Roy replied to Labidi-Maïza's critique curtly, implicitly dismissing her fellow participant's views as those of a foreigner. "In *French* social life," Roy retorted, "we don't discuss our religion or our politics at a dinner party. . . . We are asked to be discreet in regards to these subjects which, in France in any case, are intimate subjects." With these words Roy gave remarkable power to her rather strange equation between a bra strap and religious beliefs by articulating her position as that of the French community at large.

The notion that religion is an "intimate" affair, comparable to showing a "*string*" (the word used in French for thong, an example which Roy summoned more than once) at a corporate meeting is patently bizarre. Rather than offering a reasoned argument, or a claim backed by research and evidence, Roy's efforts were closer to those of misdirection. She forced Labidi-Maïza and Baubérot to engage in a nonexistent debate by establishing its terms far away from any evidence-based accounts of the varied intentions, desires, and contexts that shape the wearing of religious clothing. Baubérot tried to assist Labidi-Maïza in getting the discussion back on track, but Roy had effectively hijacked the terrain.

A year later, Baubérot posted a thoughtful piece on his blog in which he took another elite voice in France, Élisabeth Badinter, to task for claims similar to Roy's. One of France's wealthiest citizens, with a fortune exceeding €1 billion, Badinter is also a philosopher who in recent years has become well known both for her insistence on the complementarity of the sexes and her defense of laïcité, in particular against the threat posed to it by the increasing visibility of Islam. Baubérot carefully dismantled Badinter's claim that religion "must remain an intimate affair." Such an account of laïcité in France, Baubérot argued, completely misunderstands the laws separating church and state. While many in France have come to equate laïcité with the prohibition of the sight of religion in public life, Baubérot demonstrated that this was far from what the architects of the 1905 law separating church and state had in mind. He pointed to Article II of the law, which allows "recognized religions" to operate chaplaincy services "'in order to ensure the free exercise of religion in public establishments, such as high schools, middle schools, elementary schools, hospices, asylums and prisons'" (Baubérot 2011). What is more, while some deputies in 1905 had proposed the banning of priests' cassocks and nuns' habits from the streets—describing them as "'provocative,' contrary to 'liberty and human dignity,' a proselytizing costume that made the priest a 'prisoner, slave' and separated him from other men"—such a proposal was quickly defeated. Those who insisted that the law had no business regulating dress in this way argued that "'following the separation, the cassock would become clothing like any other'" (ibid.).[30] The architects of the law, it would seem, could foresee the eventual banalization of Catholic materiality.

The host's refusal to pursue Baubérot's comments regarding the sight of nun's habits in hospitals suggests that he did not necessarily appreciate Baubérot's historical clarification. If priests' cassocks once appeared to imprison and enslave those who wore them, then they would look much closer to the modes of Islamic dress that have received similar critiques in French law and discourse and that Labidi-Maïza had been called upon to explain. Here lurked the specter of Catholicism as simply one among many oppressed religious cultures. Roy's attempts at misdirection become more understandable in this light. By inviting this unusual voice into what could have been an academic discussion, employees at the Collège effaced the overlaps between Catholic and Muslim clothing. Through Roy's efforts, the debate effectively equated headscarves with bra straps, thereby relegating them to intimate attire that has no place in the public sphere. In contrast, Catholic religious garb was made to stand in for normative attire appropriate in French public life. Instead of opening up analyses that would point to connections between historical and present-day debates over religious clothing in France—and thereby articulate overlaps between Catholicism and Islam in France—this normalizing debate closed the space of opening, reducing Islam to a particular, intimate claim and relegating it outside that which is "very French," while simultaneously using the monastery as a metaphor for the French public sphere.

In his account of the monastic life, or *cenoby* (Latin), Agamben makes reference to the phrase "the habit does not make the monk." For him, the staying power of the adage reflects the ambiguity of the desire for a totalizing overlap between the two meanings of habitus—dress and way of life. In a fascinating contemporary expression of the desire for this overlap between dress and way of life, as a life coach from the fashion world Roy aims to teach her clients that their clothes and appearance can create the kind of (successful capitalist) life they want to live. And yet, Agamben argues that the original phrase that served as the inspiration for the night's discussion points to the impossibility of the monastic desire for a mode of living "in which it would not be possible to distinguish between dress and way of life" (2011, 16).

Occurring in a space that claims to be the renaissance of a medieval monastic project, the debate presented the current moment as a time of decline from an earlier moment of coherence. A summary of the event found on the Collège's website for example, states: "In our occidental societies marked by cultural and religious diversity, religious clothing is making a striking and contradictory comeback. A source of inspiration for designers, confused with the search for identity among certain communities, religious clothing seems to have lost its sacred origins for the benefit of a commercial or societal function." Similar to Pierre Nora's contrast between lieux de mémoire and milieux de mémoire, the framing of the debate could only make sense in light of the widespread assumption that, in the medieval past, social life—and especially religious life—could not be distinguished from "the rule," to use Agamben's term, or the customs and culture it inhabited. Agamben overturns this myth by pointing to its incompleteness in precisely those places in which the rule was imagined to be most totalizing: the monastery. "The distance that separates the two meanings of the term *habitus* will never completely disappear," he argues, "and will durably mark the definition of the monastic condition with its ambiguity" (ibid.).

Those who are able to occupy the unmarked habitus of the nation, Roy insisted, are those who are able to bridge the supposed gap between the Catholic and secular, refusing other forms of difference within this potential space of opening. Recall how, to many of my interlocutors at the Collège, Catholicism's recent renewal in Paris has been reflected in the increasing visibility of Catholic dress in the streets. Certainly, monks', priests', and nuns' habits are common sights in Paris and, as I described in the introduction, they generally cause little in the way of consternation. The curatorial practices of renaissance, encounter, and opening underway at the Collège allow Catholic materiality to move between the marked and the unmarked to appear as nothing more, and nothing less, than that which is "very French." This mode of opening effectively closes the possibility of including those who do not fit into the limited expanse of catholaïcité. While space is made for particular feminist visions that emphasize essential differences between men and women, Islam is foreclosed as that which is always other.

2

CRYSTALLIZATION AND RENAISSANCE

WHEN I BEGAN WORKING AT THE Collège, I was surprised that I never received any formal training on the story of its birth. Employees and managers did not offer orientation sessions or documents that laid out the main points I had to repeat to visitors. Instead, after I had heard numerous accounts—from the priests who told the story with pride to visiting family and friends, from the institution's directors as they shepherded potential donors around the space, from other mediators as they attempted to engage visitors with the exhibits—I also began to pass this shared story on to others. As Frigide Barjot's "bravo" directed to the former archbishop of Paris as the "reason we have this place to celebrate Christian culture" suggests, the narrative centers on Cardinal Jean-Marie Aaron Lustiger.

In the 1960s, I would begin, the young chaplain Lustiger often passed by the building in which the Collège is now housed during his regular walks from Notre-Dame Cathedral to the Sorbonne. Lustiger experienced the then-decaying space on the rue de Poissy as a source of inspiration. Long before his rise to the head of the French Catholic Church, he began to imagine the Collège as a site of renaissance—a space that could once again serve the purpose for which it had originally been intended. Given the cardinal's long-standing desire to return the site to its thirteenth-century calling, he jumped at the opportunity to buy the building back from the city when the occupant—by the late 1990s, a police training school—wished to divest itself of the site. This story was continually confirmed to me as I participated in activities at the Collège. During one guided tour, for example, the docent began by explaining that "at the end of the 1960s, while serving as chaplain at the Sorbonne, the Cardinal had the intuition to do something [at the Collège] for the diocese." When it became available toward the end of the 1990s, she explained, "he spoke with the experts and learned what they had to do for the restoration." In response to my question of what is the Collège, one priest I interviewed explained that it "was born in Lustiger's spirit."[1]

Given its seemingly universal acceptance, I told versions of this story several times a week in my work at the Collège. Its power and poignancy resided in Lustiger's apparent long-standing interest in the project of the Collège, and in his prophetic "intuition" that the site was uniquely situated to bring something special to the archdiocese. Weeks before I left Paris in the summer of 2010, however, I was able to examine Lustiger's archives. During my initial visit, the archivist was quick to explain his surprise that, in response to my requests, he had been unable to find among the cardinal's early papers examples of references to the Collège. This was a space that, as everyone knew, the archbishop had imagined turning into a Catholic cultural center for decades before finally being able to see his dream nearly to completion (he died in 2007, a year before its opening to the public). The archivist explained this gap as a problem of collection.

In his account of the formation of archives, Jacques Derrida argues that these houses of memory wield a number of different powers, "of unification, of identification, of classification"—and also "the power of cosignation" (1995, 3). Derrida means this term quite literally, as the "gathering together [of] signs. . . . Cosignation aims to coordinate a single corpus, in a system or a synchrony in which all the elements articulate the unity of an ideal configuration" (ibid., 3). When he did not find reference to the Collège in the cardinal's early writings, the archivist assumed this to be a problem of cosignation. The written record of Lustiger's thoughts on the Collège must exist; their absence in the archive merely demonstrated how much work still needed to be done to successfully consolidate his life in its proper home in the archive.

My examination of the rather mundane discussions of the Collège in the archives, however, showed that Cardinal Lustiger first began to imagine that the Collège could "do something for the archdiocese" not in the 1960s but in the 1990s. What is more, in these early musings, the cardinal did not imagine the Collège as a space of "culture and exchange," but as an administrative center in which various wings of the archdiocese could be brought together near the Notre-Dame Cathedral. When the Diocesan Council expressed reticence at the costly renovation of the building, a judicious suggestion helped to reposition the Collège as a space of "culture" in order to increase its chances of receiving funding from the secular state.

Why, then, did the cardinal construct such a narrative to begin with?

Why did the archivist and so many others participate in its retelling, even in
the face of evidence to the contrary? In telling and repeating such a story, I,
Lustiger, and my interlocutors engaged in the work necessary to transform a
project whose history is decidedly contingent into one that appears natural.
Or, put another way, the construction and repetition of this narrative reveals
the labors of turning moments of rupture into expressions of continuity.

While the Collège is often framed as a site of renaissance—as the repetition
of its thirteenth-century predecessor, and a self-evident articulation of the
overlap between French and Catholic culture—its rocky beginnings betray
the numerous other paths Lustiger and the Collège could have taken. They
reveal the formation of the Collège as a creative and pragmatic act of curation that unsettles claims of continuity.

As the instigator of the Collège, Lustiger is key to this book. But his
relevance goes beyond the strategic efforts he undertook to bring the Collège into being. Throughout his remarkable career, Lustiger embodied two
paradoxical identities central to the privilege of Catholicism in France: the
republican cardinal and the Jewish cardinal. The aura surrounding these
two identities, like the Collège, hinged on the ambiguity between narratives of rupture and continuity. Lustiger garnered himself the reputation of
"republican cardinal" through a series of controversial acts that many saw
as the work of a radical figure, bent on transforming long-standing institutions to suit his own particular vision. Yet Lustiger also harnessed the power
of his reputation as a "prophetic" or "apostolic" figure of rupture in order
to make a case for continuity over time, aiming to reduce the narrative of
rupture with a Catholic past that orients stories of France's secularization.
Similarly, his reputation as a "Jewish cardinal"—while clearly a reference
to his own conversion from Judaism to Catholicism as an adolescent—was
powerful because of the particularly fraught nature of this mode of conversion in European Catholic history. While appearing to embody this complex expression of rupture, Lustiger also reduced the radicality of this shift,
insisting that he remained both Jewish and Catholic. He argued that his
conversion was an expression of continuity rather than change, using the
term "crystallization" to account for his dual identity.

I understand Lustiger's ability to effectively use these paradoxical identities of rupture in order to make claims of continuity as the result of a series
of curatorial efforts by a variety of actors. Lustiger was not the only one to
curate the particular relationships between the past and the present that
undergirded images of the cardinal. Rather, the choices available to him
were, in many respects, shaped by decisions that had preceded him. I bor-

row the term "curating" from the anthropologist of Christianity Joel Robbins's (2010) account of evangelical Christians' attempts to create a temporal arrangement of radical rupture. Robbins (2003, 2007) has based his call for the creation of an anthropology of Christianity in part on his critique of anthropologists' "continuity bias" that, he argues, has prevented them from taking Christian conversion seriously. For Robbins, it is in part anthropologists' penchant for seeking out continuous cultural forms that prevented them from making space for the radical ruptures many Christians, particularly in postcolonial spaces, insist separate them from their pre-Christian pasts. Robbins has also argued, however, that occupying a position of rupture is not an easy task. It does not merely occur in the mind, as an ascent to a new set of beliefs, but requires practices that repeat the sensation of rupture in tangible and material forms.[2] In his research among the Urapmin of Papua New Guinea who converted to Christianity en masse at the end of the 1970s, Robbins found that the "purity" of a position of rupture is, in fact, impossible to maintain: "A key dynamic of the break is one of at once seeking to reject the past and at the same time curating it so that its rejection can continue to motivate commitment to the event of conversion in the future. That is to say, for many Pentecostals vigilance against the past and against the still-current propensity to sin helps to steer Christian practice, and hence, breaking with the past becomes . . . a meaningfully endless process" (2010, 647).

I find the term "curating" useful in understanding Lustiger's creation and repetition of the story of the Collège. His invention was not based in cynicism but in the challenges of attempting to draw lines of continuity between two elements often perceived to be insurmountably different: the past and the present. The contrast between the claims of rupture identified by Robbins and the work of continuity I address here can in part be explained by the distinction between Protestant (and, in particular, Pentecostal) and Catholic approaches to time. As Robbins (2012) has highlighted, Pentecostals tend to see the most authentic signs of God's presence as those that are expressed spontaneously and unexpectedly, such as when someone speaks in tongues or is moved to witness the power of God in their lives. In contrast, Catholics tend to see the most authentic expressions of God's grace in the regularized, predictable rituals and objects that gain their power precisely through their direct connection to the institution of the Church that has held a continuous, unbroken linkage with the most significant moment of rupture—the Christ event—over the millennia. Rebecca Lester has described the labors of continuity thinking by exploring how Catholics learn to attribute what might be experienced as a moment of rupture as, instead, "reading the future into the past" (2003, 208). In her study of young Mexican women who choose to enter the cloistered life of a nun, she describes how "the new nuns learn to construct an understanding of their selves as continuous across different temporal spheres, alongside (and perhaps *in spite of*) certain experiences of discontinuity" (ibid., 202).

The tension between catholaïcité and secularized Catholicism that I explore throughout this book is in part driven by similar temporal debates. An understanding of France today as an expression of secularized Catholicism operates through a narrative of rupture. Whether dating that rupture to the French Revolution of 1789 or the law of separation of church and state first initiated in 1905, voices in France that celebrate (or lament) a secularized Catholicism see these as powerful moments of rupture that forever altered what was thinkable and doable. Voices that understand France to be defined by catholaïcité, on the other hand, engage in the fantasy of continuity, imagining and postulating connections and homogeneity across the longue durée (long term). I argue that neither continuity nor rupture can fully account for the complexity of the practices that are found in any given local context. Claims of continuity or rupture may best be understood as performative ideals to which to aspire, and as such they require ongoing and ever-transforming curatorial practices. Claims of continuity, however, struggle in particular with histories of violence. Maintaining narratives of moral continuity over a longue durée marred by destruction and inequality requires careful curation.[3] As the story of Lustiger's prophetic desire to bring the original project of the Collège back to life and its repetition by those around him suggests, these are labors that cannot cease. Through his persistent curatorial efforts, Lustiger pushed back against interpretations of his actions as those of rupture and insisted instead on tales of continuity. These efforts, moreover, not only emphasized his own power and charisma; they helped to reaffirm the privileged place of Catholicism in secular France.

THE REPUBLICAN CARDINAL

Cardinal Lustiger died within weeks of my first arrival in Paris in the summer of 2007. On the morning of his funeral I made my way to Notre-Dame Cathedral. As I approached the square in front of the cathedral, Place Jean-

Paul II, I was surprised by the size of the gathered crowd. Thousands of Parisians stood quietly under cloudy skies as we watched the funeral proceedings on a giant screen. While I observed the moment with interest and had carefully followed the media's focus on him in the preceding week, it was not until after I returned to Paris in the fall of 2008 that I realized just how important Lustiger would be to my research. During the two years I spent at the Collège, Lustiger's name came up often and almost never in a negative light. Many of the volunteers who worked there explained that they had been inspired to donate their time to the space in honor of Lustiger. One woman told me that her volunteer work at the Collège was the result of a promise she had made to herself when he died. Employees often made sure that visitors knew that the site was Lustiger's final project as archbishop. Taking a cue from my interlocutors, I realized I needed to learn more about the late cardinal. The more I learned, however, the more I found myself confounded by this paradoxical figure.

The French Catholic public was rather shocked by Pope John Paul II's decision to name Lustiger as archbishop of Paris in 1981. A Benedictine abbot from Normandy, Don Grammont, had been the pope's preferred candidate, but he was ill and declined to move to Paris. The vicar of Christ had to name his alternate for the position, the relatively unknown bishop of Orléans, Jean-Marie Lustiger.

Lustiger quickly made a name for himself, however, pushing through a number of institutional and cultural projects. These included the Catholic television station, KTO; Radio Notre-Dame; a diocesan website; a weekly publication entitled *Paris Notre-Dame*; a political organization that hosts monthly breakfasts for politicians; a public theology school, the École Cathédrale; and a new diocesan seminary called the Faculté Notre-Dame. A group of priests educated at the Faculté Notre-Dame came be known as "LuLu's boys" ("LuLu" being a diminutive form of a number of French names that begin with *L*), and some held important positions at the Collège while I was there. Both the Faculté Notre-Dame and the École Cathédrale came to be housed in the basement of the Collège after its renovation.

What made these acts even more impressive was that he accomplished many of them over and above the resistance of his colleagues in the Conference of Bishops of France. Through his efforts Lustiger came to be widely admired but also widely criticized. Few remained indifferent to the "bulldozer" (another of his many nicknames). Those who had the opportunity to work closely with Lustiger confessed that he was not always the easiest man with whom to work. His ideas, according to one of his assistants, once fully formed, would brook no resistance. "He was rarely open to the ideas of others," another mentioned with a surprising degree of admiration. "He was exacting and demanding of those who worked with him"; he was "hard." According to one obituary, Lustiger

> could be authoritarian, provocative, impulsive, quick-tempered, and unforgiving. He could be unfair. . . . He end-ran his own diocesan seminary by building two others. . . . And he treated the French Conference of Bishops as if it were a *parvenu* on history's stage, of no ecclesial or theological importance. His episcopal colleagues responded by never electing him president—an unheard of *gifle* [slap in the face] for a cardinal, to say nothing of the archbishop of Paris. (On the other hand, Lustiger made it very clear he could never accept, so why offer?) [Englund 2007, 12–13]

Despite these critiques, all of the voices I encountered insisted on the profound influence Lustiger's ideas and character had had on their lives and, importantly, on the life of their city. His successor as archbishop—André Vingt-Trois—was, by all accounts, a far less charismatic individual. His presence around the city was rarely remarked upon in the media and in person he appeared a quiet, unassuming man. He served, however, for several years as the president of the Conference of Bishops of France, a position requiring careful calibration of a variety of different interests. In a presentation at a colloquium devoted to Lustiger held at the Collège on December 9, 2008, his former personal secretary, Father Rougé, acknowledged that the cardinal had been an "independent" archbishop—a *franc tireur* (sharp shooter) who had often been "abrupt" with the episcopate. "Lustiger could have never served as president [of the Conference of Bishops]," one insider told me. "He had no flair for negotiation and compromise, for weighing different voices and ideas, as does Vingt-Trois. For Lustiger, there was but one voice of French Catholicism: his own."

Many of his collaborators contributed to the work of transforming these acts of rupture into those of continuity. In the guided tour of the Collège I described at the beginning of this chapter, for example, the docent used the word "intuition" to account for the impetus behind Lustiger's desire to do something at the Collège. At the colloquium, contributors lauded Lustiger's political acumen while also insisting that he did not "do politics."[4] Instead, Rougé argued, "he was too . . . besotted with proclaiming the Word of God, to mistake the register" of his language (Rougé 2010, 10). Another participant offered a contrasting view that appeared controversial in the context of the colloquium. This speaker—Dominique Wolton, a media scholar most famous in this space for having produced along with Jean-Louis Missika a lengthy autobiographical interview of the cardinal—stood out as the only one to offer a different perspective to what appeared to be the party line. Wolton insisted that Lustiger was always "doing [politics]: in Paris, in Rome, and elsewhere" (Wolton 2010, 34). Even Wolton reduced the hard edge of his claims, however, when he concluded by suggesting that Lustiger was, ultimately, a "secular man inhabited by the breath of God." At various points in Wolton's speech, members of the audience gasped audibly and clucked their tongues in disapproval.[5]

I see in this tension between Lustiger as an "authoritarian" "franc tireur" and as someone "besotted with the Word of God" or "inhabited by the breath of God" precisely the sort of curatorial work that goes into maintaining claims of continuity in the face of unexpected change. While the former terms make space for the strategic efforts of individuals in producing novel experiences and practices, the latter offset these labors onto sources outside of individual control. In so doing, they impute a coherence onto what otherwise might appear random or contingent. Continuity thinking is often aided by schema that downplay human strategy—displacing it to the work of God, providence, a transcendent concept, or human nature.[6] I want to emphasize that in pointing to this tension, I am not refusing the possibility that the Word of God motivated Lustiger's efforts as archbishop. Both accounts of the archbishop may be true. I am interested, however, in the debate that persisted—and in Lustiger's efforts to reduce the gap—between them.

Lustiger often worked to downplay the presumed gap between the "registers" of politics and Catholicism in France. In the words of his former secretary, for Lustiger "the novelty of our spiritual situation, in a secularized Christian country, with the mix of true serenity and the dramatic emptiness of this secularization, seemed to him to call for a new evangelization but also a renewed connection with political realities" (Rougé 2010, 10). In the account of another contributor to the colloquium, in light of this ambiguity between secularism and Catholicism, Lustiger took a position that, in many respects, contrasted with more conservative Catholic voices that see modern democratic forms as, in essence, moving away from the Christian message. Lustiger turned to voices such as Jacques Maritain who saw democracy as "giving political form to some of the most central truths of Christianity" (Portier 2010, 18). For Maritain, Christianity could become more itself in and through the democratic project.

Lustiger tended to emphasize the other side of this equation—that democratic norms could become their fullest selves in and through the Christian message. He insisted that the roots of the freedoms and liberties that defined democracy—including the separation of temporal and spiritual powers—were, in fact, Catholic. For Lustiger, "it was gradually, through the providential work of the centuries, that collective consciousness has opened itself to the truth of the message of Christ, from which a civilization of autonomy could arise somewhere between the seventeenth and the nineteenth centuries" (Portier 2010, 20). Similarly, at the colloquium, Monsignor Eric de Moulins-Beaufort argued that his former colleague "was very conscious that the trinity of liberty, equality, and fraternity was deeply rooted in Christian thought, and therefore in the Christianization of our country" (de Moulins-Beaufort 2010, 42). For Lustiger, the liberties associated with modernity were the truest expression of the Christian message.

With such arguments, Lustiger made a powerful case for catholaïcité in France. Asad has noted the plethora of voices that have made similar claims. Many, such as political philosopher Larry Siedontop, describe "secularization as Christianity's gift to the world," and see Christianity as "connected to its secular successor by the values of equality, freedom of choice, and conscience" (quoted in Asad 2018, 13–14). Media coverage of the life of the cardinal in the week preceding his funeral hinted, however, that a tension between Catholicism and secularism persists in France. Public reflections on his life, in fact, tended to bring these tensions to the fore. In and among numerous special editions of newspapers and magazines that celebrated his life, for example, pundits debated whether or not the president of the secular republic should cut short a trip to the United States in order to attend the funeral. What might such an act signal regarding France's laïcité?

On the morning of the service, an op-ed in *Le Figaro* quoted an adage I had not heard before: "Paris vaut bien une messe" (Paris is well worth a mass). It is originally attributed to Henry IV (1553–1610) upon his renouncement of Protestantism just ahead of his coronation as king of France in 1594. *Le Figaro* referenced the saying in order to explain why Sarkozy had indeed felt it necessary to return to Paris for Lustiger's funeral. "[Sarkozy] decided that he couldn't not be present for the funeral of the most famous French cardinal. 'He decided that his absence was incompatible with the role he intends to play with regard to religions in France, especially Catholics,' explained a government minister" (Jaigu 2007, 6).

Interestingly, a variation on this phrase arose surrounding the funeral of another important figure in France in the late twentieth century. Ahead of his death in 1995, the Socialist president François Mitterrand had declared, "Une messe est possible" (A mass is possible). Following this rather ambiguous declaration, just as with the presidents who had most recently died before him—Charles de Gaulle and Georges Pompidou—Mitterrand was given a double Catholic funeral, a public one at Notre-Dame (presided over by Lustiger) and a private one in a church in his home commune of Jarnac. This model had not proved the least bit controversial when applied to de Gaulle and Pompidou, but a great deal of hand-wringing accompanied its use with the first Socialist president of the Fifth Republic. While committed Catholics protested that a well-known agnostic should not benefit from the ritual of mass at his death, committed secularists lamented that the principle of separation of church and state was being buried along with him. In her rich analysis of the event, Danièle Hervieu-Léger argues that this debate displayed a fascinating paradox in which contradictory evaluations of a "deficit of Catholicism" (on the part of the president) and an "excess of Catholicism" (in the rituals of the state) reigned (1996, 24). This convergence between a deficit and an excess of Catholicism, to my mind, speaks again to the power of banality, of Catholicism's ability to move flexibly between the background and the foreground depending, in part, on the perspective of the beholder. For Hervieu-Léger, these funerals, while appearing to point to the ongoing power of Catholicism in France, in fact highlighted the limits of the Church's power. "The 'Catholic monopolization' supposed in the funerals," she argues, "could only be . . . the paradoxical symptom of the formidable secularization of the French religious landscape" (ibid., 29).

Here, Hervieu-Léger, as in much of her work (see, for example, her 2001 book *Religion as a Chain of Memory*), interprets contemporary events through the framework of secularized Catholicism. Catholic rituals may remain, but they have been forever altered through secularization. The revival of a sixteenth-century phrase—"Paris is well worth a mass"—in order to explain Sarkozy's decision to attend the funeral of Lustiger, however, suggests that the alternative interpretation of contemporary France—one that emphasizes the power of catholaïcité—is also possible. If, in the sixteenth century, at the height of violence between Huguenots and Catholics, Paris deserved a king who would attend a Catholic mass (rather than a Protestant service), it seemed that in the twenty-first century the city deserved a president who would attend the funeral mass of the archbishop.

Asad has argued that the effect of "secularists claiming a Christian heritage" is "the political exclusion of all those who cannot claim that heritage" (2018, 14). It would seem that Catholics making similar claims produce similar effects. The article in *Le Figaro* went on to acknowledge that the leader of France and the leader of France's Catholics had often disagreed.

> Nicolas Sarkozy had often battled with Monsignor Lustiger. For the former archbishop of Paris, the former Minister of the Interior and of Religions made too large a place for Islam in France, helping it to develop through the means of the state. He had reproached Nicolas Sarkozy for making it "a state religion," instead of defending the thousand-year-old tradition of Christianity in France. But Nicolas Sarkozy redeemed himself during his campaign for the presidency. Where he affirmed, on numerous occasions, that Christianity "participates in an essential manner in the national identity." [Jaigu 2007, 6]

Lustiger knew well the powerful role of state support in curating religious affordances in the national landscape. The French state's efforts have been central to the reproduction of Catholic privilege in France. His account of catholaïcité, however, deemed any space made for Islam in French public life a movement away from the "essential manner" of France's national identity.[7]

These concerns were evident when, in 2003, Lustiger addressed the Stasi Commission charged with addressing the so-called "crisis" of laïcité in France at the time.[8] Despite its numerous recommendations—many of which, such as the incorporation of holidays associated with other religions into the French republican calendar, may have helped to address the inequalities that accompany Catholicism's privileged banality—the government took up only one: the ban on headscarves in French public schools. Lustiger discouraged the members of the commission from taking up the headscarf ban, but his suggestion was not made in the interest of creating a more inclusive public sphere. A full transcript of his remarks appears as the concluding piece in the publication of the proceedings of the colloquium devoted to him at the Collège under the title "Our Laïcité." The title accurately conveys the curatorial efforts he engaged in during his speech. He insisted upon the essential link between Catholicism and secularism in France, while powerfully refusing Islam any place within it.

Lustiger began with a short history lesson, reminding the committee that the term most commonly used to designate "religion" in France— culte—does not "designate an abstract or general notion, likely to integrate any given content, but fundamentally Catholicism, the model upon which Protestantism and Judaism were restructured" in France under Napoleon's concordat that aimed primarily to reestablish the relationship between the

Catholic Church and the state following the revolution (Lustiger 2010, 159). The Catholicization of Judaism under Napoléon I described in the introduction is certainly in line with this account. In the words of Lustiger, it was "a secularized and nationally institutionalized Catholicism that, in the thinking of the Emperor, served as the juridical model for all religions" (ibid.). Because Catholics initially resisted a key component of the 1905 law—the formation of *associations cultuelles* (religious associations)—at the behest of Pope Pius X, Lustiger argued that the laws of laïcité came more fully into effect only with the 1923 compromise that created a solution more agreeable to "both parties."[9] For Lustiger, "it was in this manner" of back and forth between republican and Catholic voices that "bit by bit the law of 1905, with the agreements of 1923, was codified and recognized as it would appear to us today as the foundation of the 'French compromise'" (ibid., 161).

Here, Lustiger made a fairly straightforward argument for catholaïcité. Rather than the ultimate expression of the rupture between church and state, laïcité is instead forged both by making Catholicism into a model for other religions and through an ongoing series of compromises between the state and the Catholic Church. Some religions—such as Judaism and Protestantism—are partially incorporated into this history through their "Catholicization." Notably absent from this partial incorporation, however, is Islam. Lustiger continued by insisting that "no matter what, for our part [presumably, here he is speaking on behalf of the French Catholic Church] we think that we must not touch this compromise. I see that the most wise and informed republican forces take the same position. Because touching this equilibrium would challenge, with unpredictable consequences, that which today constitutes the unity and identity of France" (ibid., 165). To add a law banning headscarves, in other words, would bring Islam—even as adversary—into the compromise that, according to Lustiger, has heretofore been defined by an ongoing conversation between Catholicism and the French state.

In case his meaning was unclear, Lustiger went on to invoke demographic fears that underscore many Islamophobic visions of France and Europe. "As for immigration, that which will change everything is still to come. This immigration is already more enormous than one thinks one can tolerate, but . . . it will undoubtedly amplify in the next twenty or thirty years." And while he discouraged politicians from using xenophobia and racism as political tools, he added that "no *limes* could ever prevent the large movements of populations" (ibid., 167). A footnote explains that a "*limes*" is a fortified wall built to prevent "barbarians" from entering the Roman Empire.

As he moved toward his conclusion, Lustiger went so far as to argue that the state is completely "disoriented" in the face of Islam because none of the "earlier" groups of migrants proved so resistant to "integration." He then made his call for the exclusion of Islam from the "essential character" of France all the more explicit: "Islam alone can reform Islam. Or Muslims alone can reform their religion. Our country can supply them the conditions for this evolution, if they want it. Therefore, we must remain on our own terrain, with the rules that we have fixed, without all of a sudden putting in place a new religious politics for which we have neither the experience nor the juridical tools, and which could . . . destroy our interior equilibrium" (2010, 170). With this disturbing conclusion, Lustiger made two curatorial moves. First, through the persistent use of the third-person plural, Lustiger drew powerful lines of inclusion and exclusion. For Lustiger, Islam remains and should remain outside of the history of catholaïcité; France can merely supply the "conditions" for the "evolution" that Islam must undergo "alone." Second, he warned the commission against the risks of radical rupture. If laïcité has been formed slowly over time in conversation with Catholicism, Lustiger argued, then to insert Islam into this ongoing conversation would mean transforming laïcité in potentially destabilizing ways. Instead, he insisted, "we must sufficiently believe in the strength of our civilization and our culture, not through chauvinism but through trust in reason and humanity—confidence in the fundamental ground of human rights, the dignity of the person, respect for liberties and the common good, public order and the rule of law that exist in this country" (ibid., 171).

It is remarkable here to see Lustiger so effectively using the language of secular republicanism in France to make a case for catholaïcité, the privileged banality of Catholicism in France, and the denigrated place of Islam. In the early twentieth century Carl Schmitt (1922 [1987]) famously argued that many of the transcendent ideals that inform the sovereignty of modern nation-states were secular transformations of Christian means of mediating access to God. For Lustiger, these secular ideals could also serve as effective allies in underscoring Catholicism's privileged and unquestioned place in France and in Europe.

While continuity thinking is clearly deeply imbricated within Catholic practice, it is also powerfully present in the work of nationalism.[10] Another way in which Lustiger put his identity of rupture to the service of claims of continuity was precisely through the articulation of nationalist visions. In an article published in *Paris Match* at the time of his death, for example, the cardinal was described as "a 'model' of the secular school, viscerally republican and proud to be French" (Pigozzi 2007, 45). Lustiger's curatorial efforts—as his contributions to the Stasi Commission make clear—aimed at linking the continuity of the nation to that of the French Catholic Church. In an op-ed Lustiger published in the centrist paper *Le Monde* in 1996 he declared that "there is not a France born at the baptism of Clovis and another France born at the victory of Valmy. Clovis and Valmy belong to the memory of everyone, and everyone can claim them" (Lustiger 2007, 11).

Selective memory is key to the curatorial work of continuity and rupture alike. In this example of selective remembering, Lustiger offered up a model of continuity thinking over the longue durée that contrasted with a similar and widely cited claim made by French historian Ernest Renan, a key figure in secular republican thought.[11] In his account of the curatorial efforts necessary to the production of the nation over the longue durée, Renan emphasized the importance of selective *forgetting* in the creation and reproduction of nations: "The act of forgetting, I would even say, historical error is an essential factor in the creation of the nation, which is why progress in historical studies often constitutes a danger for nationality. Indeed, historical enquiry brings back to light the deeds of violence that took place at the origin of all political formations, even those whose consequences have been the most beneficial" (2018 [1882], 251). Originally delivered as a talk at the Sorbonne in 1882, Renan's "What Is a Nation?" overlaps and contrasts with Lustiger's curatorial efforts in significant ways. For Renan, "no French citizen knows whether he is a Burgundian, an Alan, a Taifal, or a Visigoth; every French citizen has forgotten the St. Bartholomew's Day massacre, the massacres that took place in the Midi in the thirteenth century" (ibid.). Here, Renan referenced two moments of potential dismantling of the nation: a day of horrific violence on August 24, 1572 when up to 30,000 Protestants were killed by Catholic groups and the horrific Albigensian crusade against the Cathars from 1209–1229.

In each of these accounts, Lustiger and Renan take up examples that, if remembered or forgotten, would aid in forging the nation of France. Lustiger described two narratives of the "birth" of France, one dating back to the baptism of King Clovis at the end of the fifth century and the other dating to a victory by the French revolutionary guard against Prussian troops attempting to enter Paris in 1792.[12] In so doing, he takes France's most powerful claim of rupture and of movement away from Catholicism—the Revolution—and makes it contiguous with the rupture that had Catholicized the region centuries earlier. Moreover, in creating such a perfect parallel to Renan's critique, Lustiger once again displayed his prowess as a republican cardinal.[13]

Through these curatorial efforts, he transformed events of rupture into those of continuity, arguing that the source of France's continuity was, in fact, its Catholicism.

THE JEWISH CARDINAL

As my exploration of Lustiger's archives reveal, narratives that insist upon continuity inevitably leave traces of rupture and disconnection. Acknowledging these moments of rupture is particularly fraught in the case of Lustiger because doing so potentially disrupts another of his curatorial efforts: his account of his conversion to Catholicism. Throughout his life—despite protests from the Jewish community and from many Catholics—Lustiger insisted that he renounced nothing in being baptized and that he was simultaneously Jewish *and* Catholic. In an interesting parallel to the choice of the term "renaissance" to describe the Collège, Lustiger saw his baptism not as an act of conversion but as one of "crystallization." His Jewishness, which had been "given to him by his parents and by God" could not be lost (Duchesne 2010, 10). In a 1982 interview in an Israeli daily newspaper, Lustiger described the reasoning he had offered to his distraught parents to explain this process of crystallization. "I said to them, 'I am not leaving you. I'm not going over to the enemy. I am becoming what I am. I am not ceasing to be a Jew; on the contrary, I am discovering another way of being a Jew.' I know that Jewish people think that's a scandalous way to talk, but that's what I experienced" (ibid., 11). So significant was this blended identity for the cardinal that he requested that upon his death the following epitaph be displayed in the Notre-Dame Cathedral:

> I was born Jewish.
> I received the name
> Of my paternal grandfather, Aaron
> Having become Christian
> By faith and by Baptism,
> I have remained Jewish
> As did the Apostles

Partway through *The Jewish Cardinal*, a French biopic celebrating his life (Cohen 2013), Lustiger visits his dying father to find him quietly chuckling.

The film depicts their relationship as fraught, and it is the first time the father has been shown smiling. Lustiger inquires as to what is so funny, and his father explains that he is laughing at the joke that is currently circulating about his son. "Do you know why the new chief rabbi is Sephardic?" the father begins.[14] "No, why?" Lustiger responds. "Because the archbishop is Ashkenazi." They both laugh. The film is filled with many such unsettling jokes. While the biopic clearly cannot be mistaken for a transcript of the life of the cardinal, it offers fascinating insight into the popular image of Lustiger and his legacy in France in the twenty-first century.

As the joke and the film's title suggests, the biopic explores the second key paradox that Lustiger maintained throughout his life. The French title—*Le Métis de Dieu*—makes the paradox even more explicit. A direct translation might be rendered as "God's Mongrel," implying that Lustiger was of "mixed race." The term "métis" brings to mind colonial fears of miscegenation and nineteenth-century race science.[15] Born to Polish Jewish immigrant parents in Paris, Aaron Lustiger announced his intention to be baptized Catholic, along with his younger sister, at the age of fourteen. The year was 1940 and his parents, Charles and Gisèle, had sent Aaron and his sister to live with a Catholic family in Orléans to protect them from the Nazi occupation and French collaboration. In 1942, Gisèle was betrayed by a neighbor in Paris, sent to Drancy, and, in the following year, killed at Auschwitz.

For many French Jews, Lustiger's insistence that he was both Jewish and Catholic was untenable. The biopic offers a scene in which their concerns are articulated. The incoming chief rabbi accompanies his soon-to-be predecessor to meet Lustiger following his appointment as archbishop. The exiting rabbi explains that he did not want to "quit public life without asking you, on behalf of our community to stop proclaiming yourself Jewish and Christian in every interview." An awkward silence follows. "One is either Christian or Jewish, Monsignor. Not both" the rabbi insists. Lustiger takes offense, explaining that he will not deny his ancestors merely to please the rabbi. After an emotional exchange, the retiring rabbi departs and Lustiger turns with warmer words to the incoming leader of France's Jewish communities to confirm that he is indeed the first Sephardic chief rabbi of France. Riffing on the film's earlier joke, he explains, "I am the first Jewish Cardinal of France. As pioneers, I hope we'll get along." Rabbi Sirat smiles and responds that, while he's sure that they will get along, "I don't think you're a pioneer. I'd say an exception instead."

Many Catholics were also made uneasy by Lustiger's refusal to renounce his Jewishness. In the words of one rabbi I met in Paris who was engaging in a series of Catholic-Jewish dialogues, "for Jews, Christianity is not a theological problem. For Christians, Judaism is a theological problem for the Christian world. That is to say, the survival of Judaism appears as a theological problem, a question." He described how, traditionally, Catholics have referred to the "mystery of Israel" or the "Jewish question," demonstrating how—given their assumption that Christianity "accomplished" the prophecies of Judaism—Christians have struggled with the ongoing presence of Jews.

According to numerous scholars of Christianity and Judaism, the "problem" posed by Judaism within Christianity more particularly dates to the decision by early Church leaders to claim (portions of) the Hebrew Bible as their own. In so doing, in Englund's (2014) words, "the church condemned herself to an ongoing, conflicted internal dialogue with 'Judaism,' whose fundamental purpose was to defend and illustrate the Christian appropriation not only of Hebrew texts (Torah and the prophets) but also of many central Jewish theological concepts: 'God,' 'Israel,' 'messiah,' the end of days, and on and on. Indeed, it became standard Christian procedure to state the *invalidity* of these concepts in the forms they took in Judaism." Paula Fredriksen (2002) demonstrates in more precise and nuanced terms how, as Christianity shifted from another sect of Second Temple Judaism to a distinct religion, a variety of ways of relating to Second Temple Judaism remained open. Some Christian apologists, such as Valentinus (100–160) and Marcion of Sinope (85–160), rejected or reduced the significance of the Hebrew Bible and its God for Christians. The ideas of the second-century thinkers (such as Justin Martyr [100–165], Tertullian [155–220], and Irenaeus [130–202]) that would emerge victorious in the fourth century when such debates were violently closed down, however, took the Hebrew Bible and its God as a Christian text and God, and insisted that Jews had done wrong by both.

Like all accounts of the relationship between the past and the present, this mode of supersessionist appropriation has required curatorial efforts throughout history, leading to the integration of anti-Jewish claims into numerous Christian texts, prayers, and practices over the centuries. Englund points to David Nirenberg's (2013) work that painstakingly reveals the layers of "anti-Jewish myths" written not only into Christian thought but also into philosophical texts from the Enlightenment onward. The effective erasure of such practices is apparent in the way many Christians today are unaware of the Jewish origins of numerous Christian concepts. At one conference devoted to the idea of salvation in Catholicism and Judaism I attended at the Collège in 2010, one Jewish thinker had to continually correct a Catholic theologian who kept insisting upon the uniqueness of Christianity. Again and again, the Jewish thinker would clarify for the audience that the ideas taken to be distinctly Christian had a long history in Judaism prior to the life of the Jesus.

Thus, when Lustiger argued that Judaism and Catholicism could continue to comingle not only alongside one another but also within himself—no less than the leader of the French Catholic Church—he continued centuries of curatorial efforts that had gone into the supersessionist appropriation of Judaism. Most recently, his Judeo-Catholic identity might be understood in light of the local history of Catholic philo-Semitism in Paris. The Catholic Renewal of the interwar period not only turned to various Catholic mystical and artistic traditions to reimagine the present, it also glorified suffering as a means to overcome the deadening rationality of modern secularity. Jews and Judaism provided a model for this suffering, particularly for a subset of Catholic converts from Judaism who participated in the Renewal. Moore (2013) has offered a powerful assessment of the potentially radical nature of the new tradition forged by these converts. Her account focuses on a key figure in this movement, Raïssa Maritain (the wife of Jacques Maritain), who converted to Catholicism from Judaism along with her sister Vera and her husband (who had been Protestant) in 1906. Moore demonstrates how Maritain saw suffering Jews as models for the agonized Catholicism she so cherished. The symbol of the suffering Jew, Moore acknowledges, "is one of the most obviously problematic and complicated legacies of the revival, trafficking in essentialism and stereotype, valorizing suffering instead of his-toricizing and analyzing it and working to eradicate it. It requires historically oppressed communities to bear the symbolic weight of human anxiety about finitude and suffering" (2013, 13).

Despite this clearly problematic relationship with Judaism, given the context of genocidal violence, this group did offer a radical alternative in important ways. While many anti-Semitic writings of the time made use of the stereotype of the Jew as an arch capitalist, unassimilable into European nations, Maritain and others in the Renewal offered up an important alter-native to the claims of Jews as irredeemably other increasingly made by both fascist and democratic voices during the period. What is more, Moore argues, the group was united by their stridently antibourgeois stance. Choosing to live lives of austere simplicity, participants in these artistic, intellectual, and cultural circles offered critiques of wealth, inequality, and the isolation of domestic, bourgeois spaces. In this respect, Lustiger departed significantly from the politics of the Catholic Renewal. While he offered another example of conversion from Judaism to Catholicism that continued to uphold Judaism as a positive model, his embrace of the wealth that permeates the Catholic Church in Paris was central to his tenure as archbishop.[16]

For his part, Lustiger described his conversion not as part of a Catholic philo-Semitic heritage but—as is the case in numerous conversion narratives—as a highly individuated moment of discovery. Lustiger's parents had immigrated to France during the 1920s.[17] Many Eastern European Jews at the time saw France as a safe haven. In the words of Raïssa Maritain to a close friend in 1938 in the face of public pronouncements of anti-Semitism, "'that such abominations can be thought and uttered in France—it is not possible to be comforted. I confess, I have the strongest desire to leave, because if injustice is everywhere in the world, here in France, it is more intolerable than elsewhere, because we've put too much hope in this country'" (quoted in Bensoussan 2010, 6). The widespread anti-Semitism in France at the time of the Holocaust casts doubt on Lustiger's account of his conversion-as-crystallization. The fact that his twelve-year-old sister also decided to convert along with him while both were living in hiding with a Catholic family further complicates the power dynamics entailed in his narrative. That Lustiger's sister was generally absent from public discourses regarding him—and, indeed, he is not even depicted as having a sister in the biopic—highlights the powerful ways in which she troubles his account of his crystallization.

While the European Holocaust is widely seen as a rupture that inspired a significant transformation in Catholicism's relationship to Judaism, in *From Enemy to Brother*, John Connelly provides a history of this shift in ways that pay heed to the contingent, winding, and unwieldy efforts that mark rupture and continuity alike. The major figures in the debates that led to the formation of *Nostra Aetate* (In Our Time)—the Vatican II document seen as the ultimate expression of Catholic reconciliation toward Jews—were, in fact, very particular Catholic figures. "From the 1840s until 1965, virtually every activist and thinker who worked for Catholic-Jewish reconciliation was not originally Catholic. Most were born Jewish. *Without converts the Catholic Church would not have found a new language to speak to the Jews after the Holocaust*" (Connelly 2012, 5, emphasis in original). Changes in the Church's relationship with Jews were the result of the efforts of Catholic converts who had themselves suffered the effects of the Church's anti-Judaism. Rather than a radical rupture following the horrors of the Holocaust, Catholic attempts to forge a new relationship to Judaism arose out of the ongoing efforts of converts who forcefully transformed an institution that had shown little interest in such changes only a few decades earlier.[18]

Connelly argues against interpretations of nineteenth- and twentieth-century anti-Semitism as a new, racist, secular expression of hatred entirely divorced from the Christian anti-Judaism that preceded it. Many who make this argument do so by taking for granted the retreating power and significance of Christianity during this period. While scientific racism certainly contributed another layer to anti-Jewish thought, "religious forms of Jew hatred did not disappear" (ibid., 8). I depart from Connelly, however, in his suggestion that secular racism was more open to re-analysis than Christian anti-Judaism, because "religion is not about grounding in fact. Christians believe in 'things not seen'" (ibid.). Karen and Barbara Fields (2014) have developed the concept of "racecraft" to demonstrate how folk categories of race—whether secular or religious—operate as "invisible ontologies" that, while based on purportedly visible characteristics, take their meaning in connecting these visible signs to invisible traits. Furthermore, they argue that racecraft repeatedly proves impervious to re-analysis, no matter the evidence offered to counter it.

These debates point to the ambiguity between continuity and rupture in addressing the history of anti-Semitism in Europe. Can its ongoing presence be seen as the continuous expression of an anti-Judaism woven into the very fabric of Christianity? Does the so-called scientific articulation of anti-Semitism reflect the power of catholaïcité, in which Christian concepts continue to undergird secular thought? Did *Nostra Aetate* indeed move Catholicism away from its anti-Judaism? Have European secular states overcome their "scientific" or "racist" expressions of anti-Semitism?

Lustiger's curatorial work in this regard both emphasized continuity over time and downplayed any essential connection between Christianity and anti-Judaism. In the biopic, when Lustiger learns that he has been appointed archbishop of Paris, Lustiger shakes his head in astonishment and declares: "It's as if the crucifix had suddenly put on the yellow star." Remarkably, these words are not liberties taken by a filmmaker. Lustiger uttered the phrase on numerous occasions. In an article in the daily tabloid newspaper *Le Parisien* published following his death, the phrase is described as a personal "slogan" (Baverel 2007). I first encountered it in the opening pages of Lustiger's interview-biography *The Choice of God*. The interviewers explain their interest in the cardinal as stemming from this phrase: "From where did the desire to know more of this man arise? From a phrase caught in the air from a television news program: 'it's as if the crucifixes began to wear the yellow star'" (Lustiger 1987, 11).

In the same 1982 interview with the Israeli newspaper cited above, the journalist also took note of how extraordinary the phrase was. He wondered if Lustiger might repeat it again in the interview. Lustiger demurred, suggesting it would "hardly add anything." The journalist then attempted to make sense of the bizarre phrase. "By that remark you were paying homage to the Jews who were persecuted and who had to wear the yellow star?" (Duchesne 2010, 29). In response to the reporter's prompting, Lustiger replied, "Yes, in spite of themselves and without knowing it, they became the image of innocence in this world. . . . Since they were persecuted unjustly, they bore the figure of innocence and right. Some people deny what happened, the concentration camps, and so on. By doing that, they not only reveal their bad conscience but also their secret desire to deny innocence and to avert attention from it" (ibid.). Lustiger's words do little to clarify what it means for a crucifix to wear this sign of innocence and innocent suffering. Is it possible that, with this phrase, Lustiger attempted to call attention to the role of Christianity in Jewish suffering? Such a reading becomes unlikely given Lustiger's response to the journalist's next question as to whether or not the Catholic Church has "a moral obligation toward the Jewish people." "Of course," Lustiger replied. "But I have always felt like that, and so would anyone, I think. . . . I would add that every time there has been persecution of the Jews, there has also been rejection of Christianity" (ibid.). Here, we see how claims to continuity—the persistence of a "true" Christianity over and above its violent regressions—can effectively diminish the significance of violence and overlook the actions of many key figures within the European Roman Catholic Church throughout its history. The "innocent" suffering of Christianity conveyed in the crucifix does not bear the blame for anti-Semitism or for violence against Jews.

This is not to suggest that Lustiger did not struggle with the violence of the history of Christian anti-Judaism. In a review of Connelly's *From Enemy to Brother*, Steven Englund recounted numerous conversations he had with the cardinal in which Lustiger lamented that "the church, over her two thousand years, had treated the Jews in such a way—including praying for their conversion—as to make Jesus's message all but unhearable to his own people, and virtually guaranteeing that they would stay insulated against it, and against him" (Englund 2014). Even in his laments, however, Lustiger maintained his supersessionist assumptions, finding the Church's anti-Judaism reprehensible because it prevented Jews from hearing the message of one of "their own" and thereby implying that, without Christian anti-Judaism, more Jews would have converted to Catholicism.

In his role as archbishop Lustiger tended to favor theological rather than historical interpretations of Catholic anti-Judaism. For example, in the interview biography with Missika and Wolton, Lustiger declared that "if the Jews are the object of a particular persecution, it is not only because Christians elaborated a particular polemic regarding them, it is because they carry in them the most sacred and the least bearable: the surety of divine election. That is why anti-Semitism cannot be completely assimilated with racism or xenophobia. It is one of the most serious spiritual stakes of history" (Lustiger 1987, 109). To suggest that anti-Semitism is rooted primarily in the question of divine election is a remarkable claim of continuity and one that downplays the political, historical, and violent efforts that have been necessary for its production and reproduction over the centuries.

I encountered an explicit critique of Christian anti-Judaism in the summer of 2010 when I attended a lecture at the Museum of the Memorial of the Shoah in Paris. The title of the panel discussion that night was taken from a special issue of the museum's journal that had just been published: "French Catholics and Protestants after the Shoah" (Delmaire and Bensoussan, eds., 2010). The auditorium was filled to about half capacity and stacks of the very thick journal sat for sale on a table off to the side. I picked up a copy and immediately recognized Cardinal Lustiger on the cover. He stands in his bishop's robes, a small covering on his head, hands awkwardly folded below his chin. It is similar to the photograph of him that graces the cover of *The Choice of God*. Here, though, he stands in front of the electric fences and factory-style buildings of Auschwitz.

I had heard mention of Lustiger's visit to the former concentration camp but never seen an image of it before.[19] The picture is arresting. The dark and dramatic folds of the archbishop's vestments stand in sharp contrast to the grassy field filled with weeds below him. It is an incongruous image, and one that calls to mind the history of the Catholic Church's role in contributing to Europe's attempt to rid the world of its "Jewish problem." What is particularly interesting about the choice of this picture for the cover is that Lustiger is mentioned only a few times throughout the many essays found within. The choice suggests that the image is one that is emblematic of attempts by Christians and French citizens to come to terms with the Shoah.

At the conference that night, three historians worked to counter some of the myths surrounding the deportation of Jews in France under Vichy. One point they returned to frequently was that it was Jewish organizations and individuals who worked to find ways to hide one another when it became clear that the Vichy government was willing to collaborate with the Nazi regime. It was often Jewish resistance groups, in fact, who provided money to the Christian families who came to be known *les justes* (the righteous). The second point that the evening's speakers emphasized was that Protestants were overrepresented among les justes relative to their small share of the French population. The explanation offered for this disparity was not that Protestants were more ethical than Catholics but that, in the context of France, Protestants also knew something of the experience of religious oppression and, therefore, were more likely to be sympathetic to their Jewish compatriots.

The discussion was both rich in terms of historical detail and enlightening in its analysis of the material. The scholars chose their words carefully; they spoke respectfully and with appropriately reflective tones. In this regard, it contrasted sharply with many of the debates and lectures I witnessed at the Collège, such as the debate on religious clothing. The conversation continued until late into the evening. It was nearly eleven o'clock when the moderator concluded the discussion and members of the audience rose to gather their belongings. We were stopped in our tracks, however, when one elderly man stood, his hand raised, asking to be given the chance to speak. Employees at the Collège, at times, held their breath when members of this generation would stand to speak at conferences and colloquia, fearing that their words might diminish the sophisticated atmosphere they worked hard to create. Here, at the Museum of the Memorial of the Shoah, however, deference seemed to be offered to those who had been alive during the events at the core of the institution's foundation and memory. The man's hands shook slightly as he thanked the speakers for their important research. The pitch of his voice altered when he expressed his curiosity as to why they had not confronted the larger question of the role of Christianity in the Shoah. He pointed out that the Nazis had not invented anti-Semitism and that it had been found in Christianity long before then. His next words surprised me when he explained that he was tired of seeing images of the cross. It was everywhere, he insisted, and he wondered why people didn't spend more time talking about what role it played in what had been discussed at the museum that night.

A few people in the audience applauded in response to the man's words. The moderator thanked the man for his thoughts but also attempted to defuse the critique. He reminded the man that anti-Semitism and Christianity were not identical and that the evening's discussion had revealed how many Christians had played important roles in countering the actions of the Vichy government and the Nazis. The conference had not been easy and the burden of the discussion hung in such a way as to make the man's questions feel like more than the room, collectively, could bear to confront late at night in the slowly emptying auditorium. However, his words continued to reverberate in my mind for months following the lecture. His question— Why must he look at the cross all the time?—struck me as a searing critique of the privilege of Catholic materiality in France. It asked why Catholic signs and institutions were able to escape confrontation with the historical acts of violence in which they had participated, and why they continued to maintain their privileged space despite this history.

The man's powerful questions pointed to another expression of privilege: the insistence upon the righteousness of signs that may, in fact, be viewed very differently by those against whom they have been used to enact great harm. Critiques of material expressions of privilege have gained some traction in the United States in recent years, as African Americans and Indigenous peoples have demanded the removal of statues glorifying civil war "heroes" and colonial "settlers" from the public sphere. The crucifix is clearly a more complex and multivalent symbol than many of these statues. However, as I explored in an analysis of the 2010 European Court of Human Rights (ECtHR) decision in *Lautsi v. Italy* (see Oliphant 2012), its underdetermined nature allows it to be used in the forging of a variety of political claims. One lower Italian administrative court that encountered this case— which addressed the legality of hanging crucifixes in Italian public-school classrooms—before it arrived at the ECtHR offered an extraordinary summation of Christian history. The judge claimed that "with the benefit of hindsight, it is easy to identify in the constant central core of Christian faith, despite the inquisition, despite anti-Semitism and despite the crusades, the principles of human dignity, tolerance and freedom, including religious freedom, and therefore, in the last analysis, the foundations of the secular State" (*Lautsi v. Italy*, The Facts, I. 15. 11.6).

With jarring audacity, this account foregrounded three historical reasons why the crucifix may be read as a symbol of violence, while simultaneously insisting upon the ease with which it stands for the tolerance presumed to be at the foundation of Europe's secularism. The judge managed to both call attention to and deny the legitimacy of the history of violence that the crucifix symbolizes for some of its viewers. As in the debate around religious clothing at the Collège, Catholic materiality can be summoned to support the privilege of Catholicism through encouragement—such as emphasizing the crucifix's "tolerance." Doing so, however, often requires overlooking or dismissing the exclusions and violence suffered by those who do not engage with these material forms in their banality.[20]

Since at least the third century, Catholic writings and doctrine have depicted Jewish suffering in this world as punishment for the rejection of Christ. Furthermore, institutions and practices from the parish to the papacy contributed to the maintenance of Jewish destitution (Connelly 2012, 2). In Europe the cross has long stood as a powerful symbol not only of the supersessionist appropriation of Jewish concepts and the effacement of that supersessionist appropriation but also of the actions, practices, and laws that had violently excluded Jews to the margins of social life over the centuries.[21]

The power of Catholic materiality also plays a significant role in Lustiger's account of his conversion in *The Choice of God*. In contrast to the archivist who accepted Lustiger's narratives, interviewers Missika and Wolton pushed Lustiger to account for his sudden desire to convert while hidden with a Catholic family under the Vichy regime. For a "little Parisian," responded Lustiger, Orléans was a "garden" in which he "shared everyday existence with convinced Christians. They knew perfectly well that we [Lustiger and his sister] were Jewish and showed, in my view, an exemplary discretion regarding us" (1987, 54). Thus, he insisted, it was without any pressure from the family with whom he lived that one day

> I entered the cathedral that was on the daily route to high school. At the center of a square . . . an enormous edifice, of a bare and austere beauty, always under repair. I entered on a day that I now know to be Holy Thursday. I stopped at the southern transept where there glowed an abundance of flowers and light. I stayed for a long moment, transfixed. I didn't know why I was there, nor why things were happening as they were inside of me. . . . The next day I returned to the cathedral. I wanted to see this place again. The church was empty. Spiritually empty also. I underwent the proof of this emptiness: I didn't know it was Good Friday. I can only describe the materiality of things, and at this moment I thought: I want to be baptized. [ibid., 56]

Given that Lustiger's sister joined him in his decision to be baptized against their parents' wishes, the interviewers felt compelled to push him further and pointed to the possibility of proselytism. "You insist a lot," Missika noted, "and I can understand why, on the fact that there had been no proselytism in the home in which you were welcomed. . . . Isn't successful proselytism exactly the one which is forgotten?" (ibid., 60). In response, Lustiger refused to budge, as was the case throughout his life.

While Lustiger downplayed the explicit proselytism he likely encountered in the home in which he and his sister had been placed, he nonetheless acknowledged the implicit proselytism made possible by his repeated exposure to Catholic materiality in France. His story points to the potential effects of the curatorial efforts that preceded him. It was his daily walk to school as a child in Orléans—like the daily walks past the Collège he would one day claim to make as chaplain in Paris—that allowed him to admire the cathedral again and again. Like the proselytism so effective that it is immediately forgotten, the infrastructure of Catholicism permeates the French landscape in ways that appear natural. Monumental edifices recede into the routines of daily life, but in particularly fraught and difficult moments—such as when two young adolescents are separated from their family and home during a time of war, deprivation, and violence—they may suddenly move to the foreground and beckon one to enter.

The ubiquity of Catholic symbols does a great deal of work in limiting and framing what is considered normative and desirable in France. In *The Choice of God*, Lustiger offers up another memory that "shows," in his words, "the strange relationship between a young Jewish child and Christianity" (ibid., 29).

> The scene appears bizarre to me today, because I am incapable of recovering the sequence that could explain it. We were on summer vacation, at the seaside in Brittany. My mother had let us go, me and my sister, in a little tranquil creek where few people passed. There was very fine sand there. I entertained myself—really, I do not know why—by making crucifixes of sand and I had drawn a banner above on which I had marked INRI, but I didn't know why![22] I did not know, I assure you, what I was doing represented. A woman passed with a little boy; the little boy approached, looked and asked his mother: "What did he write there? Why did he write that?" And the woman replied with a strange, stupid remark: "INRI, because his name is Henri." [ibid., 29–30.]

This odd tale becomes legible in light of the proselytizing effects of Catholicism's privileged banality in France. The way Catholic symbols bubble up into Lustiger's childhood consciousness evocatively displays how they permeate everyday life in France. Children who do not attend church and whose families are not Catholic are, nonetheless, exposed to signs whose meanings may be unclear, but whose power and significance are palpable. The woman's response to his drawing in the sand, moreover, suggests that those who are, perhaps, more familiar with such symbols are no more cognizant of all of their connotations.

In the story above, Lustiger's sister is, once again, only briefly mentioned. As was frequently the case, she barely registers in his recollections from childhood. She plays a complex role in his account of conversion-as-crystallization, given that her conversion provides further evidence of explicit proselytism. Equally powerful however, was how Lustiger proved susceptible to the implicit proselytism of the curatorial work that had preceded him. Certainly, the power of Christian materiality is not determinative. Many pass by France's tens of thousands of churches without feeling compelled to convert to Catholicism. But Lustiger's conversion is made palatable precisely by the way in which it displaces the act of proselytism from the family with whom he lived to the landscapes he inhabited, naturalizing his transformation from Judaism to Catholicism as the result of his ability to recognize the "essential" role Catholicism plays within the French nation. As a Jewish child of immigrants, Lustiger appeared to understand one clear path to fully inhabiting the nation of France, of occupying the "we" in "Our Laïcité," rather than the "they."

CURATING A RENAISSANCE

I conclude this chapter by returning to Lustiger's archives to explore the contingent and strategic efforts necessary to bring the Collège into being. Lustiger was clearly motivated by the idea of rehabilitating this space. He knew what a powerful contribution such a building would make to the already extensive Catholic materiality of Paris. The archives reveal that such an opportunity to contribute to the normalization of catholaïcité—and to the work of implicit proselytism—was not one that Lustiger was willing to forgo, no matter the resistance he encountered.

In the documents to which I had access, the Collège is first mentioned on June 21, 1994.[23] This initial description of the space is found in the minutes of the monthly meeting of the Diocesan Council for Economic Affairs. Discussions had already begun between the city of Paris and the archbishop,

whose interest in the site arose after another fell through. Minimal renovation costs were imagined, and a grant from the Minister of Culture's Commission of Historical Monuments was deemed a likely scenario. No mention
is made of a cultural center at this point. Instead, the Collège is one of a few
buildings located near the Notre-Dame that could host organizations connected to the archdiocese, specifically those connected to "youth, solidarity,
and pastoral action." Later meetings and letters from 1994 and 1995 show
that an architect employed by the state had toured the site and offered an
estimate of the costs of the renovation. The Diocesan Council was clearly
less than excited about the architect's expensive assessment. Minutes from
various meetings suggest ongoing, slow-moving conversations with the
city and concerns within the archdiocese about the cost of the building's
renovation.

In February 1995, a letter marked "Urgent" was faxed to the economic
adviser of the archdiocese. It is here that the first mention of a cultural center at the Collège is made. On the fax cover sheet attached to a letter about
the funding of the Museum of Jewish Art and History, an adviser to the
archbishop typed:

> For your next visit with the Mayor, for your information, you will find
> attached to this letter, a note . . . indicating the acceptance of a plan for
> the city and the state to equally split an investment estimated at 196 mil-
> lion francs [approximately €29 million]. Perhaps we could be interested
> in developing in the Bernardins program more of an idea of a Center of
> Sacred Art as an all-encompassing concept, including teaching, docu-
> mentation, and research. . . . In terms of a comparison, would a schema
> of 33 (city) + 33 (state) + 33 (other financing) be an element of negotiation
> worth researching?

The Museum of Jewish Art and History, to which the writer refers as a
potential model for the Collège, is found in a seventeenth-century man-
sion in Paris's Marais neighborhood, known as the Hotel de Saint-Aignan.
Also expropriated during the Revolution, it was divided into workshops
and living quarters. Several Jewish families lived here in the nineteenth century. Many of those who occupied the space during the Vichy regime were
arrested and deported; thirteen perished in Nazi death camps. In 1986, at
the behest of Jacques Chirac, the mayor of Paris at the time, the Hotel de
Saint-Aignan was made available for a museum devoted to Jewish "civilization." It inherited collections from Jewish groups who had recovered and

conserved Jewish material forms in the immediate aftermath of the Holocaust. Its administrative council includes six representatives of the Ministry
of Culture and Communication, six representatives of the City of Paris, and
six representatives of Jewish organizations.

For the writer of the note to the archbishop, it was the museum's "cultural" focus that appeared to offer a solution to the Collège's funding problem. If the state had seen fit to invest in the creation of a Jewish "civiliza-
tional" or "cultural" museum, then might it be similarly open to funding
such an initiative for the Catholic Church? The Museum of Jewish Art and
History did not merely receive funding from various levels of the state,
its very structure of governance reflects the cooperation of these different
groups. No mention of this shared governance model, however, was made
by the writer, nor has it been taken up in the structure of the Collège. More
importantly, of course, this suggestion overlooks the memory of violence
that had also shaped the decision to make a historic building available for
a museum devoted to Jewish "civilization." In this brief fax cover letter—in
another example of appropriation—the writer suggested that the Collège
might be reconceived as an artistic and cultural center in order to improve
its chances for access to public funds to cover the costly renovation.

The impacts of this judicious suggestion cannot be immediately found
in the archives. A few weeks after its receipt, a summary of a Diocesan
Economic Affairs meeting on March 7, 1995, highlighted the significance
Lustiger attached to the renovation of the Collège. According to the summary, "Cardinal Lustiger opened the meeting by reminding participants that
today's debate on the economic stakes of the diocese for the period 1995–
2000 need to be positioned in a much longer-term perspective. What are the
possibilities for action for the Church at the end of the century? What is the
symbolic value of the different possible choices? He reminded participants
that financial considerations must be thought of in the longue durée and
that, in this spirit, an occasion like the Bernardins may not come again."

Here, once again, we can see the efforts that go into claims of continuity. In attempting to garner support for the purchase of the Collège—even
before he had defined its purpose—Lustiger argued that owning the space
would be of important symbolic value. The ensuing debate "underlined the
very seductive character of this project [of the Collège], with its symbolic
value for the Church of Paris tied to the character and placement of the
building." However, according to the summary of the meeting, "a reser-
vation was nevertheless stated" in which "the financial feasibility cannot
really be examined except in relation to negotiations with the state and the

City." For members of the Diocesan Council, the desirability of the project—however valuable its symbolic capital might be—lay in direct proportion to its capacity to drain the finances of the archdiocese. As the Diocesan Council debated the merits of the renovation, they did not appear to concern themselves with the use to which the space would be put. However, as I carefully read over the minutes from meetings debating whether or not to go forward with the project of the Collège, I realized that the faxed letter had at least one powerful effect. From that point forward, the Diocesan Council began (although not universally) to take up the language of a "cultural" and "artistic" center at the Collège, however ambiguous such an idea remained.

In June 1995 the director of economic affairs for the archdiocese sent a letter to the director of architecture of the City of Paris impressing upon him the desire of the archdiocese to engage in the "basic" rather than "ideal" restoration plan, which, the letter stated, would be more than sufficient to meet the needs of the diocese as well as the building's security. Even while foregrounding concerns about the costs of the renovation, the director of economic affairs took care to present the project as one of art and culture. "The Collège des Bernardins presents a historical, cultural, and religious interest of the highest order; the ground floor . . . constitutes the longest gothic room in Paris with the chapel-sacristy adjoining. Not only does the proposed program favor the conservation and restoration of an element of artistic heritage, but it will reestablish, to the extent possible with historical evolution, the initial vocation of the Collège des Bernardins: activities of study, teaching, research, and learning, a space of welcome and encounters, choral chants and sacred music, colloquia and exhibitions of religious art."

Here, the space now referred to as a nave was described as a large gothic room. The letter-writer was clearly uncertain how to refer to the space now described as the sacristy, referring to it as both a chapel and a sacristy. The concept of what would come to be known as "renaissance" is rather hazy, emphasizing religious, rather than contemporary art and music alongside of study and research. The writer even took the time to limit expectations around a renaissance, recognizing that "historical evolution" would constrain the re-establishment of the "initial vocation" of the Collège. Even in this laundry list of possible functions, however, one can observe the power of the idea that the secular state would be more likely to support a "cultural" rather than a "religious" venture. Here, in other words, employees at the archdiocese were behaving as secularized Catholics in order to secure a project that would eventually be used to reinforce narratives of catholaïcité.

Various documents suggest that the archdiocese failed to convince city

officials to opt for the basic renovation plan. In the minutes of a meeting of
the Diocesan Council dated January 1996, the Diocesan Council notes that
a plan costing more than F123 million has been "imposed" by the Commission of Historic Monuments. The City has suggested they could try to pursue a project costing F100 million that would exclude the renovation of the
sacristy. In order to make even the more limited project tenable, however,
members of the council insisted they would have to succeed in receiving no
less than F20 million from the state, and F50 million from the city, as the
participation of the archdiocese was limited to F30 million. At the time, no
such agreements, apparently, were forthcoming and the Collège dropped
out of all official discussions between January 1996 and September 1999.

In the summer of 1998, Lustiger contacted a successful businessman in
Paris, Bernard de Feydeau. In a filmed interview posted on the Collège's
website while I was there, but since removed, de Feydeau explained that he
had never met Lustiger when the cardinal contacted him. Lustiger asked de
Feydeau to look into the challenges that would accompany the realization
of his vision of the Collège. According to de Feydeau, after he explained to
the cardinal the numerous obstacles in their way, Lustiger simply declared,
"Si c'est possible, faite-le" (If it's possible, do it).[24] Two years later, de Feydeau was officially appointed as the new director for economic affairs for
the archdiocese.

After de Feydeau had taken on this position, conversations between the
City and the Diocesan Council recommenced. As letters passed between the
archdiocese, the mayor of Paris, the president of the region of Ile-de-France,
and the minister of culture and communication, the terms used to describe
the plans for the site remained very much in flux, variously described as "a
cultural building open to the city" and "a new institute of theology." Apart
from demonstrating the endless strategizing that goes into complex projects
with multiple funders and interests at play, these letters also highlight that,
ultimately, it was *not* necessary for the Collège to be presented as a cultural
project in order to receive government support. When considering the possibility of subventions to support the renovation, transforming the space
into a theology institute owned by the archdiocese seemed a perfectly tenable option for the secular government to entertain. While some state officials cited the revival of its "original vocation," many of them understood the
site to be the new home of École Cathédrale rather than a broader cultural
project. Even with this restricted vocation, the region of the Ile-de-France
was willing to sign on to a subvention of F18 million to support the renova-

tion of the "Bernardins Convent" in June 2000. Eventually, a shared funding model was agreed upon, with the state, city, and region sharing €14.5 million of the €52 million renovation, €16.5 million provided by a mixture of corporate and private donors, and €21 million provided by the archdiocese through long-term loans the archdiocese was mostly able to pay back through subsequent real estate transactions (de Feydeau 2017, 71).

In contrast to numerous anthropological accounts of secularism that emphasize its totalizing nature, it is significant to note how the secular state serves as an imagined, rather than real, disciplinary force within the French Catholic Church. Although some within the organization saw the idea of a "cultural" center as a strategic means by which to encourage the French state to participate in the cost of the renovation, such definitions ultimately proved unnecessary. The terrain upon which the French state operates appears equally unstable. Rather than consistently constraining the space of Catholicism in French public life, as has been the case historically, today the secular state at times appears to support its privileged banality.

***

One quiet day at the Collège, I filled the morning by reading *The Choice of God*. Leaning against one of the pillars in the nave and rather deeply engrossed, I was startled when a volunteer complimented me on my choice of reading. Standing up and closing my book, I smiled and thanked her. Returning my smile, she described to me how she had been present during one of his viewings of the Collège during its renovation. Already retired from his position as archbishop of Paris, he came to the site to view it once all traces of the fire station and police academy had been removed, but the building had yet to take on its "renaissance" form. Deeply satisfied with what he saw, he declared, "It seems the thirteenth century has quite a bit to say to the twenty-first."

Claims of continuity must be forged time and again against evidence to the contrary. In order to buttress claims of renaissance, Lustiger had to continually curate connections between the past and the present. Neither rupture nor continuity can be taken for granted—both necessitate social action in order to define that which is natural and that which is novel. In the case of Lustiger and the Collège, crystallization and renaissance are claims about the place of the past in the present that must continuously be forged. As a figure who embodied powerful expressions of rupture, he was well versed in the curatorial work required to reframe change as an expression of continuity. As a figure representative of the very partial ways in which difference might be incorporated into catholaïcité, however, Lustiger's crystallization also buttressed the power of Catholicism's privilege through the supersessionist appropriation of Judaism and the violent rejection of Islam.

II
MEDIATING
CATHOLIC
PRIVILEGE

WALLS THAT BLEED

IN THE SPRING OF 2010, I sat down for a conversation with one of the priests who work at the Collège. "Do you know what President Mitterrand responded when asked by a reporter 'what is Europe?'" he asked. I shook my head "no" in response to his question about the Socialist French president whose Catholic funerals had caused so much concern a few decades earlier. With a knowing smile, he said, "The Cistercians."

In making such a statement, President Mitterrand was likely being asked to justify something like the idea of Europe at early stages of its unification. To do so, the former French president had turned to the Catholic medieval past, and in particular, to the Catholic medieval monastic body that had built the space in which we sat. I have never been able to find evidence that Mitterrand made such a statement to reporters. What matters, of course, is that the priest felt the story was a self-evident anecdote to share with me in our discussion of the Collège. While it was the first time I had heard this story, I had been conducting research among elite Parisians long enough to know to smile and nod knowingly, rather than to ask the priest for clarification of its meaning. As in numerous other practices associated with the work of normalization, part of his purpose in telling me the story was to see if the narrative was self-evident to me as well. If I could respond with a knowing smile then I might be trusted to understand the broader argument he wanted to make about the Collège.

In addition to serving as a litmus test, the priest's story also demonstrated that my interlocutors were not the first in France to express desires for the medieval past. Medieval Catholicism has served as an object of desire in France since at least the nineteenth century.[1] With this story, the priest expressed an approach to French history in the style of the longue durée. As I demonstrate in chapters 1 and 2, Collège employees and Cardinal Lustiger both made use of the term, which comes out of the work of Fernand Braudel

(1958).[2] Many scholars focused on a variety of periods have taken up the concept, including the medieval historian Jacques Le Goff. In 1995, Le Goff participated in a colloquium devoted to the display of contemporary art in medieval spaces, particularly to the unveiling of stained-glass windows produced by the abstract painter Pierre Soulages for the St. Foyes Abbey in Conques in southern France. The published proceedings of the event are entitled "On the Pertinence of Putting a Work of Contemporary Art in a Space Full of History." In his opening words, Le Goff described thinking of history in the longue durée as recognizing that "the past is not dead. The past continues. Potentialities long dormant rise up. New creators enrich the monuments of the past" (Soulages and LeGoff 1995, 11).

In light of Le Goff's definition, the longue durée appears to offer a particularly powerful account of continuity over time. Indeed, under his direction, the Annales School (an influential approach to social history in France focused on the medieval and early modern period) began to incorporate the work of archaeologists in order to think about trends and changes beyond the typical distinctions between modern and medieval. In a 1983 article, Le Goff argued for an alternative understanding of the Middle Ages as beginning in the third and ending in the mid-nineteenth century. Modes of periodization that institute a hard-and-fast divide between the medieval and the modern have been interrogated for the global and local inequalities that they have supported (see, for example, Chakrabarty 1997, Kathleen Davis 2008, and Johannes Fabian 2002 [1983]). What interests me here is how and with what effects material forms come to stand in as evidence for temporal—and therefore political—claims. In expressing his support for Soulages's contemporary stained-glass windows in a medieval abbey, Le Goff declared that "the defense of heritage . . . does not consist in preserving the monument as mere vestige, in keeping it dead, even if it were a glorious death. The beauty of the dead, as it has been said, even if it is to be preserved, must not be the sole or the main tool of the champion of heritage. Defending heritage, conserving heritage, means helping it to continue to live" (Soulages and Le Goff 1995, 11). I want to highlight how, here, Le Goff is making an argument for the vibrancy of material forms. While, as a medieval historian, he certainly has emphasized the "life and historical meaning" (ibid., 12) of heritage spaces, his preference for the longue durée draws him to those spaces that appear to carry the past into the present.

Much of the success of the Collège has similarly resided in the apparent vitality of the space in which it is housed. For numerous visitors, the renovated thirteenth-century building has offered visceral access to the medieval past that so many have desired to bring into the present. There is, perhaps, little that is surprising and much that is understandable in such desires. In February 2019, the *New York Times* magazine ran a riveting account of the recent "discovery" of two Rembrandt paintings that touched on yearnings for Europe's past made available through its material forms. The author described how the renowned art dealer Jan Six—himself the aristocratic descendant of a family whose founders once posed for Rembrandt—gave him a "remarkable little demonstration" when showing him through the family home filled with Rembrandts.

> He turned off the lights and lit candles, and in an instant the paintings were transformed. They took on new energy; the golds and reds and flesh tones became warmer. The flicker of the flames seemed to breathe life into the two-dimensional figures. Six's eyes gleamed as he saw that I had registered the point: These paintings were made for candlelight. Six was helping me to experience the world of 17th-century Amsterdammers in the most tangible way: the minute differences in ways of seeing and feeling that separate one historical epoch from another. [Shorto 2019]

Despite the material forms we have inherited, the past remains intangible, elusive, and beguiling, not entirely distinct from other intangibles, including gods, spirits, and the dead.[3] Accessing it requires what anthropologists and scholars of religion refer to as forms of mediation. I follow Angela Zito's dialectical definition of the term, which highlights how "people are constantly engaged in producing the material world around them, even as they are, in turn, produced by it" (2008, 726). People produce social worlds not only by creating new tools and material forms but by engaging with and transforming those they have inherited from the past. The nature of mediation between the past and the present in any given place or time is never fully predetermined by these forms.

By focusing on the Collège's contemporary art programming in this chapter and the three to follow, I am following the work of scholars who have approached religion *as* mediation. Birgit Meyer encourages scholars to see religion

> as a medium of absence, that posits and sets out to bridge a gap between the here and now and something "beyond." It is in this sense that religion, in "making the invisible visible," involves "multiple media" for "materializing the sacred" (Orsi 2012, 147). Here media are understood in the

broad sense of material transmitters across gaps and limits that are central to practices of mediation, encompassing modern mass media as well
as other and older media. One of the advantages of an understanding of
religion as a practice of mediation is that it no longer takes the practices,
objects and other forms through which religion becomes manifest in
the world as secondary to beliefs, meanings and values, but as necessary
forms though which the "beyond" becomes accessible or the "invisible"
is "shown." [2015b, 336–37]

In employing Meyer's work, however, I also want to expand her understanding of the "invisible," "sacred," and "beyond." Rather than a mediator
of God's absence alone, religion needs to be approached as a mediator of a
host of absences, including the past. As my original guide's response to what
she referred to as the "crypt" demonstrates, the past, too, must be made visible. The reconstruction of the Collège and its contemporary arts programming are not only aimed at making God present. They also aim to make a
certain idea of the past present. Claims about the relationship between the
past and the present in ways that undergird Catholic privilege may also be
reproduced by media that link up spaces and those who occupied them in
the past with those of the present. Many of those who visited the Collège
took visceral pleasure in accessing a medieval space that appeared to have
been lost to time until it insisted upon its renaissance. In so doing they
were demonstrating that religious mediation may not only connect God and
humans; it may also connect humans with human sensoria, and materiality
of the past.

   In this chapter and the next I explore two distinct ways in which the past
is mediated through the Collège's contemporary art programming. First, I
discuss processes—like those engaged in by my guide, the priest who shared
the story of Mitterand, Pierre Soulages, Jacques Le Goff, and Jan Six—that
enliven Catholic materiality. Second, in chapter 4, I analyze processes and
practices that *aestheticize* it. Enlivening and aestheticizing are two distinct
modes of mediation. In the former, human agency is displaced onto material
forms that appear to demand and constrain human action in ways shaped
by the original purpose to which the object was put. In the latter, material
forms mediate the past by reducing the moral demands of the past in favor
of a distanced and learned appreciation for the manipulation of the material forms. In this chapter I explore how, when considering the relationship
between religion and the secular in Europe—and the kinds of exclusions
we see repeated, time and again—we need to approach the enlivening of

material mediations of the past with caution. Put another way, we cannot allow ourselves to presume that the revival of a medieval Catholic space in which to engage with contemporary art is a neutral decision that will have neutral effects.

THE POLITICS OF A VANISHING CATHOLICISM

During the first, provocative contemporary art exhibition put on at the Collège, the enlivening of the space itself had the effect of heightening its potentially exclusionary nature. Many visitors, expecting to have their desires for visceral access to France's medieval past met and celebrated at the Collège, found their encounter with the three-part installation by the Italian arte povera artist Claudio Parmiggiani to be unsettling.[4] Many expressed their discomfort by arguing that before them was not the work of an artist but the work of vandals, specifically the work of those living in Paris's banlieues. In so doing, they linked the exhibit to the work of particular kinds of outsiders: the first-, second-, and third-generation Muslim immigrants with connections to former French colonies.[5]

While the leap from a contemporary art installation in a medieval space to complaints about young Muslims in Paris's suburbs may appear rather abrupt, numerous far-right movements in France and elsewhere demonstrate how adulation of the medieval past can be used in support of exclusionary visions of Europe and France in the present.[6] The fact that so many visitors made such a comparison in ways that appeared legible to others around them points to the powerful role that medieval Catholic materiality can play in reproducing a particular idea of France. When the Parmiggiani exhibit appeared to disrupt their fantasy of France—a place in which the Catholic medieval past could unproblematically be reborn in the present— many visitors associated it with the practices of those they had learned to consider irredeemably other. Upon discovering material forms they considered to be out of place in this space, visitors associated that matter with France's Muslim population.

The exhibit's opening occurred early in my acquaintance with the Collège. I was not one of the select few to receive an invitation to the *vernissage* (opening) on November 22, 2008, but I inadvertently crashed it while attending a conference, "Anthropologies of the World and Christian Thought," held in the third-floor auditorium. Approximately fifty people milled about somewhat awkwardly in the nave at the midday event. Many were clearly shocked by what confronted them.

The installation had three parts. Most visibly, the north half of the nave contained row upon row of approximately eight-foot-tall and one-inch-thick glass panels that the artist's assistants had smashed and shattered with mallets on site, leaving a mixture of jagged pieces scattered on the floor and cracked fragments that continued to stand. Along one side of this "sea of glass," the artist constructed on site a "library of shadows."[7] Using soot from a controlled fire lit inside the newly renovated Collège, Parmiggiani created traces of the destruction of a library of books.[8] Finding the false wall that the restoration architects had built along one length of the nave abhorrent, Parmiggiani decided to cover it with, in the words of the exhibition curator, "the most authentic signs of passage, of the secret and moving life of things" (Grenier 2008, 34). Finally, in the sacristy, Parmiggiani stacked bells that once hung in village churches throughout Italy on the floor.

Eventually, the artist gave a short speech. Following his words, a woman in her late sixties caught my eye and approached me. "You're young, aren't you?" she asked me. I shrugged. "Perhaps this is something generational. Do you like this? Do you understand it?" she demanded angrily. In response, I suggested that it was indeed interesting and asked her what she thought of it. She laughed and responded, "What is there to think?" She shook her head. "No, it is not art—it's not possible." She and her companion looked at each other, shook their heads again, and headed briskly for the door.

Her response was hardly atypical. When they encountered extensive layers of broken glass and the appearance of burned books, many visitors felt excluded from the community they had hoped to inhabit. That community was, of course, no longer present in the flesh. Among these vaults, they wanted to walk where the monks once walked. By aiming to create a community with specters from the past—rather than residents of the present—the project underway at the Collège leaves open the space for particularly exclusive visions of Paris, France, and Europe.

The renaissance of this space for many of the visitors who came through its doors proved so powerful because it appeared to "bring back" a Catholicism they presumed had otherwise vanished from public life in France. I encountered such claims frequently both within and beyond the Collège. For example, in response to my question of where one sees Catholicism in Paris today, a young man named Paul—seated across from me in a café in the sixteenth arrondissement just before Christmas in 2009—declared, "I don't." Turning to his fiancée seated next to him, he added, "The only

Catholics I see are us." A successful professional in his late twenties, Paul had a gentle way of enforcing traditional rules of French *politesse* throughout our conversation. It was he who ordered the wine that we shared, he who tasted it, and he who offered it to us, pouring equal portions into our glasses before his own at regular intervals. He spoke directly, without exaggerative adjectives, and in a soft and steady tone, even when he was passionate about a subject. His manner affected both his fiancée (Andrea, an American woman) and me. Neither of us moved to touch the bottle of wine, and we both tended to quiet our voices and words following his interjections. "I don't see Catholicism in France, not anymore," Paul continued. "I think it was different when my parents were young. I don't see Catholicism in France. What I see are other religions." Andrea hesitated before expressing her disagreement.

"But I see it all the time . . . you know, like those posters in the metro?" she asked, turning to me, another foreigner. I immediately knew the posters she was describing: advertisements for Catholic charities I too had noticed on the subway during this Christmas season and the one prior. Seeing that Paul was unconvinced by her interjection, she changed her tone slightly. "It's true that I'm more aware of the Muslim presence in France. It's more visible, because of the dress and so forth." Paul nodded. "And it works better too," he added. When I asked him to elaborate, he explained that in France Muslims are more religious than Catholics. "They follow the rules, and they practice their religion as they are told. The same is not true for Catholics. They have had to assimilate so they aren't different from anyone else. But it means we are losing our identity in France." Still hesitating to accept Paul's position entirely, Andrea wondered if the visible presence of "other" religions in France would help to "bring back a more traditional Catholicism." Paul smiled doubtfully.

Paul's insistence that Catholicism cannot be seen in Paris anymore is just one example of the commonly held assumption that Catholicism has vanished in France.[9] Indeed, the most frequent response I received to my explanation that I was in Paris researching Catholicism was sarcasm and surprise: "You managed to find Catholics in France?" many would inquire with a smile and a raised brow. In the words of a writer for the Jesuit review *Esprit*: "The decline of European Catholicism is, at the same time, spectacular in terms of its figures and discreet as a felt and lived social phenomenon. . . . In Western Europe . . . and in France in particular, the Church finds itself in a worrying state of anemia and decline, quantitative and qualitative. We are attending a sort of adieu to Catholicism, an adieu that is done without alarm, drama or nostalgia. Catholicism is certainly not yet dead. . . . And yet, in Europe, it sometimes seems close to retirement" (Schlegel 2010, 78–79). These words gave me pause when I first read them browsing through journals and magazines at a public library in a western suburb of Paris. Many of the voices I encountered expressed a great deal of regret for this "adieu," mourning Catholicism's seemingly unstoppable decline. And yet, few of those who regretted Catholicism's apparent vanishing would have disagreed with Schlegel's words. The taken-for-granted nature of this vanishing, I argue, has powerful effects. It makes Catholic materiality appear unthreatening in ways that encourage both its enlivening and determinations of the kinds of matter that belong in such spaces.

Many visitors to the Collège brought strong predetermined notions of what kind of art was appropriate to "such a space." One afternoon in mid-December one of the mediators, Charles, who had quickly become a friend, emphatically explained to me that the Collège was not a church. Over the following weeks, I realized that the building's lack of sacred status was one of Charles's favorite points to make. That day in December he insisted that "The priests and monks who come here would agree with me—it is not a place of worship." Soon we found ourselves discussing the topic with a few visitors who strongly disliked the installation. One man made reference to Cardinal Lustiger and insisted that the cardinal had intended the space to be sacred. He was certain, moreover, that Lustiger would have been horrified by the decision to fill the nave with broken glass in its first few months of existence. Charles stood his ground and insisted that Lustiger did not intend the Collège to be an *endroit de culte* (religious space, or space of worship) and, therefore, nonreligious artworks could be displayed.[10]

Charles was right in arguing that Lustiger had intended the Collège to exceed the boundaries imposed upon religious spaces in France in the present. But this does not mean that the space cannot be thought of as sacred. With France serving as a primary example, Émile Durkheim (1995 [1912]) demonstrated long ago that sacred spaces are merely those separated out as distinct from the everyday and that rituals of all kinds—secular and religious—are practices that serve to affirm the power and righteousness of the gathered community. Moreover, it is quite possible that Lustiger was at least aware of the decision to exhibit a work by Parmiggiani at the Collège. As employees explained to me, all four of the exhibitions displayed in the first two years of the Collège's operation had been chosen at a very high level within the institution long before the space opened to the public. Although retired as archbishop at the time, Lustiger was still involved in

conversations surrounding the Collège. And while they had given Parmiggiani carte blanche—the artist had free rein to produce a work of his
choosing—it would have been difficult for employees or directors to claim
that the installation Parmiggiani produced had come as a surprise. As the
catalog published to accompany the exhibit demonstrates, broken glass,
burned books, and silent bells had played important roles in Parmiggiani's
repertoire in the past.

Given that visitors had arrived at a space that not only had been inhabited by Cistercian monks centuries earlier but, even more importantly, was
currently owned and operated by the French Catholic archdiocese, it is
not surprising that they had anticipated something very different than the
Parmiggiani exhibit. The remarkably diverse array of objects, images, and
spaces associated with Catholic traditions, however, makes it difficult to
discern what, precisely, they might have expected.

Art historian Hans Belting uses the term "cult" to describe images and
objects including icons, relics, depictions of the saints, and crucifixes that
allowed for irregular and limited access to the divine on holy days when
they were paraded through the streets or held up for adoration in churches.
His use of "cult" avoids the term "religious" and the very particular meaning
it—like art—took on in the modern period. Both religion and art now refer
to autonomous processes that are widely seen as separate from political and
economic life and unessential to broader social forms. Both religion and art
are, instead, admired for the potential spiritual "add-on" that they provide
to modern life.

Historically, however, cult images played a powerful political, economic,
and social role. According to Belting (1994), the power of cult images was
twofold. First, legends surrounding their origins tended to connect them
with the work of God. Their power resided not in the skill of the artist but
in the manner in which the artist's hand receded and that of God was felt.
Images such as the *Veronika* (literally, "true image"), which, according to
legend, was initially formed when Jesus wiped his bloody face while wearing a crown of thorns on his march toward death, leaving an imprint of his
face upon the cloth, are exemplary in this regard. Copies of this image had
to be produced with careful precision in order to downplay their human-
created nature and allow viewers to be as close to the "original" as possible.
Second, the power of cult images also resided in their role in the formation and reproduction of communities and relations of power. Generally
withheld from view most of the time, they were only displayed in limited
ways on occasions of significance. A ninth-century council at Carthage

ruled that churches required relics—the "corporeal remains" of saints and martyrs (Geary 1994, 41)—in order to be properly consecrated, ultimately leading to a scramble for relics during the medieval period. Questions about their authenticity—or about the legitimacy of their theft from other towns and churches—tended to be confirmed by the extent to which they brought renown, wealth, and pilgrims to the communities in which they came to be housed (see Geary 1991 [1978]).

These two distinct but interrelated effects and affects of cult images demonstrate how Christian art never served only to make the invisible visible, or to allow communion with God. Christian objects and images were equally significant in fomenting particular notions of communities and relations of power. Even when, during the Renaissance, Christian objects shifted from "cult images" to "art images," and came to exist under "the sphere of the artist who assumes control of the image as proof of his or her art" (Belting 1994, 16), such practices remained embedded in regimes of power, such as those of patronage. Thus, while the Collège does not point to God's presence in the way that the Eucharist, a relic, or an icon might, it serves to affirm the power and privilege of particular visions of community in ways reminiscent of cult images and objects. Moreover, reactions to the Parmiggiani exhibit suggest that, despite the decline of the cult image and powerful critiques made of the art image in recent decades, viewers remain attentive to the politics of the production, display, and reception of objects, spaces, and images, Christian and otherwise.

On Tuesday, December 16, 2008, I arrived at the Collège at 2:45 in the afternoon, just in time to witness an exchange between a man and a woman in their seventies and several of the mediators. The man reacted immediately and explosively to the work yelling, "This is a disaster, not art!" to one of the mediators. "It is sacrilege," he continued, "and not at all appropriate in this place!" Unable to stand before it, he stalked off to the bookstore. His wife, however, remained behind. Overwhelmed by the work before her, she exclaimed, "But it is the only thing you can see when you enter!" again and again as different mediators attempted to engage her in conversation and debate.

"Are you here to defend this?" another man teased a mediator who was standing to the side of the drama that unfolded before us. Before the other mediator could respond, the joker continued, "But is it possible to defend?" At this point, the angry man had looped around the bookstore and returned to retrieve his wife. "No, it is not possible!" he responded to the joker's remarks, attempting to bring him onside. Two women in their late fifties entered. "But what is it?" they demanded to know in undisguised shock. As the mediators were still ensconced in a rather passionate debate with the first couple and the joker, I attempted to explain the installation as best I could to the new arrivals.[11] I described how the work was created and pointed to its three different elements. They allowed me to speak but their brows remained arched in confusion. "Yes, yes, but what is it? Is it art?" I smiled and nodded in response.

Right from the vernissage, I encountered visitors who explained precisely how "out of place" the work was by equating it with the actions of those in the banlieues. One man who referred to himself as a "Catholic intellectual" was shocked to learn that the same artist was responsible both for the bells and the broken glass. While he insisted that "the bells are us," he saw the broken glass as a bleak expression of violence. He explained that, as a historian who works at a university outside of Paris, for him, "broken glass symbolizes the violence of protests in the banlieues. It is reminiscent of historical violence but also of today's violence. It is disturbing to see in this place." On a particularly busy and passionate day in mid-December, a couple demanded to know whether the work was indeed done on purpose. Feigning confusion they asked, "Oh, it was not an act of vandalism by the youth of the banlieues?" In France, "youth" is often used as a code word for Muslim immigrants living in the suburbs. In late January, a clearly enraged man responded curtly to Charles's offer to provide some reflections on the exhibit: "Just explain it!" His friend, in an attempt to lighten the mood, exclaimed, "It's just like in the banlieues!" In a slightly more casual tone, one woman asked me, "Is this artistic?" When I responded in the affirmative, she looked surprised and added, "One really has the impression that vandals came in the night!" Early on in December, a man asked if the artist had been offering a commentary on the youth who spend their time breaking glass in the banlieues. "When they destroy things, is it art? Is that what the artist is saying?" In the words of one remark in the comment book, or in French the *livre d'or* (book of gold), "when the youth 'offer' this sort of art in the streets of Paris, we put them in prison." Another, equally unsettling, remark declared, "So this is this what's called inviting the destroyers of the banlieues to the good neighborhoods where the prices are higher."

What made these remarks such powerful forms of critique? The specter of the vandal from the banlieues acted as a stable signifier of not only that which is other but that which threatens to thwart expressions of "true" French culture. This sense of people and things out of place offered a means by which those who despised the exhibit could lament how the Collège,

which they sought in order to affirm an idealized vision of France, appeared
to participate in practices that were contributing to its demise.

Having rejected the artist as a con artist and an immigrant vandal, most
visitors did not take the time to explore what his intentions might have been.
Had they done so, they would have been surprised by what they learned.
While many visitors saw the broken glass and burned books as an inappropriate expression of violence in the space of the Collège, the artist's account
of his work suggests that the installation was, in fact, created in sympathy
with it. According to the Press Release for the exhibit, "the power of the
space will be matched by the power of the work: by recalling the intellectual
and spiritual memory of the Collège des Bernardins, but also through the
staging of destruction and oblivion, Claudio Parmiggiani offers the public,
more than a work of art, the experience of a revelation" ("Exposition Claudio Parmiggiani" 2008). The exhibit's curator, Catherine Grenier, produced
much of this text. As the director of modern and contemporary art at the
Centre Pompidou, Paris's national modern and contemporary art museum,
Grenier came in to act as curator for the exhibit at the request of the artist.

Given that the Collège boasted impressive individuals with ample contemporary art experience among its employees, I was curious why an external
curator was deemed necessary (the two exhibits that followed Parmiggiani
did not have external curators). One of the arts coordinators bristled slightly
when I asked her to explain. As the time of the exhibit approached, she
recounted, Parmiggiani had requested that Grenier be brought in to act as
an "intermediary" between him and the Collège. He wanted to be sure that,
in her words, "we took his point of view—the point of view of the artist—
seriously. I was a bit surprised, because it was almost an act of defiance vis-
à-vis the Bernardins, as if it was obvious that we would misinterpret, or do
poorly by his oeuvre." Parmiggiani's hesitation shows that while employees
feel the Collège's place in the contemporary art scene is self-evident, the artist was less certain. His request to bring in Grenier revealed his doubts that
employees at the Collège could move beyond the limitations, perhaps, of an
endroit de culte and successfully inhabit the norms and practices of a space
of contemporary art display.

While Parmiggiani used the services of a curator to bridge a perceived
distance between himself and employees at the Collège, he found linkages
between his work and the medieval space far more palatable. He described
the relationship between the installation and the space in the following terms
in a video recorded at the Collège and projected on a wall during the exhibit:
"The space is the blood of the oeuvre." He went on to compare himself to

a "beggar" or a "pilgrim" seeking spaces that will provide "shelter" for his
works. "I search for shelter for my work by trying to guide it into spaces with
blood that will give it life. I find this blood in spaces that contain it in their
walls, in the thickness of their bodies. You have to feel that these spaces carry
culture in their breast, that they are pregnant with culture, of the feeling of
the beauty of culture." As a "beggar" or a "pilgrim," Parmiggiani claimed to
stand outside of the space and time in which he lives, needing to seek "shelter" in those places that carry the past within them and allow him to access
the proper space and time in which he and his art should reside.

    Such declarations reveal the vibrancy the artist attributed to the medieval
space, encountering it as brimming with "life" and "culture." This, indeed, is
one way of accounting for the capacity for the medieval to be reborn in the
present: medieval objects remain enlivened with the past, carrying it into the
present. All humans need to do to access the past is to listen to these spaces
correctly. That Parmiggiani purposefully excluded staff at the Collège from
the exhibit further amplified his claim that certain *spaces*—rather than those
who inhabit them—are living beings with a vibrancy that can then give birth
to or "shelter" other sentient objects, such as his works of art. In this respect,
Parmiggiani betrayed a view of objects akin to that described in many of the
texts associated with the new materialism. For Parmiggiani—and, often, for
many of the visitors as well—the medieval vaults served as what Jane Bennett (2012) would call an "affective catalyst." With this term, Bennett wants
to point to "the agency of things that *produce* (helpful, harmful) effects in
human and other bodies" (xii). In other words, Bennett and others writing
in this vein aim to decenter agency away from humans alone and explore
the possibility of a host of actors—including objects—producing effects and
affects in the world.

    For scholars of religious media, such notions are far from new. And yet,
my research at the Collège has encouraged me to approach the enlivening
of objects with caution. While many of those writing in the new materialist
movement see an emphasis on the agency of objects as a means of opening
up more inclusive encounters within various social worlds, at the Collège I
found that displacing agency from humans onto objects could also support a
very different kind of politics. I want to focus attention on the human efforts
that go into enlivening and enchanting particular material forms. In emphasizing the long-dead Cistercian monks and the stones that make up the walls
they built, artists, employees, and visitors at the Collège sought to reduce
the significance of living human action in this space. When the employee
I interviewed insisted that employees were "charged" with the project of

renaissance, for example, this work of displacing agency from living actors to the dead and the stones provided powerful evidence of ideological claims of the place of the medieval in the contemporary.

In the video of the artist that played throughout the exhibition, Parmiggiani described how the idea of the "book" served as the foundation of the project, even in the slabs of glass, which "resemble the pages of a book, a destroyed book, a city annihilated, a metaphor of the library of Alexandria, which evokes another tragedy: that of our current situation."[12] He went on to explain how a destroyed city, a burned library, and silenced bells all express a similar idea: "a profound feeling of melancholy that follows the ruin, the echo of a destruction." The artist never explicitly stated what had been ruined or destroyed, but his poetic descriptions clearly lamented the loss of a medieval Catholic past. He described church bells as, at base, "an emblem of the voice, of a language of a community, a society, a voice that assembles, but also a voice that guides, a civil and moral voice. In this space, this voice is extinguished, dead—a faraway echo."[13] The first page of text in the catalog begins with a quote from Parmiggiani from 2006 that similarly mourns a particularly Catholic loss. "At the birth of time, art was prayer. There remains very little of this infinite beauty. Now we aren't even capable of prayer. We walk like the blind among the ruins" (Grenier 2008, 33). Even in his act of mourning a time now destroyed, however, Parmiggiani managed to uphold the project of simultaneously inhabiting the medieval and the contemporary so key to claims of the renaissance of an enlivened Collège.

Herein lies a central paradox of the Collège's temporal contortions. As I demonstrate in chapter 1, a great deal of work goes into branding the Collège as a renaissance of the medieval past. Yet, part of what makes the Collège so tantalizing is the impossibility of resuscitating the medieval in the present. According to the French theorist of heritage spaces Roland Recht, historical objects "are no longer that which they once were, but their materiality, and their phenomenal existence make us believe the opposite" (2008 [1999], 16). The power of the Collège was not nearly so apparent during its existence as a fire station, however. It was only through the renovation and the use of a variety of discursive and affective means by which to emphasize its vitality that the Collège came to provide artists and visitors alike with tangible access to what Benjamin described as an "aura" (2002 [1936], 104): an object whose power resides both in its connection to the past and in the loss of that past to which it refers. As Parmiggiani's poetic laments demonstrate, the notion that the medieval past is distant in ways that cannot be recuperated is equally powerful in underscoring the visceral and beguiling attraction of the

Collège, I argue that the tantalizing nature of the Collège is situated here—in the paradox between the audacious claim that the past can be reborn in the present through the enlivened materiality of this newly renovated heritage space and laments for an idealized past that can no longer be found. This loss means that humans alone are unable to resuscitate that past; it must be mediated through other means. Put another way, in order for them to be properly modern subjects, visitors and artists at the Collège cannot themselves recreate that past. Such labors have to be displaced onto the material forms themselves.

Even if employees were offended by Parmiggiani's use of an external curator, his value as an inaugural artist cannot be understated. A few weeks after the opening of the exhibit, Paris's weekly arts and culture magazine *Télérama* offered the exhibit two out of three "Ts." While the exhibit may have failed to achieve the highest rating, for a space owned by the archdiocese to even be included on the list of must-see exhibits represented a significant coup. "On the occasion of the reopening of the College des Bernardins," the brief review read, "we must salute the great intellectual integrity of the commission given to the Italian artist Claudio Parmiggiani, who presents a suite of works . . . around spirituality and confidence" ("Claudio Parmiggiani" 2009, 30). The magazine followed up these positive words with a quote from Parmiggiani found in the catalog. "Certain places have an energy, they palpitate; others don't. If one were to make a hole in the wall of any medieval cathedral, blood would flow; if one were to make a hole in the wall of a museum, nothing would come out. I always want to create a heart that beats in the thickness of the walls. " Not only did the magazine offer glowing admiration for the artist, by repeating Parmiggiani's words it also engaged in the work of enlivening the Collège.

THE POLITICS OF ENLIVENING
CATHOLIC MATERIALITY

If medieval churches bleed, but nothing comes out of a museum wall, then the enlivening of the Collège through the Parmiggiani installation made a case for the necessity of the Catholic Church in the cultural life of France. Despite the tension Parmiggiani created within the institution, his words and efforts repeated the work in which many employees engaged. He offered the Collège authenticity as an evocative space in which to exhibit contemporary art, while also locating this legitimacy in the Church's medieval past. In an interview, Grenier explained how "the elements of the religious and then civil history of the Collège nourished [Parmiggiani's] imagination. . . . He began with the idea of the book and of the memory of the vocation of the diffusion of knowledge of the Collège, which was lost and then reborn today" (Folscheid 2008, 6).[14] The exhibit for many visitors appeared to work against what they thought the Collège ought to affirm: the visceral power of Catholic materiality. Parmiggiani's words, however, suggest that he had far more in common with visitors than they imagined.

To understand the "tragedy" of the current moment as the loss of an imagined Catholic past is not only poetry; it is a powerful political and ideological claim, and one that potentially accords with Pope Benedict's sense of crisis. That viewers misinterpreted the artist's act of mourning by blaming the destruction they saw on the "youth" in the banlieues speaks to the exclusionary nature of the vision of France conveyed in such accounts of loss. Some visitors noted how the combination of burned books and broken glass brought Krystallnacht to mind. These visitors, however, were less numerous than those who made reference to the banlieues. When visitors critiqued an artwork they saw as destroying the vitality of the Collège—the living presence of an idealized French past—by attributing it to immigrant criminals, they were expressing how much the Collège should, in their eyes, stand in for "true"—that is, white, Catholic—French culture. At a time widely considered to be one of crisis of French identity and the republic, these visitors to the Collège were repeating widely held notions that immigrants were the root cause of this crisis. These responses and expectations, moreover, were not spontaneous but were learned through other encounters with other mediating forms.

In chapter 1, I note how the French writer Michel Houellebecq's bestselling novel *Submission* similarly laments a crisis in French identity. The text offers a fascinating parallel to the merging of anxieties about Muslims in France and laments for France's medieval Catholic past that I encountered at the Collège. The narrator, François (the old French word for France and French), is a literature professor and specialist in the work of the nineteenth-century decadent novelist Joris-Karl Huysmans.[15] François leaves Paris in the aftermath of crippling riots and the end of a relationship with one of his students. He heads into the French countryside without much of a direction in mind. He ends up in the town where one of his former colleagues has gone into hiding in her family home. His colleague's husband implores him to visit Rocamadour, where "you'll see what a great civilization medieval

Christendom really was" (2015, 129). He takes the man's advice and, while there, he learns that the Muslim Brotherhood has won in the second round of the presidential elections. He casually acknowledges this fact and then turns with more attention to the Black Virgin at Rocamadour in ways that echo those of my guide in the cellar, and Parmiggiani's account of the space of the Collège.

> Every day I went and sat for a few minutes before the Black Virgin—the same one who for a thousand years inspired so many pilgrimages, before whom so many saints and kings had knelt. It was a strange statue. It bore witness to a vanished universe. The Virgin sat rigidly erect; her head, with its closed eyes, so distant that it seemed extraterrestrial, was crowned by a diadem. The baby Jesus—who looked nothing like a baby, more like an adult, or even an old man—sat on her lap, equally erect; his eyes were closed, too, his face sharp, wise, and powerful, and he wore a crown of his own. There was no tenderness, no maternal abandon in their postures. This was not the baby Jesus; this was already the king of the world. His serenity and the impression he gave of spiritual power—of intangible energy—were almost terrifying. [2015, 133–34]

In his review of *Submission* for the *New York Times Sunday Book Review*, the Norwegian novelist Karl Ove Knausgaard describes this scene as the only one in the book in which "there is no trace of satire. The description of the statue's unearthliness, its dignity and severity, its almost disturbingly powerful aura, is exquisite in a novel that otherwise seems to shun beauty or not to know it at all. And the attempt to approach its mystery is genuine" (Knausgaard 2015). For Knausgaard, what makes the novel shocking is how no one is particularly surprised or dismayed when the Muslim Brotherhood comes into power. The novel, says Knausgaard, is about "an entire culture's enormous loss of meaning, its lack of, or highly depleted, faith, a culture in which the ties of community are dissolving and which, for want of resilience more than anything else, gives up on its most important values and submits to religious government" (ibid.).

And yet, it is not just any "religious government" to which France "submits." The novel is shocking and was widely read as a warning of France's imminent demise because it was a Muslim—and not a Catholic—government that came to power. Indeed, in the novel, it is the decline of Christianity in Europe that is taken to be the source of France's crisis. "'Europe,'" François is told by the Muslim Brotherhood member now presiding over the Sorbonne, "'which was the summit of human civilization, committed suicide in a matter of decades'" (2015, 209). In the concluding paragraph, François notes that the new president of the Sorbonne "was the first to admit the greatness of medieval Christendom, whose artistic achievements would live forever in human memory; but little by little it had given way, it had been forced to compromise with rationalism, it had renounced its temporal powers, and so had sealed its own doom—and why? In the end, it was a mystery; God had ordained it so" (2015, 226).

The historian Judith Surkis's (2015) review of *Submission* is far more critical than that offered by Knausgaard. She argues that Houellebecq has long been "preoccupied by a chauvinistic view of French men's national decline and derogatory ideas about Muslims." She points to how the majority of the novel is devoted to describing France's decline through the less-than-subtle lens of François's diminishing libido. As François comes to accept the power of the Muslim Brotherhood in France, he is finally able to regain erections, in particular once he has been established in a polygamous marriage to teenage girls. Surkis highlights research demonstrating how long-standing Orientalist fantasies about Muslim women continue to be revealed in searches for internet pornography in France. Houellebecq does not offer an inclusive vision of a multicultural France but a "clichéd reduction of Islam to male sexual domination and female sexual pliancy." While Parmiggiani likens spaces such as the Collège to the last remaining fertile ground in France, Houellebecq's François—despite his desire to approach the mystery and aura of the medieval past—does not encounter them as enlivened. For François, Catholic materiality has lost its vitality, and so he must seek the return of his libido in submission to Islam.

Houellebecq's concluding words resonate in perhaps surprising ways with those of Marcel Gauchet (1985), a theorist who has argued that it was Christianity that initiated the process of the "disenchantment" of the West.[16] I want to highlight that, however much its institutions and practices have transformed over the centuries, the Catholic Church in France has not "renounced its temporal powers," nor "sealed its doom." At the Collège, according to Parmiggiani, the Catholic materiality that so often goes overlooked takes on a powerful, living presence. Catholic materiality does not always recede into private spaces, or ubiquitous obscurity. At times, it can also push through to the foreground, its objects and images appearing to act in ways that disenchanted minds are supposed to abhor.

The Parmiggiani catalog also betrays the powerful influence of other material and cultural forms in shaping desires for the Catholic past. The first page of the catalog displays the work of an artist who is not Parmiggiani. It opens with an image of a painting by a fifteenth-century Italian artist, Andrea Mantegna. The painting depicts the early Christian martyr Saint Sebastian. What is remarkable about the image is that it goes completely unremarked in the catalog. No acknowledgment of the title, the artist, or the date of production is included. The work and its relationship to Parmiggiani are presented as self-evident.

I recognized the image only because, a month earlier, I had attended an exhibition of Mantegna's works at the Louvre. In mid-October 2008, I had participated in a "Song and Liturgy" weekend at Saint Roch—the seventeenth-century self-coined "church of the artist" located one block north of the Louvre. Following two intensive days of learning new liturgical chants from contemporary composers, and performing them at mass late on Sunday morning, a small number from the group wrapped up the weekend with a visit to the famed museum. The choir director also worked as a community liaison at the Louvre, bringing underprivileged and underrepresented communities into this sacred national institution.[17] She was more than happy to act as our guide, leading us from the church, through the Tuileries garden, down the Pyramide, and into the Louvre. Upon arrival, there was little discussion. Despite the many options of what one might see in the French state's seemingly limitless collection of treasures, it was the Mantegna exhibit that those in the group most desired to experience.

Among those who attended were the composer, a young monk who had written the accompanying lyrics, a monk associated with St. Roch who was dressed in in a long black robe with a rope tied around his waist and a large wooden cross hanging around his neck, a smattering of men and women mostly in their fifties and sixties, the choir director, and me. While the exhibit began in brightly painted, well-lit rooms that displayed the artist's early explorations of Greco-Roman motifs, it quickly departed into more somber tones marked by sharp distinctions between light and shadow. In these rooms, the subject of the paintings was decidedly more Christian, without, however, entirely abandoning references to antiquity. The visit was a lengthy one. The group spent a great deal of time in front of almost all of the paintings displayed, remarking on and pointing to the paintings' minute details, debating the various meanings implied by the choice of colors, or by the inclusion of such and such a saint, and often deferring to the knowledge of the monks when in doubt.

One painting in particular seemed to move those in attendance. It was a much larger exploration of the same subject detailed in the painting reproduced in the Parmiggiani catalog. The oil on wood painting included in the catalog normally hangs in the Kunsthistoriches Museum in Vienna. In the exhibit, it was displayed alongside this similar image of the same subject in more monumental proportions owned by the Louvre. The expression of anguish on the martyr's face, the perfection of the minute but detailed city that ascends behind him, and the crumbling remnants of antiquity at his feet awed the group. They were not alone. Curators of the exhibit placed both paintings in a central, culminating position, assigning the larger one a number so that those who chose to follow the exhibit with an audio guide would stop, learn, and reflect on the work's magnitude.

It was not a coincidence that Parmiggiani, the curators at the Louvre, and the musicians from St. Roch all took the time to admire (and demand that others admire) Mantegna's paintings of St. Sebastian.[18] Exhibitions are planned long in advance, and those working at various cultural institutions in Paris tend to be well apprised of the upcoming events occurring at other spaces. The decision to open the catalog with the Mantegna image may well have been informed by the knowledge that the two exhibitions would coincide. Even if not, the choice points to the role that museums have long served in making Catholic material forms available for a variety of modes of engagement. The convergence of interest around these works at this particular time shows how the enlivening of Catholic materiality occurs through an array of social forces beyond the objects alone.

Indeed, visitors often made explicit the ways in which their expectations of how art ought to look had been shaped by museum visits—including disappointing ones—over the years. "AN IMMENSE SCANDAL," one remark in the comment book declared. "After the Louvre and Versailles . . . today, the Bernardins. The Devil does his work in the light of day. What sadness." For the writer, the former palace turned treasure-trove of the state that is the Louvre, the monument to monarchical glory that is Versailles, and the newly renovated space of cultural Catholicism that is the Collège all belong to a shared sacred space that, in recent years, has been tainted by contemporary art. Only a few months earlier, a Jeff Koons exhibit at Versailles had induced a level of outrage similar to that seen in response to the Parmiggiani exhibit at the Collège. Famously, the Pyramide structure that streamlined access to the Louvre was much critiqued when it was first added to the museum's courtyard in 1989.

The Pyramide, similar to the Parmiggiani exhibit, brings to mind a potentially violent history without offering the tools to confront or critique it. While the Louvre stands in the minds of many as a powerful expression of the wealth of European culture, objects expropriated and stolen by colonial officials around the world undergird its collection. The Pyramide sculpture could point to this exploitative and appropriative history, reminding viewers of the colonial foundations of many museums. Similarly, as visitors noted, the Parmiggiani exhibit could have referenced Krystallnacht. However, encounters with these violent histories are ultimately elided by other discourses surrounding these material forms. While the critic's words disparaged the exhibit, the "scandal" he identified in the incorporation of contemporary art into Paris's museums demonstrates the success, rather than the failure, of the arts project at the Collège. The ease with which the critic incorporated the Collège into one of numerous sacred—and not just religious—spaces that have been tarnished by contemporary art shows how quickly the Collège was able to integrate into Paris's cultural scene.

Further evidence of this success arose as the exhibit continued and received very positive reviews in the French press. Other visitors began to arrive who "loved" the work immediately, and who required no explanation from the guides and mediators. Their delight in the installation was matched only by their condescending enjoyment in reading remarks left by more hostile visitors in the livre d'or. The mediators were relieved to have an occasional reprieve from the work of managing outrage, and many employees at the Collège appeared heartened that they had succeeded in attracting a more "contemporary" public (I will explore further the particular notion of "publics" operating at the Collège in the next chapter). In terms of their ultimate effect on the Collège, however, the detractors and celebrants may not have been so far apart as they appeared. Those who appreciated the exhibit generally saw its power arising from the relationship between the installation and the thirteenth-century stones. Those who disparaged the contemporary art they encountered did so—like Parmiggiani—by celebrating a medieval past that appeared vastly superior to the contemporary scene. In so doing, both celebratory and angry visitors supported the temporal contortions underway at the Collège, allowing the institution to benefit from derision and praise alike.

* * *

In this chapter, I highlight the deeply paradoxical, enchanted, and contradictory relationships to objects brought by viewers and artists alike to the Collège. By equating Parmiggiani's mournful work with Muslim vandals from the banlieues, visitors were not only emphasizing the outsider status of these imagined actors. They were also critiquing what they understood to be evidence of a problematic relationship with objects. The broken glass suggested a violent and disrespectful relationship to objects, particularly in a space made sacred by its heritage status. And yet, as I describe in the introduction, Charb and the Je suis Charlie campaign insist that appropriately modern subjects know better than to be beholden to objects. They should, moreover, understand the importance of blasphemy and sacrilege. Just as the Collège is made tantalizing by the paradox between a past reborn and one that exists at an unbridgeable space of rupture, visitors' references to Muslims imply an anxiety surrounding practices that enlivened the Collège, or with the pervasive feeling that this was a space whose vitality could be damaged by matter out of place. I will offer one more example of responses to this exhibit to clarify my point.

Parmiggiani had intended for the work to be interactive. Specifically, he hoped that visitors would walk through the path surrounding the broken glass, following a circumambulatory tour. While it was the artist's assistants who had smashed the glass, once it fell to the ground it took on the power of art: once created it cannot be altered. The pieces of glass on the floor could not be moved. Because glass fragments filled the floor of this potential pathway, managers at the Collège, fearing the possibility of injury, installed a security wire in front of the glass, barring entry.

On the final day of the exhibit, however, the mediators, volunteers, and employees were allowed to make the tour as originally intended. The experience was a moving one. Certainly, the exhibit was shocking upon first glance. But, like the observers of modernity described by Susan Buck-Morss (1986), those of us who worked with the exhibit everyday felt less and less shock at the sight over time. Buck-Morss describes the effects of repetitive shocks as producing an "anesthetic" response. I found, however, that many of those working at the Collège in fact developed an intimate and affectionate relationship with the exhibit. Even employees and volunteers who had expressed a great deal of reticence in its opening days and weeks had come to feel at home with the broken glass. The opportunity to walk through it as the evening light settled through the nave allowed us to experience it anew. We could feel the sharpness of the glass beneath our feet, and a loud crunching sound reverberated through the nave, as though we were walking on very cold snow. After a moment's hesitation many of us bent down to pick up some of the smaller pieces of glass, knowing that they would vanish over the weekend. One volunteer described to me a few months later how the fragments now occupied a central space in her home and how she had altered the track lighting in her ceiling to bounce off of the glass like crystal. My pieces survived the trip back to the United States and, more often than not, they gather dust on my desk. Every now and then, however, I find myself reaching for them to help propel me back to that space and time, as I work to make sense of the emotions that filled it.

Very few people remained numb to this exhibit, as emotions tended to abound in the space. These affective states, I have argued, did not arise naturally from the objects themselves. Rather, they were the result of fragmented efforts over numerous centuries that contributed to the enlivening of the space of the Collège and its cultural project. When confronted with these visceral emotions, many visitors lashed out and insisted that Muslim vandals—those who are widely considered to have "medieval" or less-than-modern relationships with objects—must have caused these strange feelings and anxieties surrounding them.

I see in the mediators' final encounter with the installation and our desire to preserve and display its ephemeral fragments—as well as in the impassioned responses to the work and the space—the privilege of the banality of Catholicism in France. Here, we were engaging with objects in ways that gave them the sort of agency secular modernity typically denies. In the emotion-laden encounters with the exhibit I have described, visitors expressed a great deal of anger toward and attachment to the objects they found at the Collège as well as toward the space itself. While Charb's critique would have us believe that only Muslims are inappropriately attached to objects, images, and spaces, my interlocutors suggest otherwise. Mediating forms are powerful. They can be made to do a great deal of work in the world; they are a form of politics. Muslims who protested *Charlie Hebdo*'s cartoons did so because they know all too well the power of mediating forms. They have the power to include and exclude as they produce and reproduce visions of the past and present of France. They cannot be taken lightly.

4

LEARNING HOW TO LOOK

IN 2018, NINE YEARS AFTER THE SECOND contemporary art exhibit displayed at the Collège—entitled *Suite Grünewald*—opened, I visited the Collège during a brief trip to Paris. While there, I was delighted to run into one of the volunteers who had worked at the Collège since its inauguration. When I reminded her that I had witnessed or worked on the first four exhibits at the Collège, she smiled and said, "ah, *Suite Grünewald*, that's the exhibit that has really stayed with me. It was so powerful, both technically, and in term of *sens* (meaning). It was really special." As the volunteer's memory suggests, *Suite Grünewald* was by far the most popular exhibit of contemporary art at the Collège in its first two years of operation.

Created by the French artist Gérard Titus-Carmel between 1994 and 1996, the work had never been exhibited before its display at the Collège from March 19 to August 9, 2009. Originally planned to end in June, it received such positive responses that employees decided to lengthen the exhibit through the summer. These favorable responses can in part be explained by the fact that both the artist and the historical work of art that inspired him are well known in France. Titus-Carmel's works are part of the permanent collections in a number of museums; he also represented France at the 1997 Venice Biennale. *Suite Grünewald* was a detailed exploration of a late medieval *retable* (altarpiece), the Isenheim Altarpiece, created by Matthias Grünewald (1470–1528) between 1512 and 1516 and now housed at the Unterlinden Museum in Colmar, a small city in the French province of Alsace. In 159 drawings and one large oil-on-canvas painting, Titus-Carmel deconstructed and reconstructed Grünewald's altarpiece through a variety of techniques.

But it is not only the renown of the artist and the work upon which he reflected that can explain the exhibit's popularity. Significantly, it was the only artwork I saw at the Collège that made explicit use of Christian motifs.[1] As such, it appeared legible to an audience that had been discomfited by Parmiggiani's broken glass. While, as I argue in chapter 3, Parmiggiani's installation in fact supported and reproduced the project underway at the Collège through narratives that enlivened the space, many visitors were far more at ease engaging with a work whose various components could be affixed to the wall for the intimate viewing of images that were recognizable, and recognizably Christian.

Because the exhibition was extended unexpectedly, many of those who had been hired to work as mediators were unable to stay on through the summer. In the scramble to find replacements when many of the mediators could not afford to continue to work at the Collège as interns for such little pay through the summer, I offered a convenient solution. The fact that I spoke English as well as French also proved useful, as the Collège had started to appear on numerous tourists' Parisian itineraries.

As I began to stumble my way through my new métier, I was surprised to discover that part of my labor was to model a mode of viewing the work not as Christian but as art. Through a variety of subtle means, the other mediators and I showed the viewers how to look at *Suite Grünewald* in a very different manner than how Belting described people's responses to cult images (see chapter 3), or what the French theorist Jacques Rancière has categorized as an "ethical" regime of art. In using this term, Rancière aims to point to objects, images, and spaces whose significance is determined by criteria external to them. These criteria are external because they extend beyond an object's material or technical properties to ask questions regarding its origin, truth-content, purpose, or use (2004, 16). In this way, as Alena Alexandrova (2017) has argued, Rancière's ethical regime holds much in common with Belting's cult images.

While viewing *Suite Grünewald* at the Collège, visitors were encouraged to encounter this work as what Belting describes as an art image, or Rancière associates with the "aesthetic regime" of art. In the aesthetic regime, artworks are judged by criteria internal to them, as art objects establish their own criteria for inclusion and judgment. These internal criteria are only possible because of the widespread notion in the modern period that art is absolutely singular and that it cannot be judged pragmatically (2004, 18). Pierre Bourdieu's *Distinction* (1977) demonstrates the differences in socio-economic class that tend to align with those who offer aesthetic judgments and those who use external criteria as a basis for judgment. Thus, when visitors at the Collège were encouraged to take up aesthetic modes of viewing, they were not only being asked to engage in a particular regime of art but one that tends to require elite education and cultural capital.

Art viewing has a long history within the Roman Catholic Church, one marked by a great deal of ambivalence. Amid the institution's powerful role as patron, figures such St. Bernard worried about the power of fine materials and images that might distract Christians from their reflections on the Word of God.[2] This history of ambivalence, I would argue, has continued through the transformation of Catholic materiality from cult to art images. Numerous studies explore how Christian viewers have encountered works of modern and contemporary art as blasphemous, sacrilegious, or iconoclastic.[3] Others have addressed what James Elkins (2004) has called the "strange place" of Christianity in contemporary art, or what Alexandrova (2004) has identified as the complex "afterlife" of Christian motifs in modern and contemporary art.[4] Still others make a case for the potentially "spiritual" implications and effects of modern and contemporary art.[5]

Here, I am interested in a different sort of relationship between modern and contemporary art and Christianity: how secular artists produce Christian art, not by virtue of an explicit or implicit spirituality but through their participation in the reproduction of Christianity's privilege. Just as scholars and intellectuals may inadvertently support the reproduction of catholaïcité through their use of Christian concepts as a model for a variety of political projects or as universal tools of analysis, so artists and curators may undergird Catholic privilege by way of its banality in using Christian motifs as foundations for their art and exhibitions, however critical they might otherwise be. With *Suite Grünewald*, this was accomplished by putting aside the question of whether the work might be perceived as a form of blasphemy or devotion. Instead, the artist and mediators encouraged the various publics who entered the space to engage with the work in aesthetic rather than ethical terms. The Parmiggiani installation mediated the Catholic past by enlivening its phenomenal forms. In this chapter I explore how visitors were encouraged to engage with Titus-Carmel's reflections on a historical cult image by aestheticizing it. In so doing, I argue, viewers further amplified the privileged banality of Catholic motifs, recognizing them as significant not in light of a particular religious (or ethical) claim but as the ground for the "high" culture that populates many of the city's museums.

THE CATHOLICISM OF THE
AESTHETIC REGIME OF ART

The late medieval altarpiece that Titus-Carmel explored in *Suite Grünewald* sits at the cusp of the transformation from cult to art images. It came to be widely known and beloved, however, in the nineteenth century. Following the violence of the revolutionary period, during which many of the country's churches saw a great deal of destruction and expropriation, the medieval Gothic cathedral began to serve as a model, not only of architecture but of republican democracy itself. During this period, medieval art and architecture was reassessed as an expression of French genius prior to the modern era.

In the summer of 2016, Prime Minister Manuel Valls justified local "burkini" bans cropping up around France by arguing that "Marianne"—a symbol of France for much of the twentieth century—went bare-breasted. Many noted how, in his attempt to justify oppressive regulations, Valls had confused his symbolic women. Representations of Marianne did not tend to depict her bare-breasted. The painting to which he referred when making this argument was created by Eugène Delacroix (1798–1863) in 1830. Entitled *28 July, Liberty Leading the People* and created to celebrate the 1830 Revolution, the painting foregrounds a bare-breasted woman as a symbol of liberty, rather than as Marianne.[6] Stephanie Glaeser (2004) has pointed to how this painting includes the subtle but powerful presence of the Notre-Dame Cathedral in the background. This was not uncommon for the period when medieval Catholic materiality—rather than women's bared breasts—came to stand as a symbol of France. Indeed, while painting *28 July*, Delacroix may have been reading the works of Victor Hugo (1802–1885), who, according to Glaeser, also "equated the Gothic cathedral with aesthetic [and political] liberty" (2004, 460).

Importantly, such ideas did not remain confined to art and literature; they were also made concrete through the work of the state-established Commission of Historical Monuments. State-employed architects played a key role in transforming Paris during this period, and many of them, such as Eugène Viollet-le-Duc (1814–1879) and Victor Baltard (1805–1874), did so by integrating neogothic and historicizing forms into the cityscape. Baltard, for example, was responsible for many of Paris's most famous modern edifices that point to the medieval past, including the church St. Augustin and the Central Marketplace, Les Halles (whose destruction in 1971 has been much regretted ever since). Baltard is famous for taking the medieval structure of rounded vaults and applying it through the use of steel and glass. Of course, the powerful flexibility of steel made the vaults unnecessary, but this contemporary take on a medieval form was deployed frequently in Paris during its massive reconstruction in the mid-nineteenth century led by the prefect under Napoleon III, Georges-Eugène Haussmann (1809–1891). This period, known as the Second Empire (1852–1870), is considered to be a key moment in the formation of modern French political formations (see Hazareesingh 1988 and Harvey 2006). Under Haussmann's destructive remaking of Paris, the state agents charged with modernizing the city also designed dozens of historicizing Catholic churches, with the state often paying for their construction (see Boudon 2001).

Many of the churches built during the period stand at the meeting point of major roads, and their names are given to the nearest metro station. Despite the monumentality of many of these edifices, they often go unseen by residents of the city. It is the very ubiquity of neomedieval Catholic infrastructure in Paris, I argue, that, over time, allows sites designed to be particularly visible to fade into the background of an urban landscape. That is, the state-funded destruction and reconstruction of Paris, which produced a significant number of the city's churches, allowed Catholic structures to play a foundational role in the "look" of Paris as what David Harvey (2006) has called the "modern city *par excellence*."

It was in this context of the celebration of the medieval in nineteenth-century France that Grünewald's particularly grotesque depiction of Christ on the cross received renewed attention.[7] The image is indeed arresting and rather brutal. Lesions, cuts, and thorns mark the entirety of Christ's taut pale skin, stretched nearly to the point of tearing between the corners of the cross. The nineteenth-century novelist and art critic Joris-Karl Huysmans (1848–1907)—whose writings were the focus of the scholarly work of François, the central character in Houellebecq's novel I recount in chapter 3—described the Isenheim Altarpiece as a sight that viewers are unlikely to forget (fig. 4.1): "There, in the old Unterlinden convent, he seizes on you the moment you go in and promptly strikes you dumb with the fearsome nightmare of a Calvary. It is as if a typhoon of art had been let loose and was sweeping you away, and you need a few minutes to recover from the impact, to surmount the impression of awful horror made by the huge crucified Christ dominating the nave of this museum, which is installed in the old disaffected chapel of the convent" (Huysmans 1976, 3).

The curatorial work of writers, artists, architects, and legislatures past and

FIGURE 4.1. Mattias Grünewald, Isenheim Altarpiece (central panel), 1512–1516.

present has its effects. The admiration of nineteenth-century writers such as Huysmans subsequently encouraged art viewers and artists to engage with the Isenheim Altarpiece. Numerous modern and contemporary artists have reproduced Grünewald's Christ, including George Grosz (1893–1959) in *Shut Up and Do Your Duty!* (1927) and *Silence!* (1935–36), and Sue Coe (1951–) in *Rape, Bedford* (1984) and *It's Not Safe!* (1987).[8] Grosz's pieces take up Grünewald's Christ in order to question the obligations of young men as wartime soldiers.[9] Coe's terrifying drawings use Grünewald's representation of suffering to depict and protest sexual violence against women. Titus-Carmel's work shares the most with *Homage to Grünewald* (1974) by James Rosen (1933 –), in which the central panel of the Isenheim Altarpiece is re-created as a shadowy fading away of the original. Some members of those I will call the "spiritual public" (described below) directed me to Emil Nolde's (1867–1956) polyptych *The Life of Christ* (1912) as an interesting comparison with Grünewald. Nolde's work, however, is quite different. Rather than taking up the Isenheim Altarpiece in particular, Nolde's painting draws on Christian iconography more broadly and depicts Christ's crucifixion without explicitly referencing Grünewald's depiction of the crucifixion. Alexandrova argues that Nolde is one of the few modern artists who engaged with

Christian motifs in a "religious" manner (2017, 44). Visitors likely pointed me to the image because it similarly makes use of abstraction while exploring Christian motifs.[10]

Thus Titus-Carmel was working on well-trodden ground in *Suite Grünewald*. According to a filmed interview available on the Collège's website during the exhibition, he first became acquainted with the Isenheim Altarpiece in reproductions found in a black-and-white art history dictionary ("Gérard Titus-Carmel au Collège des Bernardins" 2009). He was particularly affected when he saw the work in color—still as a reproduction—for the first time. Already impressed by the retable's "significance and its dramaturgy," he was surprised to discover that the work was marked by, in his words, "an immense economy of color." Black, red, and white were the only colors to be found in the central tableau. In the mid-1990s he visited the museum that houses the Isenheim Altarpiece for the first time. The museum's director offered him the chance to visit the work alone, after the museum had closed. This intimacy gave him the opportunity, as he explains in the video, "to become, not friends with the tableau, but almost" (ibid.).

Busy with other projects, Titus-Carmel did not return to the Isenheim Altarpiece for a year and a half when he found himself making a quick drawing of Mary Magdalene. A pencil drawing, the image is a rather precise reproduction of Mary Magdalene as she appears in Grünewald's painting (see fig. 4.2). Upon completing the drawing, he wondered why, of the five people depicted in Grünewald's tableau, he began with her. "Mary Magdalene," he realized, "intrigued me technically. First of all, the folds of her robe, her crimped hair" (ibid.). But also, he described, it is in Mary Magdalene that one finds movement in the tableau. Her emotive hands, kneeling figure, and supplicating gestures mount upwards towards Christ. In contrast, the figures of Christ, St. John the Baptist, and St. John holding the Virgin Mary appeared static. Mary Magdalene, explained Titus-Carmel, is where "the tableau called out to me—a phrase, by the way, that I detest" (ibid.). In other words, he aimed to respond to the work as an aesthetic or art image, focusing on its formal and expressive elements, rather than on its situated moment of production, its iconographic elements, or earlier moments of viewing. And yet at times, and despite himself, the work "called out" and demanded other kinds of attention.

After completing six drawings of Mary Magdalene, Titus-Carmel went on to address each of the other figures in the work. In subsequent series, he examined the hands of the figures surrounding Christ—the praying hands of Mary Magdalene and the Virgin, the pointing finger of St. John the Baptist

FIGURE 4.2. Gérard Titus-Carmel, *Suite Grünewald* (Number 5), 1994. Acrylic and acrylic wash. Photo by the author. © 2019 Artists Rights Society (ARS), New York/ADAGP, Paris.

as he intones in Latin "Illum oportet crescere me autem minui"[11]— as well as Christ's hands, feet, and chest. The artist repeated the figures and gestures numerous times using different materials and techniques, including acrylic, collage, pencil, ink, sanguine, and watercolor. Some drawings are highly detailed "copies" of sections of the altarpiece; others are far more abstract

FIGURE 4.3. Gérard Titus-Carmel, *Suite Grünewald* (Number 150), 1994. Acrylic and collage. Photo by author. © 2019 Artists Rights Society (ARS), New York/ADAGP, Paris.

(see fig. 4.3). The repetition of various forms throughout, however, prevents these abstractions from being nonrepresentative. In the context of these repetitions, a black triangle, for example, can clearly stand in for the body of Christ. *Suite Grünewald*'s one large oil painting reproduces the central panel of the triptych in full (fig. 4.4). At the Collège, the painting hung at

FIGURE 4.4. Gérard Titus-Carmel, *Suite Grünewald*, 1994. Acrylic on canvas, 256.6 × 332.6 cm. Photo by author. © 2019 Artists Rights Society (ARS), New York/ADAGP, Paris.

the apex of the exhibition, which followed a circumambulatory path found in Paris's many neogothic churches (and which was denied to Parmiggiani's installation).

Visitors to the Collège who knew of Titus-Carmel's other works were surprised by *Suite Grünewald*'s explicitly Christian motifs. It is indeed the only work among his oeuvre to include such allusions. In other works made around the same time, such as *Forêt* from 1995, many of the same abstract forms appear but outside the context of the conversation with the Isenheim Altarpiece, they no longer imply Christian motifs. According to Titus-Carmel, the subject of the work was neither his primary source of fascination nor an element that could easily be dismissed. In the video, he describes how his interest in the Isenheim Altarpiece began with its composition, the distribution of space, and its formal devices. He acknowledges, however, that he "could not entirely abstract away from the subject matter." But the content was, in his words, "*au même titre*" (on the same level) as the altarpiece's form (ibid.).

For Titus-Carmel, the "adventure" of his work was situated here, in the "interstice" between the subject matter and the formal accomplishments of the altarpiece. His use of Christian themes appears somewhat incidental. While he acknowledges that the images found in the work were of a particular nature, his work is an example of contemporary art that engages Christian themes in ways that are neither explicitly critical of the faith nor created in the service of worship. In other words, like the resuscitation of medieval architectural forms in nineteenth-century Paris, *Suite Grünewald* makes use of Christian motifs without engaging in either blasphemy or devotion.

Employees at the Collège did not insist that the mediators impart any single reading of *Suite Grünewald* to the public. While the institution refused to determine how the work ought to be interpreted, viewing *Suite Grünewald* in the space of the Collège inevitably influenced the manner in which the work was perceived. What are the implications of an attempt to create a space between blasphemy and devotion if it is one that is hosted by the Catholic Church? By way of a brief historical detour, I want to highlight how the Collège is not necessarily unique in this regard. Rather than an exceptional form of Catholic materiality, the Collège is important because it is a particularly powerful expression of the privilege of the banality of Catholic materiality produced and reproduced in a variety of sites in France and Europe.

What is often overlooked in the history of the rise of the aesthetic regime of art is the key role played by the Catholic Church in this shift in viewing. It was the Roman Catholic Church that created the first public art museum, known as the "Profane Museum," in the Vatican Palace in 1767. In the decades to follow, a new wing of the Apostolic Palace was added to "house many of the Vatican's most important Greek and Roman statuary" and a guide in French and Italian was published in order to help visitors explore the works found within (Ruprecht 2014, 134).

In light of an ethical regime of art, members of the Catholic Church were compelled to reject pagan material forms as idolatrous. In a museum, however, such material forms could be admired through what Rancière describes as a "poetic" or "representational regime"—in which a work is admired for its mimetic features, its ability to effectively represent the world. In the space of the Profane Museum, Greek sculpture no longer had to be deplored through the lens of an ethical regime of art which would judge a work according to the purpose for which it had originally been created. This shift was only possible because the Profane Museum at the Vatican was, broadly speaking, inaugurating an aesthetic regime of viewing. The Profane Museum helped to establish a mode of viewing in which works were seen as autonomous and admired outside of their contexts of production. Commentators at the time, such as Antoine-Chrysostôme Quatremère de Quincy (1755–1849) "understood that the massive shift in ways of see-ing such objects—the shift in religious rhetoric from 'pagan idol' to 'fine art'—had served to justify these objects display at the Vatican Museum and elsewhere" (ibid., 148).

According to Rancière,

> The aesthetic regime of art did not begin with decisions to initiate an artistic rupture. It began with the decisions to reinterpret what makes art or what art makes: Vico discovering the "true Homer," that is to say not an inventor of fables and characters but a witness to the image-laden language and thought of ancient times; Hegel indicating the true subject matter of Dutch genre painting: not in stories or descriptions of interiors but a nation's freedom displayed in reflections of light; Hölderin reinvent-ing Greek tragedy; Balzac contrasting the poetry of the geologist who reconstructs worlds out of tracks and fossils with the poetry that makes do with reproducing a bit of agitation in the soul; Mendelssohn replaying the St. Matthew Passion; etc. The aesthetic regime of the arts is first of all a new regime for relating to the past. [2004, 20]

Similarly, I see the decision by the Vatican to make its collection of Greek statues available for viewing as an effort to "reinterpret what makes art and what art makes." The Roman Catholic Church—rather than being merely the victim of the looting that contributed to museums' collections (which certainly also occurred, especially in France)—played a powerful role in the creation of museums and in the initiation of the aesthetic regime of viewing.

The aesthetic regime of art would then come to be applied to Catholic images, objects, and spaces.[12] As Catholic materiality moved into museums, its ethical effects and affects may well have altered, but, I argue, its privilege was amplified rather than reduced. Since the opening of the Louvre to the public following the French Revolution, museums have served as seemingly tangible evidence for the declared superiority of Europe by curating par-ticular histories and narratives through the conjunction and comparison of objects. That museums have accomplished this feat in large part by aes-theticizing Catholic materiality and incorporating it into this narrative has long provided the Church with a powerful ground upon which to build its privileged banality. At the Collège, the mediators encouraged viewers to take up aesthetic modes of viewing that, while developed in museums, have been supported by the efforts of the Catholic Church. Allowing Catholic materiality to be viewed in aesthetic and poetic—rather than only ethical—terms has been effective in reproducing Catholicism's privileged banality.

THE REGIMES OF VIEWING
OF THE COLLÈGE'S PUBLICS

At the Collège, visitors expressed diverse responses to *Suite Grünewald*. Over time, however, I discerned certain patterns in the modes of viewing performed and reactions expressed. In exchange for allowing me to conduct research while working as a mediator, managers at the Collège asked me to assess the publics I observed and their reactions to the exhibitions. I have decided to retain the term "publics," which I used along with my colleagues in our daily work at the Collège. While our engagements with visitors were often more direct than the abstract "reading" public described by Michael Warner (1990), the broader task of imagining a larger public also informed our work. Common points of discussion among employees included lamenting the limits of the more Catholic publics and wondering how to attract a public more accustomed to contemporary art (and, therefore, presumably more likely to identify as tacitly—rather than committedly—Catholic).

The general distinction between publics made by many of the mediators and employees was between "Catholics" and everyone else. I found this dichotomous division difficult to apply. How does one recognize a Catholic? How could we identify such traits on sight? This division, moreover, took for granted a hard-and-fast distinction between religious and secular that overlooked many of the nuances in the desires, remarks, and art-viewing practices I observed. Consequently, in one conversation with a manager at the Collège, I offered an alternative way of categorizing the visitors. Rather than attempting to discern their religious orientation, I distinguished between publics by using their motivations for coming to the space and the activities they engaged in while there. I explained that I had identified three different publics: contemporary, classical, and spiritual. I later learned that managers took up my categories and applied them as their own in subsequent staff meetings.

The contemporary public was made up of those who frequented contemporary art spaces and had come after reading positive reviews of the exhibit in the press, or who were friends with or had previous knowledge of the artist. They were unlikely to participate in any other offerings at the Collège. Nor, however, were they particularly concerned with the fact that the space was owned and operated by the archdiocese.[13] The classical public came to the Collège first and foremost for the stones. That is, they came to see the medieval building in as pure a state as possible and generally resented anything that blocked their access to its historical authenticity. They presumed that the exhibitions should have a direct relationship with what they often called the "aesthetic" of the building. Finally, members of the spiritual public often came to the Collège, they claimed, *par hasard* (by accident), implying that a force apart from their own volition had brought them there. Others in this category came to the space in order to see and experience Paris's newest—in their words—"spiritual" space, or to attend a theology class.

Some visitors, of course, displayed more than one or none of these characteristics. My choice of contemporary, classical, and spiritual attempted to complicate any clear distinction between religious and secular dispositions, as many visitors confounded any such divisions. Members of the contemporary public, for example, often explained that the medieval vaults of the nave and sacristy heightened their experience of this work, whose contemporaneity contrasted with, and yet was "perfectly at home in" or "well suited to," this space. One friend of Titus-Carmel who attended the vernissage explained that she knew of the work, and of the Collège, but to see them both for the first time together "almost made her cry." Many, although certainly not all, members of the classical public wore visible markers of their Catholic faith or identified themselves as such in conversations with the mediators. However, to assume that these signs, whether visual or verbal, implied that they regularly attended mass or that what they sought at the Collège was a deepening of their faith would be misguided. I found these visitors to be particularly intriguing because, while they strongly advocated for the importance of the restoration of spaces such as the Collège, they were often less interested in engaging in conversations about faith or spirituality. Members of the spiritual public, who were generally more interested in engaging in conversations of this sort, did not always identify themselves as Catholic. Some such visitors, such as those who declared themselves to be of a Catholic "heritage," explicitly refused the word "religious" in favor of the term "spiritual."

One observation I made about all of the publics I encountered was that almost everyone who came through the doors was white. The majority seemed to be middle- or upper-class, an observation that was confirmed by my coworkers. Not all of the visitors could easily be identified as Catholic, but only rarely did the people I met at the Collège wear visible signifiers of, or declare themselves to be affiliated with, other religions.

The following account of the responses of these publics to *Suite Grünewald* is an attempt to synthesize hundreds of conversations I recorded in many pages of fieldnotes, of experiences recounted to me by other mediators at the Collège, and of comments left in the livre d'or. I have tried to encapsulate these interactions by using terms I heard visitors utter frequently and providing examples of how their visits tended to proceed. While the differences between the practices of viewing are significant, divergent practices—much as during the Parmiggiani exhibit—ultimately contributed to the authorization of the rather particular project underway at the Collège. I want to focus here on how, despite the light touch we were supposed to take as mediators, in our work we sought to encourage visitors to take up more "contemporary," or aesthetic, modes of art viewing.

In general, members of the contemporary public responded positively to the exhibit. In early July 2009, I encountered a man who told me that he had visited the exhibit four times already. Knowing that it would close in a month, he wanted to take every opportunity to appreciate the work. A few weeks prior, two young women who identified themselves as artists explained that they knew of Titus-Carmel's work. Following their careful tour, they left remarks in the livre d'or that could have been written by critics in France's contemporary art magazines. "This is a liberated and flamboyant work that will stay in my spirit," wrote one. "A magnificent exhibition that shows the surprising faculty of creation, day after day, without ceasing to be renewed," remarked the other. They included their names next to their comments.

Members of this public were easily identifiable because they, more than any other public, refused the services of the mediators. They understood what it was they were seeing, or at least needed no assistance in their *demarche* (approach) to it. In fact, they often explained that they could not have their experience of the installation altered by our remarks, which might predetermine the nature of the relationship between them and the work. This desire to be left alone was, at times, articulated explicitly. One contemporary visitor responded to my inquiry as to whether she had any questions with a breezy "no, I'm discovering." At other times, visitors' body language could speak volumes. On a warm day in the middle of the summer, I smiled at two men, both in their forties, who entered into the space. In my notes, I recognized them as potential members of the contemporary public owing to the fact that "they wore cool glasses" and they did little to acknowledge my presence. Picking up on this body language, I did not immediately approach them. They took a pamphlet displayed next to the exhibit and, after looking through it carefully, began a long, slow, and careful tour. I eventually approached them to tell them I was available to answer any questions they might have. "Forcément" (obviously), they replied, making clear their displeasure at my refusal to read their signals correctly. They pointed and whispered to one another, took pictures, and eventually paused before the large oil tableau. They scanned the brochure, flipping it over again and again. I was seated, writing my fieldnotes, just off to the side. Finally, they approached me rather begrudgingly to ask the meaning of the Latin phrase inscribed on the painting. After I translated it into French, I left them alone again to stare at the painting for some time.

In addition to refusing interactions with the mediators, this public sometimes declined even to refer to the small black-and-white reproduction of the Isenheim Altarpiece available in the accompanying brochure, often preferring to take a copy only as they departed. While they generally understood that the piece was a reflection on the Isenheim Altarpiece, they felt that to see the source would alter their appreciation of *Suite Grünewald* on its own terms. Here, they were clearly taking up an aesthetic mode of viewing, in Rancière's terms, as they desired to judge the work purely on criteria internal to the work itself. For this public, the purpose of their visits seemed to be expressed in their capacity to identify the techniques and materials that Titus-Carmel had used in each drawing. When they did approach the mediators, it was often to settle a debate about the technique used. Significantly, it was this question that the Collège had best prepared us to answer. One of the few documents we were provided was a detailed list of every technique in each of the drawings in *Suite Grünewald*, a point to which I will return below.

Members of the classical public often described their taste as "classique," in order to explain why they could appreciate an exhibition like *Suite Grünewald* but also to express hesitance at accepting it wholeheartedly. For them, the term explained why they still preferred more "traditional" paintings to the ones before them. In general, classical visitors' responses to the artist and his work improved when they understood the relationship between *Suite Grünewald* and the Isenheim Altarpiece. If, for the contemporary public, the experience of viewing the exhibit was shaped by their capacity to identify the various techniques used in its production, *Suite Grünewald* became more comprehensible for the classical public when they were able to identify the links between it and the Isenheim Altarpiece. The experience of viewing *Suite Grünewald* often became one of finding these correspondences by making the circumambulatory tour with the reproduction in hand and pointing to the connections between the two works. They would often critique the Collège for not having a larger reproduction—in color—of the Isenheim Altarpiece, a problem that I and other mediators occasionally resolved by offering them copies of images of the central panel, which we had procured for ourselves from a glossy book about the altarpiece sold in the Collège bookstore.

One day in early July, two women in their seventies arrived. They made it clear that they were here to see the "magnificent" restoration, a good indicator that I was speaking to members of the classical public. Nevertheless, they allowed me to explain a bit about the exhibit and became fascinated by the link to the Isenheim Altarpiece. I left them with the large color image of the altarpiece to complete the tour. When they reached the first of the more abstract series, they sought me out to ask me to explain what it was they were seeing. There was a linkage between the drawings and St. John the Baptist's pointing figure, but I hesitated to point it out to them, worrying that I would be crossing a line as a mediator by determining how the images ought to be read. As I pointed to St. John the Baptist's finger on their picture of the altarpiece, however, they expressed relief at the sight of recognition. The women, however, soon became nervous that their preoccupation with the exhibit would make them miss their guided tour of the space and so abandoned the exhibit promptly thereafter. Later that same month a woman arrived with a plastic sheet in which she had brought numerous reproductions of the retable. I asked her if she was "friends" with the altarpiece, having recently viewed the interview with Titus-Carmel and enjoyed his use of the phrase. She explained that she had seen the Titus-Carmel exhibit once before, but it meant and said nothing to her. It seemed to say enough, however, that she was prompted to conduct some research. She explained that the research had resulted in her developing a keen interested in Grünewald, much more than in Titus-Carmel.

At times, members of the classical public remarked on the "obsessive" nature of the work in ways that expressed concern about the reliability of the artist. One woman surprised me with the remark "What a pity." When I looked at her quizzically, she explained that "he must have been obsessed, in a fervor to produce a work this large, obsessed by the material, all those hands praying and pleading." Another member of the classical public was astounded to learn that a single artist had created all 159 drawings. Appearing discomfited at the thought, he turned the conversation in another direction, remarking that he was equally astounded by the "magnificence" of the renovation and then asked me for details about the building. This was typical for members of the classical public. When in doubt about the art they saw, they turned their attention away from the exhibit to the space in which it was displayed. The fact that these visitors were often unsettled by the idea that the artist had engaged in a sort of fevered production suggests their discomfort with certain kinds of spiritual sensibilities.

Generally, members of this public preferred the more "figurative" images—a term they used frequently—and the meaning or success of a particular drawing often resided in its capacity to most effectively appear as a copy of the original work. On occasion, members of the classical public claimed that Titus-Carmel's work helped them better to appreciate "abstraction" because they could see that he had the "ability to really draw." They often insisted that it was necessary for artists to start with copies in order to perfect their skills; it was particularly necessary, however, for abstract artists to begin with such work in order for their abstraction to be called art. "One must begin with the figurative before arriving at abstraction," one man insisted, "or abstraction loses any meaning."

Like the Parmiggiani installation, *Suite Grünewald* benefited from another exhibit held in Paris just prior to its opening. From October 8, 2008, to February 2, 2009, the Louvre, the Musée d'Orsay, and the Grand Palais jointly displayed *Picasso and His Masters*.[14] In the exhibit, some of Picasso's works were shown alongside the classical paintings that had inspired him. It quickly became a blockbuster, with the Grand Palais holding all-night hours in its final weeks of display. Many visitors made comparisons between the exhibits, either to suggest that both had helped them to appreciate abstraction or to confirm their suspicions of the genre.

Some of the more tepid remarks about *Suite Grünewald* from the classical public came in the form of a positive contrast with the Parmiggiani exhibit. "An interesting exhibition in any case," a signed comment in the livre d'or read. "At least better than Parmiggiani! A little more effort towards the sacred for the next one!" Other members of the classical public offered positive reviews of the exhibit, while still maintaining the primacy of the space. "Could there be a more beautiful screen for such a work than this Collège des Bernardins?" one visitor inquired.

Members of the third group—the spiritual public—often expressed how they were "entranced" by the piece. They admired how the artist demonstrated a very strong, in their words, "spirit." These individuals often remarked that Titus-Carmel must have really been "inside" his work in order to produce something so large and repetitive, seeming to suggest a mode of action lacking in volition, similar to their descriptions of their own arrival at the Collège. In contrast to the classical public, members of the spiritual public admired the notion of the artist "obsessed" with the work. Some described the experience of viewing the work in spiritual terms. A few weeks before the close of the exhibit, for example, a soft-spoken man wearing a cross around his neck expressed how lucky he felt to have come on a quiet day, so that he could appreciate the work as it was intended, in complete silence. Later he asked me if we sold any posters of the exhibit. I explained that we did not have the right to reproduce the images but that they were available in the catalog for sale in the bookstore. I added that he was welcome to take pictures. "My camera is here," he replied, pointing first to his head and then to his heart.

Many members of this public were familiar with the figures depicted in the work. They could easily point to the differences between the two Marys and the two Johns. Members of this public were intrigued by the images, however, not as interpretations of those created by Grünewald, or as evidence of a particular technique but as representations of the iconography of the crucifixion more broadly. Instead of looking for the correspondences with the Isenheim Altarpiece, or identifying the various methods used by Titus-Carmel, members of this public often searched for hidden religious meanings in the work's repetitive forms. At times, they would suggest symbolic explanations for why there were seven drawings in the first series and six in the second. They would focus on the details to which Titus-Carmel had paid particular attention, seeing in the different expressions of the hands of Mary different modes of prayer (some spiritual visitors saw not only Catholic prayer but various forms of Buddhist prayer as well); some even attempted to divine a particular meaning in the colors Titus-Carmel chose for each drawing. When I would explain that the artist had, quite simply, restricted himself to the colors found in the Isenheim Altarpiece, undeterred, they would offer an explanation along the lines of "but why this particular color of those available in this particular image?"[15]

For these visitors, the complex relationship between the Isenheim Altarpiece and *Suite Grünewald* was insignificant. They often saw little merit in distinguishing the iconography associated with the crucifixion from the particular representation by Grünewald that was the subject of Titus-Carmel's work. In their conversations with the mediators, roles were often reversed as this public preferred to educate the mediators about Christian iconography, details of which the mediators often knew relatively little and about which the Collège had provided us nothing in the way of orientation.

One day in late July, I approached a man furiously taking notes in front of various different drawings and asked if he had any questions. He asked me to explain the difference between two sets of hands—one pair were folded neatly (the Virgin Mary's) and the other were clasped with the fingers tensely splayed outward (Mary Magdalene's). I suggested that Titus-Carmel merely reproduced the hands as Grünewald had depicted them. The man sighed and looked at me impatiently. Trying again, I explained that one pair were those of the Virgin Mary and the other those of Mary Magdalene, and attempted to engage him in a discussion of why Grünewald might have depicted them that way. Borrowing language from Ernst Gombrich's *History of Art* (2008 [1950])—a French version of which I purchased at the bookstore around the corner from my house and often perused in the evenings—I pointed out that Grünewald depicted Mary with a certain calmness and Mary Magdalene with more of a sense of despair. Still dissatisfied with my efforts, he returned the discussion to Titus-Carmel's choices. He insisted that there must be some reason why Titus-Carmel has chosen to emphasize them so much. I nodded and listened as he insisted that there must be some "iconographic" meaning to the decisions of Titus-Carmel. He stated his intention to research this question and left in a huff. For this frustrated visitor, the artwork's meaning resided in the spiritual intentions brought to it by the artist.

A few of the more critical viewers among the spiritual public wondered about the propriety of a seemingly secular artist borrowing from Christian imagery and artworks. In early August, one man who described himself as Catholic explained to me that he has a hard time coming to terms with how contemporary artists use Catholic symbols, often for the purpose of sacrilege. Even if that were not the case here, he needed a clearer account of Titus-Carmel's intentions in order to determine his response to the work. "Is this just a technical study?" he asked me. "Is it right for the artist to do so with these kinds of images?" When I suggested that the work does suggest some careful reflection on the part of the artist, he remained unsatisfied. I suggested he look up Catherine Grenier's (who served as the curator of the Parmiggiani exhibition) book *Contemporary Art: Is It Christian?* (2003), in which she explores how, even when they are not making use of Christian images, contemporary artists may be engaging with Christian problems and questions. I hesitated briefly in recalling Grenier's last name. "It's by Catherine . . ." and paused. He raised his eyebrows skeptically—"Millet?" he asked, referring to a French curator and intellectual who published a tell-all book (2002 [2001]) about her masturbation practices as a child and her enjoyment of group sex as an adult. His wife scoffed at his inappropriate remark, told him that would be quite enough, and dragged him away. Illicit sex, of course, could easily serve as evidence of the nonnormative and highly problematic use of Christian motifs.

These three modes of viewing match up rather well with Rancière's three artistic regimes. The contemporary public clearly engaged in an aesthetic regime of viewing, insisting the artwork must be viewed and judged on its own terms, outside of the influences of the mediators, or even of the work that had been the artist's source of reflection. The classical public, in contrast, participated in the poetic regime of viewing, arguing that the power of art resided primarily in its mimetic nature, its ability to effectively imitate or resemble objects or narratives in the world. Even those who made some space for less mimetic forms of art, such as abstraction, suggested that these forms would be meaningless if the artist could not also effectively engage in a form of precise representation. Finally, the spiritual public engaged in practices associated with the ethical regime of art, admiring the work for its potential rootedness in broader, more transcendent truths. When concerned about its potential impropriety, they asked questions about the right to make use of such images.

For Rancière, the term "regime" is not historical. He is not describing a progressive movement from the ethical to the poetic and, finally, the aesthetic. Rather, the three can coexist together. "Regime" gets at how the making of images and their modes of visibility are understood and regulated by people involved in their production, circulation, and viewing. What, then, can we learn about the effects of the coexistence of these three regimes in response to the same work of art in the same place and time?

These variations cannot easily be delineated along religious and secular lines. Recall the comments in the livre d'or by the contemporary visitor who described how the work would stay in her "spirit," or the slightly negative remark by the member of the classical public who acknowledged that the piece was better than Parmiggiani's installation but who still encouraged the Collège to move a little more "toward the sacred" in its future exhibits. Did his use of the term "sacred" imply a more religious or spiritual exploration, or did he desire to see art whose classical status rendered it sacred in spaces such as the Louvre? Given the slipperiness of these categories, the *effects* of these various art-viewing practices render them, as with the Parmiggiani exhibit, not as far apart as they might appear. To my mind, the practices and responses of all three publics helped to bolster the broader project of the Collège in different ways.

First, in their engagements with *Suite Grünewald*, both the classical and spiritual publics expressed admiration for Titus-Carmel's citational practices. In other words, their account of what they admired in the piece came close to a classical concept of artistic beauty as "semblance" (Hansen 2012, 115). This desire for semblance brought the ethical and poetic regimes of viewing together in important ways. What differed significantly was their understanding of the "original" being cited: for the classical public, the source of semblance was a fifteenth-century altarpiece; for the spiritual public, the source of semblance was Christ's incarnation that made Christian iconographic representation of God possible. I understand the viewing of art with desires for semblance in mind as a means, yet again, of using Christian motifs to mediate the gap between the past and the present in ways that reproduce Catholicism's privileged banality.

This mode of mediating between the past and the present does not entail making the past present in a visceral way—and indeed it cannot do so. In his essay "Some Motifs in Baudelaire" (1940), Miriam Hansen described how, for Benjamin, "'the aporetic element in the beautiful' as semblance marks the object as not just absent in the work but always already lost. The admiration that 'is courting [the] identical object' is a retrospective one: it 'gleans what earlier generations admired in it'" (2012, 116). This desire for that "which earlier generations admired" was expressed, time and again, in visitors' engagements with the work and space alike. By admiring Titus-Carmel's capacity to reproduce medieval or iconographic images from the past, viewers celebrated his capacity to repeat what earlier generations had admired.

Second, the convergence of these three regimes ultimately brought Titus-Carmel's artistic practices closer to those of Parmiggiani. Titus-Carmel's decision to play with the interstice between the formal elements and the subject matter of *Suite Grünewald* served to place Christian motifs at the center of Europe's art historical canon. In using such motifs to create a space between blasphemy and devotion, and in choosing to exhibit it at the Collège, Titus-Carmel also participated in a political project. He insisted that Christian motifs could be abstracted and universalized—that they could be made foundational to contemporary art. Thus, while Parmiggiani worked to enliven Catholic materiality, and Titus-Carmel worked to aestheticize it, they both contributed to the project of catholaïcité underway at the Collège.

Finally, while the contemporary public may not have admired the piece for its "beautiful semblance," the effects of the practices they brought to bear on *Suite Grünewald* also reinforced the vision of the Collège, in three ways. First, in the contemporary public's refusal of the very possibility of mediation, these visitors denied the previous, culturally situated experiences of viewing (including the viewing of Christian motifs) that informed their capacity to appreciate *Suite Grünewald*. In needing no context, these viewers suggested that the images and techniques found in this contemporary work were self-evident, at least for informed viewers. In so doing, they supported the archdiocese's efforts to naturalize the place of Catholicism in contemporary France and its art forms. Second, as I noted above, the form of viewing that the Collège had best prepared the mediators to facilitate—that of identifying the various techniques used in each piece—was, in fact, that enacted by the contemporary public. It was this public, more than any other, that employees at the Collège imagined and discursively produced through their advertising, brochures, and website. By working to draw them into the space and to accommodate them once present, the Collège sought to remind this public of the unthreatening nature of their Catholic heritage. In this light the contemporary public helped to authorize the project underway at the Collège by virtue of their very presence.

By encouraging the mediators to promote the contemporary mode of engaging with these Christian motifs, employees at the Collège also contributed to the banalization of those motifs, allowing them to escape the ethical regime of art and enter the aesthetic. Thus, the third and most significant effect of the contemporary public's engagement with the piece was the way they reduced the potential ethical power of the Christian motifs undeniably found in *Suite Grünewald*. Instead, they encouraged a distanced encounter with this iconography. In the tools they provided to the mediators, employees at the Collège worked in subtle ways to reshape the viewing practices of classical and spiritual publics to engage in the aesthetic, rather than in the poetic or ethical regime of art. Such practices discouraged visitors from engaging in determinations of blasphemy or devotion. Instead, they encouraged publics to participate in the decontextualized and distanced acts of aesthetic viewing. In constructing a space for the aesthetic regime of viewing, the archdiocese of Paris created a site in which production and consumption of art that is not of the Church may occur under its purview. Participating in practices at the Collège can be both secular and Catholic in ways that— like Titus-Carmel's citational practices—do not require one, ultimately, to declare (or decide) which one is doing. This tacitness has political implications, as one is able to engage with Catholicism without defining these actions as religious and therefore as inappropriate in the public sphere in France.

As the warnings of some members of the classical and spiritual publics suggest, however, these practices also come with certain risks. When the man who suggested that the hedonist Catherine Millet might be at work in this space, he was also pointing to the possibility that the malleable place of Christian motifs in the European art historical canon and in exhibitions of contemporary art displayed at the Collège may contribute to the production of a secularized Catholicism, even in a space owned and operated by the French archdiocese.

Just as ethical, poetic, and aesthetic regimes of viewing could coexist in the space of the Collège, different exhibitions at the Collège could mediate the gap between the past and the present in quite distinct ways—enlivening Catholic materiality or aestheticizing it. That various regimes of viewing and divergent modes of mediation could all, however, end up contributing to the privileging of Catholic materiality demonstrates how employees did not need to appropriate *Suite Grünewald* as a "religious" artwork in order for it to contribute to the project of equating Catholic history and culture with that of Europe and France. This work could be accomplished tacitly and, therefore, all the more powerfully. In scholarly attempts to highlight the ongoing power of religion in social life, we must also pay heed to how this intertwining may produce highly unequal effects. Here, I have charted practices of art viewing that coproduce the secular, certain visions of Catholicism, and French culture in ways that make concerns about blasphemy and devotion superfluous. The implications of the mediation between the past and the present through the convergence of Catholic materiality and contemporary art at the Collège are subtle but powerful. In contrast to signs of other religions, Christian motifs may be made banal and, therefore, move flexibly between the ethical, poetic, and aesthetic in the French public sphere.

III
REPRODUCING
CATHOLIC
PRIVILEGE

THE IMMEDIATE, THE MATERIAL, AND THE FETISH

ACCORDING TO THE DOUBLE-SIDED EXHIBITION summary that accompanied the third contemporary art exhibit displayed at the Collège, two "emerging artists on the contemporary arts scene," Nathalie Brevet and Hughes Rochette, had been invited to "inhabit the space." With this invitation, the pamphlet continued, "the Collège wished to valorize an artistic proposition indicative of its mission: above all, to be a space of exchange and debate." With these words of welcome, the writer of the pamphlet also implicitly acknowledged that, as a site of debate, the installation—entitled *Cellula*—would likely prove controversial.

When approaching the building along the rue de Poissy from the Seine River during the run of the exhibit from May 28 to October 31, 2009, one may have noticed a red fluorescent light sculpture in the shape of the number 18 affixed on the external east-facing wall, near the door to the former sacristy (see fig. 5.1). In contrast to Parmiggiani's installation and *Suite Grünewald*, both of which occupied half of the nave, *Cellula* was displayed in the room referred to as the sacristy, located behind the bookstore. Eighteen is the sacristy's address. Two elements, however, made the sculpture difficult to recognize as an external address marker. First, its red glow stood in stark contrast to the small blue-and-white metal signs that mark most addresses in Paris. Second, the number 18 was rotated 90 degrees to the left, turning the 8—as I explained time and again in my work as a mediator for the exhibit between July and November 2009—into an infinity symbol (∞).[1]

Inside the former sacristy, Brevet and Rochette used scaffolding and plywood to create a second floor at two-thirds the height of the vaulted space. Upon entering the sacristy, visitors penetrated into the scaffolding's

FIGURE 5.1. Cellula, 2009, Nathalie Brevet_Hughes Rochette, Collège des Bernardins, Paris (Photo. F. Thibault) © ADAGP. Used by permission of the artists and F. Thibault.

dark underbelly. A flood of light, however, beckoned them to venture up the metal stairs, a climb that would invariably cause the entire structure to tremble and shake. The stairs turned on two 90-degree angles, preventing visitors from seeing what was at the apex until they had completed their ascent (see fig 5.2). Laid out at ankle-height on the plywood platform was

FIGURE 5.2. Cellula, 2009, Nathalie Brevet_Hughes Rochette, Collège des Bernardins, Paris (Photo. F. Thibault) © ADAGP. Used by permission of the artists and F. Thibault.

another neon sculpture, this one made of white fluorescent lights in hexago-
nal shapes intended to imply, as the installation's title suggested, a series of
"cells" (see fig. 5.3). The cells stayed lit, however, only when those in the room
ceased all movement. The fullest expression of the sculpture could only be
seen when visitors achieved unity in stillness.

    In chapters 3 and 4, I argue that both the Parmiggiani installation and
Suite Grünewald ultimately offered support to the project underway at the
Collège. In contrast, the exhibitions I explore in this chapter and the next
had the potential to provide far more critical perspectives on the building as a medieval space, and on the project as a renaissance of medieval
monasticism. Both, however, were met with a great deal of resistance from
visitors. In this third and final part, I explore the labor required to overcome
these critical perspectives in order to reproduce both the particular project
underway at the Collège and the privilege of Catholic banality more broadly.
These two exhibits induced visitors to confront some of the tensions that
accompany reproducing Catholic privilege. In this chapter, I explore how
Cellula encouraged visitors to consider whether the privilege of Catholicism
on display at the Collège was based on the fetishization of Catholic materiality. In chapter 6, I address a problem that haunts the privilege of the banality
of Catholic materiality: the banality of privilege writ large.

DESIRES FOR IMMEDIACY
AND THE SPECTER OF THE FETISH

———————

Even among those who had positive responses to *Cellula*, very few arrived at this conclusion without a great deal of concerted effort on the part of the mediators—labor that did not always prove efficacious. One hot summer day, I came across another mediator in tears. "Why do they hate it so much?" she wailed, clearly overcome by a day of endless "debate." Over time, a tension between two kinds of critique mounted against *Cellula* emerged. On one side, many visitors expressed concern about art that required so much effort to understand. In early October, for example, I spoke at length with one woman who acknowledged that the approach I offered was interesting but that she struggled with the apparent necessity of texts and explanations surrounding today's art. She described herself as an "art lover," who attends all the exhibits in Paris and even, on occasion, exhibits artwork herself. But, she explained, she still struggled with the complete absence of "beauty" in today's art. She acknowledged that the way we look at art from the fifteenth and sixteenth century is often simplified, given that we lack the proper "codes" to see all that is going on in the works, but "at least," she lamented, we can still just stop and admire it, because it is "beautiful." In response, I returned to her point about fifteenth- and sixteenth-century art to ask if, by foregrounding the use of texts, contemporary art might point to how all art appreciation is informed by texts of some sort. She persisted, however, and suggested that even if some paintings from the medieval period may not be described as "beautiful," they still "hit" (*frappent*) viewers who look at them. "Here, I am not affected. Even though I find it interesting intellectually," she explained, "I am left cold."

Another woman expressed her discomfort with my lengthy explanation through humor, asking if the cables hanging down from the ceiling above the scaffolding (fig. 5.3) represented the Word—were they microphones from above? Then she returned to the refrain I often encountered. "I prefer immediate responses," she explained. "This is more intellectual than artistic." A few days later, an older man who also described himself as an artist explained to me that the piece lacked the "visceral element, the direct response, the organic element of sculpture." According to one comment in the livre d'or (written in English), "explanation kills art. This time even explanation was not necessary to kill."

Not everyone made uncomfortable by the installation launched into an

FIGURE 5.3. Cellula, 2009, Nathalie Brevet_Hughes Rochette, Collège des Bernardins, Paris (Photo. F. Thibault) © ADAGP. Used by permission of the artists and F. Thibault.

explicit critique of works that lacked a visceral impact. Some articulated this desire for immediacy through their confusion. "But there's nothing to see," I often heard confused visitors whisper to one another when they arrived at the top of the stairs. Others expressed the need for immediacy through embarrassment enacted on behalf of the exhibit. As I sat in a chair at the top of the stairs one early autumn afternoon, I watched a group of women huddle midway up the steps. My smiles to encourage their entry proved insufficient, and only one ventured forth. "No, it's not finished," she called down to her friends, looking over at me conspiratorially and giggling, as if we had just walked in on someone in the act of dressing. Another day, I heard the sound of two young women laughing down below. They stopped when they arrived at the top and saw me, and quickly departed, bursting into laughter again once I was out of sight. Earlier in the afternoon, a man had laughed heartily when, in response to his question, I explained that he was standing in the installation of contemporary art he claimed he could not find. I see in these outbursts of laughter and awkwardness an admonition that the installation failed to pull visitors into its orbit or wordlessly demonstrate how one ought to respond and feel. They were embarrassed for the work because their confusion was a sign of its impotence.

In contrast to those who lamented about art that does not speak for itself, other visitors responded to the installation with vehement outrage and, on occasion, acts of vandalism. The number 18 was smashed one evening by a melon; seeds remained evident on the wall for months after its repair. On numerous occasions, visitors accidentally and not so accidentally tripped over, stepped on, disconnected, or even shattered the lights below them. Brevet and Rochette made many visits to the site during the exhibition—often to repair the installation. To have the Collège once again inhabited by broken glass almost a year after Parmiggiani's inaugural exhibit—but this time produced by viewers rather than the artists—amplified the violence of their actions. I see an articulation of privilege in both forms of broken glass. The privilege, on the one hand, of an artist to use broken glass as an artistic tool without paying heed to the myriad expressions of historical and present-day violence it might bring to mind, and the privilege, on the other hand, of visitors to dismiss an artist as a vandal and then to engage in actual acts of vandalism themselves. Indeed, one critic in the livre d'or explicitly encouraged others to destroy the work. "This exhibition is completely ridiculous! Why forbid those under 15 from entering? It is those under 15 who would have the good idea to break these neon tubes!"[2]

These responses stand in stark contrast to one another. The former insisted that the work was mute and lacked any power over the beholder. As one woman explained explicitly, because my presence was "necessary" to understand the exhibit, it obviously lacked truth. When we see something beautiful, she insisted, we have an immediate, emotional response. No explanation is needed. My presence showed that such an experience was impossible with *Cellula*. The latter set of responses demonstrated the visceral response *Cellula* could, in fact, elicit, most powerfully through acts or threats of destruction articulated against it. Analyses of iconoclasm have highlighted how such acts amplify the power of the objects they aim to dismantle by giving them a threatening, visceral voice that needs to be extinguished (see, for example, Gamboni 1997). How, then, are we to understand this tension between laments for art that lacked immediate power, and the need to destroy the very power others experienced as absent? Both, after all, see material forms as potentially capable of conveying experiences of immediacy in powerful ways.

I want to explore desires for immediacy that surfaced during encounters with *Cellula*. Matthew Engelke (2007) uses the term to describe how various Christian practices work to make God's presence proximate. Some of these desires for immediacy I encountered may have been connected to efforts to gain closer access to God, but many people had other goals and concerns. Broadly speaking, I understand the desire for immediacy as the desire for objects whose intrinsic value is located in their capacity to offer a visceral encounter with phenomena otherwise thought to be transcendent, or inaccessible in material form. Both those who dismissed *Cellula* as mute and those who felt the need to destroy it sought visceral encounters with objects of self-evident value.

This definition is in part inspired by William Pietz's (1985, 1987, 1988) account of the historical origins of the category of the "fetish" in anxieties surrounding "the problem of the social and personal value of material objects" (1987, 35) in colonial contexts of expropriation and enslavement. When a number of other concepts, such as witchcraft and idolatry, proved insufficient to account for the moral, political, and material quagmires of colonial encounters, Pietz argues, the category of the fetish arose to explain a variety of seemingly problematic material-human relationships. The fetish, in other words, is an accusation made against others that the objects they presume to carry an intrinsic value located to a transcendent origin actually lack this ground. While it often entails a critique of desires for immediacy through objects in general, the fact that those who would wield such a critique likely harbor objects of immediacy, whose value is similarly intrinsic and located in divine or transcendent origins, suggests that such desires are widely held.

The concept of the fetish, rather than a category of objects in the world, in the words of media scholar W. J. T. Mitchell, points to "objectiv*ist* projections of a kind of collective imperial subject, fantasies about other people, specifically other people's beliefs about certain kinds of objects" (Mitchell 2005, 162). Such fantasies abounded in the space of the Collège. Both the edifice itself and contemporary installation art are offered up as potential sites of immediacy *and* as spaces in which to critique such desires. Visitors to the Collège are encouraged to access the medieval past in ways that are visceral and immediate. At the same time, however, for many visitors the Collège's medieval forms serve as an implicit critique of the material practices of the present, in which people tend to give inordinate power and prestige to objects that lack transcendent value.[3] Installation art benefits from similar paradoxes. Given that, generally speaking, it cannot hang on a wall or be displayed in any straightforward way, it is often celebrated as a means of escaping both the bull market of art and the bourgeois fantasy of "beauty" or "aura" encapsulated in domesticated artistic forms. And yet, as I will demonstrate, installations also traffic in the power of immediacy. They desire to be forms whose value is self-evident. The framework of the fetish offers one means of thinking about the relationship between immediacy, materiality, and value that both the Collège and contemporary installation art attempt to address.

In using the term "fetish" here, I am pointing to how *Cellula* and the Collège may serve as objects of critique as well as sites of immediacy. *Cellula* did not simply engage with the space of the Collège. Instead, through their layered efforts, the artists worked to counter others' potentially fetishized experience of the space. Similarly, for many visitors, the mere presence of the building's medieval vaults could offer a powerful corrective to fetishized practices of the present—practices, moreover, that appeared to be embodied in works of contemporary art.[4]

This view of the present as marred by the fetishization of material forms became evident during a meeting between the mediators and managers at the Collège. During the *Cellula* exhibit, rather unusually, one of the managers sat down with the mediators so that he might offer an alternative lens through which to view the exhibit. He insisted that this reading was his alone, and he did not want us to take from the meeting a sense that his interpretation should be the only one we were authorized to pass on to visitors. Instead, he hoped that it might serve as one of several tools to help us bring more visitors into the experience of the installation. I will return to his fascinating take on *Cellula* below. For now, I want to highlight how he opened his talk by casting what he called the "narcissism" of the present as a taken-for-granted fact of social life upon which we could all agree, and which might help to explain the vandalism enacted against the exhibit. Michael Jackson had died only a few weeks prior to the meeting, and the bishop used the global outpourings of grief and the various temporary shrines devoted to him as examples of this narcissism.[5] He explained that visitors might experience *Cellula* as "violent" because, as a projection of the world in which we live, the installation presented this narcissism for viewing.

The manager saw the social world as engaged, through its narcissism, in a fetishization of material forms lacking transcendent grounds. He implied that the vandalism could partly be explained by visitors' desire to combat such narcissism. In so doing, like the iconoclasts he hoped to tame, he acknowledged the dangerous power of the modernist fetish.[6] While he wanted to offer the mediators some context for these acts of destruction, the manager in no way encouraged or excused them. Instead, as I will elaborate below, he went on to suggest that we could better avoid these acts of vandalism by encouraging visitors to view the installation in a certain light, one that would allow them to see how the installation could assist in the work of critiquing—rather than exacerbating—the narcissism or fetishism of the contemporary social world.

The artists, for their part, would likely not have endorsed such an interpretation. Brevet and Rochette never laid out their vision in any totalizing way. Instead, as mediators, we picked it up slowly in conversations with them—and with each other—and by observing them with visitors they brought with them through the exhibit. As we gathered these narratives together, it became increasingly clear that the artists did indeed see their work, in part, as that of the unmasking of fetishes. However, rather than offering a critique of modern material practices in general, the fetishism the installation aimed to critique was located in those practices that emphasized the immediacy of the medieval past made available by the Collège itself. In a variety of ways, their installation highlighted the made-ness of the Collège, refusing claims of its self-evident value and the proximity it offered to the medieval past.

When visitors claimed that there was "nothing to see" at the top of the stairs, they overlooked a number of components of the installation beyond the neon sculpture. This is unsurprising given that, with these elements, the artists attempted to call attention to aspects of the space of the Collège that generally went overlooked. After a conversation with the artists, one of the other mediators explained to me that the cables hanging from the ceiling typically held boxy light fixtures that, upon touring the space, the artists had found to be rather "ugly." By removing the eighteen fixtures, stacking them on the staircase, and leaving the cables dangling, the artists pointed to the fact that space was not "natural," but the result of a series of decisions—good and bad—made by its occupants. The scaffolding itself, of course, also brought these very recent and extensive efforts to mind.[7]

In a similar vein, the addition of a second floor actually rebuilt a vertical division of the space that had existed during its life as a fire station, when an upper floor served as an apartment for officers. In reconstructing this form, the artists could remind viewers of inhabitants beyond the Cistercians. This level served an additional purpose. The artists referred to it as a *sur-sol* (above-ground), seeing it neither as an *étage* (a floor, as in story) nor a *plancher* (a floor, as in the physical ground). Rising approximately four meters above the ground of the sacristy and stopping a few centimeters short of the wall, the *sur-sol* was also positioned to give visitors full access to the windows that begin far above the sight line when one stands on the ground level. In a portfolio of their works produced in 2018, Rochette and Brevet open their account of *Cellula* by highlighting that the "former sacristy of the Collège des Bernardins appeared buried to us, cut off from the street."[8] By bringing visitors up to this level, the artists allowed for an exchange between "the interior and exterior."[9] The mounting of the building's address in neon likewise served to further the idea of an exchange between the city and the building, pointing to the specificity and locatedness of the site and refusing it the power to exist beyond its precise geographical locale.

Cellula is the Latin term for a small room, and it served as the basis for early monastic architectural design. According to the historian Thomas Coomans, these "spaces of small dimensions" could be found anywhere—"in grottos, in tombs dug into the mountainside, even in abandoned villages" (2015, 16–17). In creating cells made of neon lights—eighteen neon lights to be precise, which was also the number of hanging lights they had removed, as well as the address of the building—atop a plywood platform, the artists could be read as pointing to the simplicity of the basic foundation of monastic life. However, according to the pamphlet accompanying the exhibit, it was the "polysemy" of the word *cellule* the artists aimed to reference. Prisoners, for example, also inhabit cells, and so the sculpture could equally refer to the brief moment in the Collège's history when it had served as a prison during the Revolution. The shape of the cell, moreover, is that of a hexagon: the general shape of France and one of the country's nicknames.[10] Here, again, the artists denied the intrinsic value or transcendent origin of the space as one that was monastic.

Perhaps most powerfully, by building this second level the artists pointed to the fragmented history of the space, including its disjointed medieval history. The artists offered visitors access to numerous small decorative flourishes in the sacristy that could not be seen very well from the ground floor, and that are absent from the nave. They used the installation to emphasize these details. The pillars in the sacristy, for example, are far more elaborately carved than those in the nave (see fig. 5.3). One afternoon, I listened attentively as Rochette offered a gallery owner a tour of the installation. He pointed to how, rather than just cutting out a large hole in the plywood to make space for the pillar, they highlighted its complex shape by imitating it. The construction of the nave and that of the sacristy were separated by a century, as it was only in the fourteenth century that a church was added to the site. The numerous distinctions between the two spaces can in part be explained by this gap in time. By the fourteenth century, the decorative flourishes associated with gothic architecture appeared more desirable, even for the Cistercians who tended to prefer simpler forms.[11]

These different elements of the installation all served to underscore the particularities of the space of the Collège. They emphasized the Collège's fragmented, shifting, and contingent history, rather than its timelessness, denying it the transcendent ground upon which its immediacy was based. The implications of their layered critique—although never uttered in these terms—was that the installation could work to counteract the fetishization of the Collège. By pointing to the vagaries of the space, and the different purposes that it had served over time, the artists forced visitors to engage with the made-ness of the space and revealed the fantasy of immediacy that undergirds the desires many bring to the Collège as a problematic expression of fetishization.

BATTLING FETISHISM WITH ICONOCLASM

The critiques of the installation made by iconoclasts (those whose visceral responses to the exhibit were violent enough to cause or threaten destruction) were a source of a great deal of stress for the mediators. However, at times, we inadvertently contributed to the tensions that helped to inspire these acts by offering up visions of the work that appeared to demonstrate our own problematic relationship with objects. Specifically, by our relating the artists' layered efforts aimed at discounting the immediacy of the space, some visitors understood us to be elevating the artists' work and the materials they used over and above the creators and the materials of the Collège.

In so doing, we appeared to display our own naïveté (depicted in visitors' occasional reference to the emperor and his lack of clothes) and the artists' vanity and presumptuousness, rather than a critical perspective.

On one relatively positive Saturday, for example, I found myself working a full eight-hour day. Many who arrived at the top of the noisy metal steps with their eyebrows raised turned out to be ready to listen and engage, and they walked away, ultimately, affected by what they had seen. Rochette had been present throughout the day, first to replace bulbs that we had haphazardly reconstructed after some earlier destructive visits, and then to conduct a professional visit with a woman from a gallery. At 3:00 in the afternoon, a large group of people mostly over the age of seventy clambered up the stairs. Their outrage had solidified long before they reached the top of the installation. By the time I met them they were livid. They were wearing the same name tags I had noticed on two women who had visited the installation earlier in the day, so I knew they were part of a group interested in St. Bernard. They seemed to be making a pilgrimage of sorts, seeking out spaces associated with the medieval saint that appeared to uphold their ideal of Europe. I backed up, attempting to position myself between the neon lights and the increasingly angry visitors.

A series of questions were fired at me, one on top of the other, so I offered to speak to the group as a whole. They dutifully but warily quieted to allow me to speak. I explained that the artists had brought us up into the vaults of the former sacristy. In many of Paris's churches, I pointed out, we did not have access to this particular perspective. Through the installation, we were able to appreciate the subtle architectural details that are unique to this space in relation to the rest of the Collège, and that are not as visible when one is situated on the ground. Cries of "ostentatious" and "pretentious" began to drown me out, and people moved about the space rather wildly, shaking the floor and the neon lights. I quickly saw my thoughtless error. While hoping to reduce their anger by highlighting the opportunity to appreciate the building they had come to see in a way not typically available, I had inadvertently suggested that the artists had somehow improved on the monks' design, troubling the transcendent origins of the space. Terms such as "ostentatious" and "pretentious" demonstrated how the visitors had interpreted me as celebrating the ability of the artists to move beyond the obfuscating techniques of the monks and reveal something new. I had established, in other words, the very narcissism they needed to critique.[12]

Thinking that Rochette had departed, I was surprised and embarrassed to see his anguished face among the crowd just at the moment when I lost any control over their movements. One elderly man had walked to the other side of the neon lights without my noticing and was now angrily marching among the fragile forms. "Sir, please stop!" Rochette cried out, reaching the front of the crowd, demanding that the man cease harming the installation. Another man divined Rochette's role in the mounting spectacle and unveiled him to the crowd as one of the artists. The man proceeded to interrogate Rochette, inquiring how he could dare to presume the right to destroy a space such as this, to enforce his questionable values on others, if he was proud of himself and what he had done, and whether he thought he had successfully fooled everyone.

The man's rhetorical questions further demonstrate how the devotees of St. Bernard saw in the artists' mode of inhabiting the space the unmerited presumptions of those who took too much pride in work ungrounded in transcendent origins. He was not alone. Words such as "pretentious" and "shameful" (and even, one on occasion, "masturbation") appeared frequently in the critiques found in the livre d'or. By asking if he thought he had successfully "fooled" everyone, the critic revealed Rochette's potential status as a swindler or a fraud. With the term "fetish," many Europeans in colonial spaces expressed frustration or concern with so-called primitive relationships to objects that refused the logics of either commodification or the sacred. Many concluded that these errors must be the result of a priestly class who had deluded the people and stood to gain economically from these social-material encounters. References to the emperor and his lack of clothes offered a variation on this theme, pointing simultaneously to the supposedly fraudulent tactics of the artists and to a broader collective delusion demonstrated in the efforts required to exhibit and mediate the work. Understandably frustrated and concerned about potential damage to his installation, Rochette refused to engage the man and his critique. The debate had ended and the pilgrims departed swiftly. While the installation was unharmed in this encounter, the wild and aggressive movements of the visitors around the space clearly demonstrated their visceral responses to it.

Another example of how the mediators' need to defend and often protect the installation could result in accusations that if anyone was engaged in the production of fetishes, it was the artists and mediators occurred in late October. I stood with Brevet and Rochette on the lower level of the exhibit, beneath the scaffolding. In our conversation, I tried to attend to their concern that few visitors were taking the time to engage with the work, rejecting it out of hand and then destroying it. I responded by describing some of the encounters mediators had with visitors who—while reticent at the beginning—shifted their perspective over time. I borrowed words from the manager in his meeting with us, contrasting *Cellula*'s participatory nature with the work by Parmiggiani, which, because it had stood *en face* (opposite) viewers in a way that could appear confrontational, few had been able to change their minds while standing before it. I pointed to how *Cellula* allowed people to move through the work, providing the time and space in which they could change their point of view. Still hesitant, they asked me to do my best to restrict the number of visitors on top of the platform in order to limit the destruction.

No sooner had a promise to do so escaped my lips than a very large private tour group arrived. Approximately forty people clamored through the scaffolding, demonstrating to us their displeasure at the sight of it. Brevet made a beeline for the stairs. Upon arriving at the apex, she attempted to position herself between the group and the neon lights. I scrambled to follow her lead, but the tour guide ignored Brevet's defensive stance and led the group around the sculpture to the far wall. There was clearly not enough space for so many people on that side of the platform, but before we could ask her to pay heed and reposition the group, she launched into a loud and lengthy lecture on the history of the building and the details of the space, ignoring the work on which they stood and that, ultimately, was giving them greater access to the details she described.[13]

Feeling embarrassed at having my attempts to comfort the artists so quickly overturned, I tried to signal with my body language that the tour guide was behaving inappropriately. When a pair of friendlier visitors arrived, interested to learn more about the exhibit, I took the opportunity to offer a competing narrative to that being loudly asserted by the guide, pointing to the various ways in which the exhibit discounted the coherence and singularity of the space. Members of the tour group, however, angrily hushed me. My stress became evident to the pair of visitors who promised to return shortly as I hustled to reclaim my spot as sentry alongside of Brevet, defending the installation against those who were clearly offended by the sight of it. Our efforts proved to be in vain as a man performing his interest in the space over and above that of the exhibit by intently staring upward neglected to notice the wires extending from the neon lights, tripped over them, and pulled them out of two of the bulbs. As Brevet looked down in despair, I took the opportunity to discipline the group, reminding them to pay careful attention where they were walking. My words, of course, were not well received. Members of the group shot back at me that they were not children, and that they had not broken anything. When I pointed to the neon lights and insisted that, indeed, something had been broken, the group broke out into laughter.

Just as our efforts to explain the artists' layered installation to visitors risked opening the artists up to charges of narcissism, our attempts to protect their work could risk transforming the material components of the exhibit into fetishes, or objects whose value we took to be transcendent and others found to be spurious. If we were to insist that something had been harmed in the breaking of a neon light, the laughter and mockery of many angry visitors seemed to suggest that we were the ones investing excessive power in "mere things." In their acts of vandalism (or threatened vandalism), visitors may be seen as attempting to remind the mediators and the artists of the base materiality of the objects used in the creation of the installation. The sculpture was "just" neon lights, scaffolding, and plywood and, therefore, could not demand their reverence. And while the artists would have objected to the idea that they were arguing for the value of neon lights, their installations created in situ could also be dismantled and objectified for other kinds of consumption. Nearly three years later, for example, the red neon address sculpture was displayed on its own as *Sans titre* (*Untitled*) in an exhibition of contemporary and modern art called *Art Paris*, held at the Grand Palais from March 28 to March 31, 2012. A series of their works were offered for sale at a gallery on the right bank a year after the close of *Cellula*. The prices of their works varied from €50 for one of multiple small works on paper to €20,000 for a life-size inflatable car. The price for one of their neon sculptures—perhaps their most consistent medium—was unlisted and could only be acquired on demand. I do not highlight the artists' commercialization of their efforts as evidence of their fraudulence. At a moment when contemporary art commands a powerful place in a variety of global markets, numerous critical installations are dismantled into discrete pieces that can be displayed and sold.

Visitors had come to the site in order to engage with it as advertised—as an immediate encounter with the medieval past. Why, then, did confronting the fragmented nature of that past appear so discomfiting? A variety of Catholic traditions allow for God's presence to be mediated by a diversity of material forms, from the humble bones of saints, or the earth surrounding their sites of burial, to more ornate objects, such as the magisterial cathedrals in which God's presence is welcomed each week during mass. These varied forms, however, have also been accompanied by anxieties about the properly spiritual approach to material forms. Iconoclasts in the eighth century and Protestant reformers in the sixteenth pronounced such concerns most vehemently. But similar critiques can also be found within a variety of Catholic writings in Europe through the medieval and early modern periods.

St. Bernard himself is one of the most frequently cited critics. In his 1125 *Apologia*, Bernard expressed concern about two forms of monastic excess: small things, such as food, drink, and clothing; and "things of greater importance," which Bernard saw, first and foremost, as located in "excessive" art (Rudolph 1990, 1–6). He desired, in the words of medieval historian Mary Carruthers, for monks to reserve the most "lavish decoration of one's own making within the 'temple' of one's soul, fiction-making which is 'supported' by the plain surfaces and clear articulation of the unadorned church and cloister" (Carruthers 2000, 86–87). I return to Bernard's minimalist aesthetics in chapter 6. Here I want simply to highlight that European Christians have long debated how material forms can effectively convey immaterial, transcendent, or spiritual ideals.

As Engelke (2007) has demonstrated, both immediacy and immateriality share an unstable and paradoxical quality and are, in fact, difficult to disentangle. Engelke describes the intertwined tensions of immediacy and immateriality as "the problem of presence." His study of the Friday apostolics in Zimbabwe—who have declared the Christian Bible to be a "mere thing" whose materiality obstructs access to the immaterial qualities that point to God's immediacy—highlights the complex imbrication of these two axes of difference: immediacy (or proximity) and distance; and immateriality and materiality. The Friday apostolics see the possibility for "spiritual immediacy" as residing in those experiences and practices that appear to have "an immaterial quality" (Engelke 2007, 7). Not all Christians are as tied to the significance of immateriality and immediacy for thinking about the relationship between the world and God. Indeed, for many, God's distance—as Max Weber (2009 [1930]) famously argued—can serve as a powerful engine for worldly action.

Within a variety of Catholic practices, various material forms can produce different types of proximity to God's presence—from the ingestible "true presence" of the Eucharist[14] to the highly mediated prayers offered to God through intercessors such as Mary and the saints (often in turn requiring further mediation: lighting candles, praying with the aid of a rosary, or giving donations before images representing these intercessors).[15] For many Catholics, mediation is not only necessary, it is also desirable. It not only aims at making God present in ways the Friday apostolics describe as "live and direct," but also allows for access to God's presence at more of a remove.

This does not mean, however, that proximity and materiality are without controversy. Idolatry is a particularly powerful Christian critique of objects of mediation because to engage in it is to anger God, making him distant to the point of desertion. For Engelke, "in Christian thought the tension between distance and proximity is often maintained through a careful differentiation between words and things. Certain words and certain things—defined as such according to specific semiotic ideologies—become privileged channels of divine apprehension. Indeed, how God's presence is rightfully mediated through language and objects is an issue over which Christians have often disagreed" (2007, 16). I am interested in the particular things that come to be understood as privileged channels not only to God's presence but also to the presence of the past and other intangibles—such as the spirit, broadly conceived, artistic "genius," or national "cultures."

Readers will notice that I am glossing over a distinction that some might insist should be primary—the distinction between working to mediate God's presence and working to mediate the presence of other intangibles, such as the past. Rather than dismissing this difference, I want instead to point to how similar practices and tensions apply to both. It would be a mistake to presume that art objects prior to the Renaissance had served as conduits to God's presence alone. Art and architecture could also point to political authority, the wealth and power of merchant patrons (Kempers 1987), and, as Belting argues, the communities in which such objects were produced and paraded. With the rise of the discipline of art history comes attention to how art objects may mediate a variety of other powerful intangibles, including artistic "genius," or the logics or essences of cultures, nations, and eras.

According to the historian of museums Andrew McClellan, this art historical approach to objects as material repositories of individual, national, cultural, or temporal genius was formed at the beginning of the nineteenth century as a result of certain political logics of the French Revolution. For McClellan, the formation of the Louvre offers the quintessential expression of "the secularizing power of the museum," in which "iconic" paintings were transformed into "art objects" (1994, 112). Like many scholars of museums—and of French history—McClellan understands secularization to operate through a form of substitution. Paintings and objects that had once served as "privileged channels to divine apprehension" could—through some effort—come to serve as privileged channels to the nation or its ideals, such as liberty.

I want to question this logic of substitution, however. Long before their apparent "secularization," Christian material forms could serve as conduits of a variety of intangible or transcendent powers. To suggest that the shift from cult images to art images can be equated with a shift from the grounding of those images in divine power to expressions of individual artistry oversimplifies this history. Christian material forms have long served multiple purposes, including battling against the temptations of idolatry or fetishism. In his book *Medieval Modern: Art Out of Time*, the art historian Alexander Nagel argues that it is helpful to look at modern works of art in relation to medieval ones because such a framework reveals the efforts that producers from both time periods have made to combat problems of the legitimacy of these objects of mediation. Nagel sees a number of modern art practices, including installations, indexicality, replication, collage, and conceptual art as having precedence in the medieval period. He sees these practices as bringing questions "fundamental to the art of both periods . . . into view," including "questions regarding the generation and dissemination of images, site-specificity and mobility; fetishism and iconoclasm; memory and anachronism; and authorship and authority" (2012, 10).

And yet, despite this complex and multifaceted history, my experiences with *Cellula* suggest that human-material encounters remain sites of profound anxiety. Pietz's study of the formation of concept of the fetish in colonial West Africa reminds us of its violent history. As it came to offer a means of explaining the primitivism of others, fetishism provided a flexible way in which to insist that it is the "non-European" who "gives false values to material objects" (1987, 42). In Mitchell's terms, the idea of the fetish "involve[s] quite general notions about the operation of 'savage' or 'primitive' mentality—that the natives are invariably gullible and superstitious; that they live in a world of fear and ignorance where these objects compensate for their weakness; that they lack the ability to make distinctions between animate and inanimate objects" (2001, 162). In a space that so effectively aestheticizes the maintenance of certain kinds of inequalities over others, the distinction between European and non-European—or between those who could participate in the project of catholaïcité at the Collège and those who found themselves excluded from it—proved to be similarly fraught. Given that, for many pundits on both the left and the right, the idea of Europe has been profoundly destabilized in recent decades, fearing one's own participation in fetishizing practices that appeared to lurk at every turn proved to be a significant source of concern. When encountering art that refused the Collège the possibility of immediacy, should viewers have worried about their own fetishizing practices? Critiqued those of the artists? Or ought they have worried about the Collège's dangerous capaciousness in including works such as *Cellula*? Given the exclusion of Muslims and very partial incorporation of particular kinds of Judaism and feminism I have described at the Collège, the risk of falling into problematic relationships with objects—and therefore potentially revealing a non-European, or non-modern status—was an ever-present threat.[16]

Humans engage with objects in ways that exceed the dichotomies of commodity or sacred object, alienable or inalienable, secular or religious, fetishized or immediate. The fact that installations such as *Cellula* led visitors more often to reiterate than to challenge these distinctions demonstrates the limits of the Collège in its inaugural years. Rather than successfully opening up space for rethinking paradoxical relationships to objects, installations more often provoked passionate desires for immediacy against the constant specter of the fetish, or, as I will now demonstrate, encouraged visitors and artists alike to draw powerful lines between the religious and the secular.

THE LIMITS OF THE RELIGIOUS/SECULAR DIVIDE

I want to call into question the clean historical divide presumed in the capacity to substitute divine transcendent origins for those more secular. And yet, it is important to acknowledge how such assumptions have long shaped human-material encounters—particularly in museums—in France and Europe. In fact, such intentions were integral to the shaping of the Louvre in the postrevolutionary period. In the space of the museum, the visceral nature of these works of art was thought to carry a potentially transformative power. David A. Bell has investigated revolutionaries' desire for the radical reformation of the French populace following the Revolution. He cites a Protestant member of the revolutionary assembly, Jean-Paul Rabaut de Saint-Étienne, who was one of many voices in 1792 who argued that "'we must make of the French a new people'" through a "'revolution in heads and hearts'" (2001, 2). Rabaut de Saint-Étienne insisted that such a transformative program would need to make use of "'the senses, the imagination, memory, reasoning, all the faculty that men possess'" (2001, 2). According to Bell, when struggling to imagine how to transform the populace, revolutionaries turned to the model of Catholic human-material encounters. Again, citing Rabaut de Saint-Étienne, for revolutionaries "'the secret was well known to priests, who, with their catechisms, their processions ... their ceremonies, sermons, hymns, missions, pilgrimages, patron saints, paintings, and all that nature placed at their disposal, infallibly led men to the goal they designated'" (ibid., 3).

Revolutionaries imagined that these same or similar objects could be used in the advancement of other goals. Their transcendent grounding in God could be replaced by a transcendent grounding in other, more humanist, ideals. It is also clear, however, that workers struggled to fit the objects displayed in the newly "liberated" space of the Louvre into their affective and transformative aims. Take, for example, a 1794 report written by the director of the Louvre to the Committee of Public Instruction explaining why the opening of the museum for public viewing would have to be delayed again.

> Art has diverged from its true path and celestial origins ... a multitude of dangerous and frivolous experiments, the results of long centuries of slavery and shame, have debased its nature: wherever one turns one sees that its production bears the marks of superstition, flattery, and debauchery. Such art does not recount the noble lessons that a regenerated people adores: it does nothing for liberty. One would be tempted to destroy all these playthings of folly and vanity if they were not so self-evidently unworthy of emulation. But nevertheless there is some point in trying to veil these vaults, to obliterate these false precepts. This is our task and we shall strive to achieve it. *It is through the overall effect of the collection that this can best be done.* [McClellan 1994, 113, emphasis in original]

The anticipation and anxiety surrounding objects that would, in the words of Minister of the Interior Jean-Marie Roland, "become among the most powerful illustrations of the French Republic" (ibid., 92) demonstrate the paradoxes of approaching human-object relationships in this substitutionary vein. Workers at the Louvre desired to maintain the visceral immediacy of these objects but aimed to reground that immediacy in the intangible ideals of the Revolution. These transcendent ideals—suddenly materialized and made proximate in this space and in the objects found within—could then be passed on to viewers in their encounters with them. In their efforts at substituting one mode of immediacy for another through the same material objects, however, the curators acknowledged that this process could prove dangerous. The desire to "potentially veil these vaults" points to the risk such objects entailed for a recently "regenerated population." It was clear that these objects could speak, but what would they say to the various viewers who encountered them? Instead of destroying these dangerous objects, workers at the Louvre aimed to capture and redirect their visceral immediacy through the effects of comparative display. Curating these objects could allow for the value of those that expressed liberty to be amplified when contrasted with those that offered only "folly and vanity."

Objects of the Italian Renaissance and those of the classical Greek and Roman past were deemed to offer the most powerful expressions of liberty prior to the French Revolution. Not all of the objects removed from churches, monasteries, and palaces would easily conform to the revolutionary narratives. Plans were made to store the more problematic objects temporarily in an abandoned convent, the Petits-Augustins on the Left Bank, across the Seine River from the Louvre. Over the next fifteen years, these two sites would become central locations for capturing and substituting the power, immediacy, or excess associated with these objects.

Since the Louvre occupied much of the curatorial attention, the little depot across the river remained mostly out of view. Its director, Alexandre Lenoir, was left with a collection of mostly sculptures, tombs, and monuments excavated from Paris's churches. As objects that glorified the power of monarchs and an institutional church now despised, it was unclear how best to fit them into the revolutionary rituals being produced at the Louvre. Lenoir took it upon himself to engage in an ambitious comparative project that would display the history and evolution of French sculpture. It was Lenoir who turned the storehouse into a museum, asking the commission responsible for the expropriated objects "would it not be possible, without altering your intentions or your patriotic wishes, to make public however many days in the week it would please you the pieces of painting and sculpture of which you are aware and have gone through the difficulty of transporting" (Poulot 1994, 160). In 1795, his plan for a Musée National des Monuments Français was approved, and he went about transforming the convent and its contents into the first evolutionary art history museum. Each century was given a room, and he decorated each room in a way he understood to be "typical" of its time.

Demanding that works cohere to the "logics" of such an evolutionary tale required a great deal of effort. In the words of McClellan, they "required historicizing and exoticizing through context to become museum objects" (1994, 155).[17] The narrative Lenoir worked to create through his contextualizing practices is now familiar, thanks in part to secularizing and modernizing accounts of Europe. Hints of French sculptural genius can only briefly be glimpsed in the "dark ages." With the advent of the Renaissance, the fruits of individual artistry can fully be appreciated. There then follows a period of excess and decline as despotic kings demand works that buttress their power, rather than advancing that of art, until the Enlightenment, when art and artists were liberated and rediscovered true artistic spirit or genius. According to narratives of the kind Lenoir attempted to materialize, Europe was secularized through processes that overcame the divine ground of images and architecture to discover a latent humanist spirit or genius. The humanist ground maintains its transcendence through its persistent but intermittent presence throughout history. "True" art always existed, even when it was oppressed or diminished by tyrannical regimes such as monarchies and the Catholic Church. In contrast to catholaïcité, such arguments see secularization at the source of Europe's continuity.

This narrative was made explicit in Lenoir's decorating practices. The room devoted to the thirteenth century was dimly lit, which Lenoir described as "appropriate to the 'timid artists' of the Middle Ages, those 'servile copyists of nature and costumes,' who had done no more than give a 'sort of form to their statues'" (McClellan 1994, 182). In contrast, in the sixteenth-century gallery, "an abundance of light encouraged the viewer to scrutinize the marbles and recognize in them the work of individual masters and the emergence of a beautiful and uniquely French style in sculpture" (ibid.).

At times, however, lighting, decoration, and comparison proved insufficient in materializing the evolutionary tale Lenoir wished to tell. In an interesting corollary to David Harvey's account of the "creative destruction" of Paris by Baron Haussmann in the mid-nineteenth century, McClellan describes the "creative restoration" of numerous objects by Lenoir. Many of the objects he received might more accurately be described as debris because of the violent way they had been removed and transported. In addition to a number of tombs and statues, Lenoir found himself among a sea of broken, smashed, and discarded semi-objects. According to McClellan, the temptation to reforge such works in creative ways was simply too great. Lenoir took, for example, a single statue of Charles of Orléans and mounted it "on a base featuring an anonymous alabaster relief of the Death of the Virgin from Saint-Jacques-la-Boucherie." He then "framed" the newly enlarged monument with "Corinthian columns and decorative arabesque moldings that Lenoir claimed were authentic but that seem rather to have been manufactured to his design by his restorer Lamotte" (McClellan 1994, 184–86).[18]

Lenoir's efforts demonstrate the very real labor required to substitute one form of immediacy with another. These were works carved in stone. Dismantling, reconstituting, and recombining these works would not have

been an easy task. Chiseling, sawing, hammering, and forging are practices
that reverberate throughout the body, require strength, and leave their traces
in sweat, scrapes, and vibrating limbs.[19] Similarly, one of the most powerful
elements of the Parmiggiani exhibit had been the way his pieces called to
mind the physicality of his labors aimed at constructing catholaïcité. The
thick glass fragments pointed to the work required to shatter them; the ash
indexed the heavy smoke that could leave behind such traces. Transforming histories that are fragmented and contingent into those that are coherent and whose logics may be accessed in visceral, immediate ways requires
powerful embodied and material work.

Clearly, it is not this fragmented, reconstructed, dismantled, and contingent history that visitors to the Collège seek in encounters with the space.
Engelke has explored the transcendent experiences of time that many Christians highlight through the reading of the Christian Bible. In summarizing St. Augustine's account of the unique temporality of the Bible, Engelke
points to how "Scripture is in time, but not wholly of time because the Word
of God is eternal. Reading Scripture, then, is an act that can take one out
of time" (2009, 159), away from the localized everyday labors of forging a
Christian account of history. As Belting has described, images, statues, and
spaces that function as "icons" operate in a similar manner. According to
Nagel (2004), within the Byzantine and Catholic traditions from at least the
eighth century, "iconic" images were understood through a very different
kind of substitutionary logic to that held by revolutionaries. Their producers aimed to replicate images that were purported to date back to the life of
Jesus, Mary, and the saints on earth. It was the artists and images that were
substitutable, and the resemblance between the images and their "prototypes" that served as the primary concern. Humans standing before icons
could venerate them in ways that would allow the devotion they offered at
particular moments in time to be passed on to those situated outside of time.
The authority of icons, therefore, rested in their ability to appear timeless.

And yet, as Engelke, Belting, and Nagel acknowledge, maintaining
practices of timeless immediacy can prove challenging. By the thirteenth
century—as painters paid increasing attention to details of dress, interiors,
and hairstyles—many such images failed to maintain their logics of substitution and, instead, betrayed the moments in time in which they were
produced. According to Nagel, anxieties surrounding the apparent shallow-
ness of painting reached their height at the beginning of the Renaissance.
Images looked increasingly distant from their prototypes, as they bore the
current but ever-changing styles of dress, hair, and décor particular to the

periods in which they were made. Nagel recounts how "a powerful strategy of late medieval devotions was to fill out narrative contexts, from the bible and from hagiographic literature, as a field for meditation, and this often involved visualizing religious subjects in familiar contemporary surroundings" (2004, 37). Thus, what appeared to be the problematic intrusion of the "secular" within paintings was, in fact, a response to the rise of new kinds of devotional practices among the elite, highlighting the complex, contested, and varied history of Catholic human-material encounters.[20]

If, during the Renaissance, shifts in modes of dress and décor betrayed in religious art proved unsettling because they provoked questions about God's presence in time and in objects, at the Collège, the artists' attempt to highlight the fragmented history of the Collège destabilized a medieval past whose presumed coherence underlay powerful ideas about France and Europe. The contrast between the nave and the sacristy emphasized by Brevet and Rochette betrayed their distinct moments of production and, thereby, reduced the immediacy and timelessness of the space so many visitors desire to encounter. One particular outcome of exhibiting such critical forms at the Collège became clear when—rather than contributing to an ongoing "exchange and debate"—they exacerbated divisions employees at the Collège hoped to reduce: those between Catholic and secular.

On the day when the devotees of St. Bernard interrogated Rochette, I had stood with him as they departed in order to apologize for how out of control the situation had become. One woman from the group stayed behind while the rest marched down the stairs, loudly remarking to one another on the audacity of the presumptuous claims to call this "art." The woman looked on at the artist as he and I discussed how to prevent similar events in the future. "Apart from all of this," she called out, dismissing the installation with the wave of her hand, "are you a believer (*croyant*)?" The question was unexpected and I looked over at Rochette, wondering how he would respond. "Je m'intérroge," he replied, stating that he pondered, reflected, and asked questions about things. "What does that mean?" she replied with no small amount of sarcasm and disapproval in her voice. But she continued before he could elaborate. She went on to suggest that, perhaps if Rochette were a believer, he would no longer be controlled by his anger because he would be filled with the love of God.

For this visitor, evangelizing offered a means by which to critique what she understood to be the dangerous material forms found in *Cellula* and, presumably, other contemporary art installations. Such works, and the texts and explanations that accompanied them, served not only to impede upon the immediacy of the medieval Cistercian past many visitors like her sought, they also risked retraining Christian gazes in ways that, once again, high-lighted catholaïcité's potential capaciousness. Warnings of these dangers could frequently be found in the polemical text that was the livre d'or. One remark, for example, referred to the use of "imbecilic literature to explain the elementary" and warned those at the Collège that they were "going too far." Another contributor pleaded, "Let's not speak of 'dialogue and exchange,' but of the 'loss of orientation' (repères). Is it parishioner money that was wasted in such a way?" According to another, "Simply reading the descriptive sheet at the entrance of the space is sufficient for understanding that the linguistic polysemy is sufficient for you to retrace your steps toward the door for fear of entering into the dictatorship of absolute relativism." The acts of vandalism against Cellula (as with the acts of vandalism found in the banlieues during the protests of 2005) should not simply be dismissed as savage or unmodern. In this case, they intermingled with complex Catho-lic critiques of the fetishisms of secular modernity seemingly embodied in contemporary art.

For their part, the artists insisted that, even though they had exhibited in medieval spaces in the past, including in one called Les Églises (the churches) in a far eastern suburb of Paris, they had never before encountered such violent responses. One afternoon, in expressing his frustration, Rochette declared that the visitors wanted to "stone us and chase us away." His use of the term "stoning" clearly dismissed those who critiqued the exhibit as irra-tional believers, engaging in medieval modes of critique. When I suggested to the devotees of St. Bernard that the artists had offered us an experience the monks would have denied us, I similarly—and inadvertently—reproduced a common trope of the secular. By reminding visitors that they were denied access to the vaults of most churches in Paris, I implied that the Christian past was one cloaked in mystifying enchantments that the enlightened age had unveiled. Indeed, a museum on the right bank of the Seine, also housed in a former church, makes such an argument in more explicit terms. The cul-minating space in Paris's industrial design museum—the Musée des Arts et Métiers—similarly uses a simple, scaffolding-like design to take viewers up to the vaults of the space. Rather than highlighting the architectural details of the church, however, these steps are used to make just such a critical comparison between a religious past and a modern, secular present. Located on each level is a mode of transportation, from bicycles to cars, until finally, hanging suspended in the vaults, an airplane. Louis Blériot designed the airplane in 1909 and used it to make a famous flight from France to England across the British Channel. Soon afterward it was donated to the museum, where it has remained ever since.

Nagel has highlighted how numerous commentators, such as the surrealist poet and writer Guillaume Apollinaire, referenced the airplane's "triumphal procession to the Arts et Métiers" through the streets of Paris in order to make negative comparisons between the processions of works that pointed to God's presence in earlier times and the twentieth century's celebration of works "invested with humanity, with millennial aspiration, with necessary art" (quoted in Nagel 2012, 36). At the museum, the scaffolding exhibit implies that the Church refused humans access to the skies, relegating them to the position of merely gazing upward. Once properly liberated from such influences, however, humanity discovered it could reach such heights on its own. These oversimplified distinctions and critiques offer little insight into the differences between a repurposed church and an airplane or a renovated Cistercian Collège and installation art such as *Cellula*. Instead, they demonstrate the Collège's failure to open up a conversation about human-object relations beyond desires for immediacy and the threat of fetishism, resulting in a return to tropes of a religious-secular divide.

BATTLING FETISHISM WITH IMMATERIALITY

One reliable solution to the quagmire of anxieties surrounding fetishes at the Collège was simply turning away from questions of materiality that foregrounded the problem of the fetish and turning instead toward the possibility of immateriality. In his attempt to assist the mediators in the task of inviting people into the exhibit, the manager suggested that the work could be read as an "echo" of the steps involved in medieval mystical experiences. He turned to the three-step model of mysticism laid out by St. Jean de la Croix, a sixteenth-century Spanish Carmelite monk, to explore how the exhibit might point to one of the most immaterial experiences in the Catholic tradition.

The first step—in the exhibit, this would have occurred beneath the scaffolding with a light beckoning upward—the manager described as that of "purgatory," in which humans see light in the darkness and desire to be penetrated by this light. The second step was that of "illumination," in which humans make the choice to reject "failure" or "sin" and to follow the path of seeking to know love. The images that accompany this step, the manager explained, were those of ascent. In the exhibit, this would have corresponded with the steps of the staircase. Once one has "decided" that which will guide one's life, the manager clarified, the illumination one seeks occurs gradually. Finally, the manager described the third step as one of "unity." In this stage, humans who are "in the light" are not conscious of being one with God, as those who are in the light cannot see it. This is the stage at which humans reach unity between what they desire and what they do. Here, the manager implicitly referred to the fluorescent lights at the apex of the exhibit that stayed lit only when there was no motion in the room. Ultimately, this account of the experience of mysticism connected experiences of immediacy with those of immateriality. While he acknowledged elements of the materiality of the exhibit—its stairs, the movement from darkness to light, the lights that did not remain lit at the apex—the material and the mediated were reduced to a metaphor for the immaterial and immediate.

For many mediators, this interpretation proved useful in engaging the different audiences who came through the Collège. Indeed, had I turned to this interpretation rather than to the artists' when confronted by the devotees of St. Bernard, I may not have put the installation at risk in quite the way I did. Over time, I found the manager's explanation particularly useful in engaging the spiritual public, which, as I describe in chapter 4, included some committed Catholics as well as those more likely to describe themselves as spiritual than as religious. Reference to mysticism proved eminently attractive to both. The contemporary audience was far more likely to be predisposed to the artists' interpretations. It was the classical public that proved most challenging. Their profound attachment to the space made it difficult to know whether they would be intrigued or disconcerted by the opportunity to encounter the building in a new way through the installation. As the responses of the devotees of St. Bernard suggest, knowing in advance how to manage the varying desires for immediacy visitors brought to the space proved immensely difficult. Encouraging viewers to relate to experiences of immediacy through an emphasis on immateriality rather than the materiality of either the Collège or the exhibit often proved to be far safer ground.

Critics of the exhibit—both those underwhelmed and those threatened by it—also found it productive to turn to the possibility of "true" art as that which indexed immaterial rather than material experiences. In one particularly memorable debate with a visitor, an older man smirked at my lengthy discussion of the polysemy of the term "cellule." He pointed out that I was not French. I agreed. "And does the equivalent term for *cellule* have so many meanings in your language?" I assured him that it functioned in a very similar way in English, but I was fascinated by the manner in which he had attempted to trump my explanation by demonstrating that words were too particular to contain the universal he presumed a work of art ought to convey. This mode of critique served to shift the focus away from the materiality of the installation or the Collège to instead highlight the broader immaterial experience that ought to be the focus.

At times the artists also insisted that they designed the exhibit to allow for immaterial experiences of immediacy. Once, they expressed the desire to me that more visitors experience the installation nearly alone, in an empty space, ripe for reflection. Clearly, despite their attention to the complex materiality of the space, the artists also desired the possibility that their work could induce more immaterial experiences. They made this desire explicit when they participated in one of the Bernardins Tuesday debates held during the exhibit. The event was devoted to the question of installations as works of art. Brevet and Rochette were joined by an art critic and a curator, both of whom had worked with the artist pair in the past. The host of the debate had a difficult time masking his reservations about the prospect that installations, or, at least, this installation, could be considered art. At one point he asked the artists about the presence of the mediators in the installation, who are there, he said, to "recount some of your intentions. But why? Are they indispensable?" he asked. "Couldn't we simply discover your work in silence?" Rochette laughed and retorted, "We would prefer that!" He explained that it was not their choice to have mediators but that the Collège was a "particular space" where visitors did not necessarily come expressly to see contemporary installation art. The mediators, however, he said, could also "erase themselves and make themselves less present." He insisted that they hoped "the public can visit this freely, without mediators, even without other members of the public, in silence."

***

To conclude, I want to highlight one additional point of concordance among those who desired art that speaks for itself and the iconoclasts who insisted its power must be destroyed. They both overlooked the powerful ways in which they had long learned to engage with a variety of media as immediate sources of French heritage. I do not want to suggest that nationalism had become the religion they shared. Sharon Macdonald (2008) has argued that heritage spaces cannot be reduced to their ideological functions alone and

THE IMMEDIATE, THE MATERIAL, AND THE FETISH

has advocated for exploring these spaces as the result of complex dialectics between curators, conservationists, and visitors. What I want to emphasize here, following the lead of Brevet and Rochette, are the vagaries but also the particularity of the heritage forms put to work in forging the nation in France.

In her fascinating account of the interconnections between monetary and political instability in France from the Revolution through the nineteenth century, Rebecca Spang (2017) explores the rise and fall of the *assignat*, a complex monetary form revolutionaries created in December 1789 in order to pay off the debts the new revolutionary state had inherited. The decision by the revolutionaries to restore the state's credit by reimbursing the nobility whose venal privileges had been abolished had the paradoxical effect of maintaining many of the class distinctions that revolutionaries had hoped to annihilate. Venal offices—powerful state positions given and later sold to those who occupied them—served as a form of immovable property because they brought in income over an indefinite period of time. By abolishing the positions, the deputies understood themselves to be expropriating private property that would need to be repaid in order to avoid accusations of despotism.

Long dismissed as the quintessential example of how markets run amuck when governments attempt to solve their problems by printing money, the assignats are for Spang one of many modes of exchange developed at a moment when the population desired value to adhere to material forms. Yearnings for these modes of immediacy did not vanish after other forms of exchange replaced the assignat. Spang insists that it was the unsettled nature of the nineteenth century in France, "a time when 'the people' regularly and violently challenged the authority of their purported representatives, when Louis Philippe's claim to the throne rested chiefly on his *not* being the 'legitimate' monarch, and when revolutions threatened to be yearly events" that "ideas like intrinsic value and innate character were both immensely comforting and under constant pressure" (2017, 259). Spang's argument holds when applied to the practices aimed at guaranteeing the immediacy of objects by employees at the Louvre and by Lenoir.

When assignats were first introduced, many expressed hope that they would be "'the signs of unalloyed value,' 'emanations of the general will,' and 'the Savior of France'" (2017, 58). What is particularly fascinating about the assignats is that they were backed by lands, objects, and spaces previously held by the Catholic Church and nationalized by the revolutionary state. The transcendent ground that proponents hoped users of the assignats would see as inhering immediately within these paper forms was none other than the immovable properties associated with the Catholic Church. It was this inherent value, moreover, that would contribute to maintaining the inequalities the Revolution purportedly destroyed.

I argue that the Collège and many other heritage sites in France not only continue to make the past present in ways that have appeared productive in the forging of the nation, they also continue to allow for the maintenance of inequality by grounding it in material forms. The democratic vision imagined and enacted at brief moments during the French Revolution was never fully implemented. A number of interests combined—and continue to combine—to resist moving French social life toward greater equality. Justification of the resulting, apparently insoluble inequalities continues to require a transcendent ground. The contemporary arts project in the medieval space of the Collège could offer a variety of alternative means of engaging with objects beyond a desire for their inherent value or transcendent ground. Such a project could, instead, offer an opportunity to confront vagaries, contingencies, and inequalities. The Collège's broader aim of aestheticizing France's distinctions by reproducing Catholicism's privileged banality ultimately discourages such opportunities. The tension between the Collège's possibilities and its limits ultimately encouraged visitors, mediators, and employees alike to turn, time and again, to the lure of immateriality in guaranteeing experiences of immediacy, discounting the need to address fragmented material pasts that might otherwise be confronted.

THE BANALITY OF PRIVILEGE

THE VERNISSAGE FOR THE FOURTH EXHIBITION of contemporary art at the Collège was a bustling event. In the preceding weeks, I had been struck by the visibility of ads for the exhibit, entitled *La pesanteur et la grâce* (*Gravity and Grace*), throughout the city. One day, I had been surprised enough to see one such poster on the billboards that advertise cultural events along the length of the Boulevard St. Germain that I slammed on the brakes of my bicycle and received angry shouts from passing cyclists as I pulled out my phone and snapped a picture. The morning of the vernissage, I had perused the internet to see how widely *Gravity and Grace* had extended into digital space. Along with the Collège and two organizations associated with the archdiocese that advertised the exhibit on their websites, the mayor's office also included it on its events calendar. I was particularly struck by its account of the Collège. With no mention of its being owned and operated by the archdiocese, the Collège was described as an "exceptional thirteenth century edifice, recently restored. . . . In 2009, more than 150,000 visitors passed through its doors." The events page for *Le Figaro* also made brief mention of *Gravity and Grace* and categorized it under "*Arts—Mixte.*" It, too, did not identify the Catholic archdiocese as the owner and operator.

That night, as I moved around the space chatting with employees, patrons, artists, and visitors, I was struck at the contrast with the quiet, midday opening of the Parmiggiani exhibit a year and a half earlier. Between attempts to speak with as many people as possible throughout the night, I also tried to comfort one of the arts coordinators who was agonizing over damage to works by a recently deceased artist. The scuffmarks that appeared on the folded panels displayed on the floor were not vengeful acts of destruction but rather spoke to just how crowded the building was that night. I stood with him as a fundraiser for the Collège offered the arts coordinator her congratulations, although the fundraiser's remarks focused more on the success of the party than on the exhibit. "There are so many people here," the fundraiser cried out over the echo of hundreds of conversations bouncing off the limestone walls. "Perhaps too many! There is no one left on the streets of Paris tonight. All of Paris is here!" She was clearly thrilled at the thought of the Collège at the center of the city's cultural life. The arts coordinator, too distraught by the potential of further damage to the art to join in the fundraiser's delight, shrugged his shoulders and, somewhat wryly, responded, "That's the Collège des Bernardins!"

The sense that the Collège had "arrived" on Paris's cultural scene was palpable. Rather than offering a source of comfort, however, the idea of the Collège as the space where "all of Paris" could be found served instead to make the stakes of this exhibit particularly high. Earlier, I had chatted with a few employees who expressed reticence about the exhibit. For *Gravity and Grace*, the Collège had invited a well-known curator named Éric de Chassey to organize a multi-artist exhibit exploring the relationship between "abstraction and spirituality." In our conversation that evening, one of the employees dismissed it as *"spirituellement nul"* (spiritually rubbish). The employees looked around the room anxiously. Even the din of the enormous crowd failed to reassure them that the exhibit would bring sufficient value to the Collège. One employee remembered that Cardinal Lustiger had once declared that contemporary art must speak to people's "sensibilities," which apparently this exhibit did not. She sighed. "But at least the arts project shouldn't *impede* the project of the Bernardins. If people come here and see exhibitions that are, for them, failures, they aren't going to come to the dialogues, the conferences." The employee's labor at the Collège was aimed at facilitating these latter activities and her frustration implied that the exhibitions had already made her work more difficult. "With *Cellula*," she complained, "we worried it would destroy our base of supporters. We worried they would take back their checks!"

While my work as a mediator for *Suite Grünewald* and *Cellula* had begun rather abruptly, I was able to spend some time preparing for *Gravity and Grace*. An arts coordinator had brought me and another mediator together for a few meetings before the opening in order to help us develop concrete outreach tools to use in our encounters with the public. He acknowledged that this exhibit might prove "difficult" to mediate. At the time I was surprised by the anxiety of both the arts coordinator and the employees at the vernissage. How could a series of (mostly) paintings prove more controversial than broken glass and scaffolding? Their concerns, however, proved prescient.

Early in the exhibit's run—April 23 to September 12, 2010—I listened as a couple in their sixties remarked on previous exhibits at the Collège. "This is where the broken glass was," the woman observed in hushed tones. "It's true, it's true," her husband clucked, shaking his head sadly. I wondered if, in comparison, the current exhibit might appear more palatable. Instead, they approached me to explain that the paintings before them were "appalling." The woman marveled at "the audacity" required to "exhibit something like this." Her husband agreed and suggested that the artists were "nothing more than thieves."

The "thieves" were five European artists working in various modes of abstraction. *Gravity and Grace* occupied both the nave and the sacristy. The works most visible to visitors upon entering the building were a series from 2001 entitled *Tours et Taxis*, named for a building in Brussels in which the series was first exhibited. Created by a Belgian artist named Marthe Wéry, who died in 2007, these folded, colorful metal panels displayed on the floor were the works attendees of the crowded vernissage had bumped into and scuffed. Rather than using a brush to move the paint across these unlikely canvases, Wéry had allowed gravity to do the work. After submerging each panel in a tray of water, and then in one of paint, Wéry lifted each panel out and allowed the paint to make its way across the surface. According to a document another mediator and I wrote to help us guide high school students through the exhibit, Wéry preferred her work to appear "incomplete" or "precarious," as she desired to "re-endanger the tableau."

The second artist exhibited in the nave was Georges Tony Stoll, who works in what he calls "the territory of abstraction." Having worked in painting, photography, and film, his installation at the Collège involved a wooden sculpture of simple, brute wood painted gold and a small painting containing a gold circle, with the brushstrokes evident to the eye. Given its size and the round gold splattering of paint in the middle, the latter drew some comparisons to the icons of the Orthodox Church. Finally, along the false wall on the right side of the nave hung five paintings by Callum Innes, an Irish artist who, like Wéry, allowed the paint to move, with the aid of gravity, across the plane of a canvas. While the thick paint used in Wéry's monochromes masked the process from the viewer, the striations in Innes's paintings emphasized their mode of production. Because of the possibility of seeing various shapes within the visible traces of the movement of paint, Innes's works were the most likely to receive positive responses from visitors.

The works of the two remaining artists were displayed in the sacristy. A French artist named Emmanuel Van der Meulen created four paintings expressly for the show. They were made in conversation with the space of the Collège, a point to which I will return below. His paintings of simple, geometrical shapes in subdued tones were hung with what felt like the lightest of touches throughout the sacristy. According to my pedagogical document, Van der Meulen described these simple shapes as "giving themselves to be seen from the start, and from there we can move on." He insisted that the role of the painter and that of the viewer were "interchangeable." The other artist in the sacristy was Emanuele Becheri, an Italian artist, who contributed a sonar installation to the show, looping the sound from a video installation of three burning flares he had produced years earlier on an LP that sat atop a wooden platform in the sacristy. Like Wéry, we wrote, he preferred to create works that were "open" and "without a final meaning." After its run at the Collège, a more extensive version of *Gravity and Grace* appeared at the Villa Medici, France's fine art institute in Rome, where de Chassey serves as director.

As an exhibition focused on minimalist forms of abstraction that emphasized the agency of materials rather than artists, *Gravity and Grace* provoked a number of questions and concerns about surface and depth and led to observations on how such questions relate to the distinction between the material and immaterial. One way to interpret critical responses to the exhibit would be to see the artists and visitors as approaching the relationship between surface and depth and the material and immaterial in distinct ways. Perhaps, in its modernism, the exhibit implicitly conveyed a "materialist" account of surface and depth, while the visitors brought with them a perspective shaped more by Catholic visions of the relationship between material and immaterial, or flesh and spirit. According to materialist perspectives, the immaterial realm of religion, ideas, and ideology exists on the surface and the material conditions of work, the nature of production, and structures of inequality occupy the site of depth. In contrast, Catholic ontologies often emphasize a worldview in which the immaterial, spiritual, or transcendent realm offers the true space of depth and the material or immanent hovers along the surface. Nirenberg's emphasis on "Judaizing" as an accusation among Christians that their opponents had "*mistaken aesthetic priorities*: a preference for the bodily meaning of scripture over its spiritual one" (2015, 12) offers one example of this mode of Catholic thought. When applied to the desires visitors brought to the space of the Collège, as well as to *Gravity and Grace*, however, this distinction between Catholic and materialist ontologies does not hold.

In chapter 5, I describe numerous Catholic material practices that make

space for both proximate and distanced access to the immaterial or spiritual. Many of these practices—such as the adoration of the relics of saints—
have also proved controversial at different historical periods. Indeed, as the
manager's preference for the immaterial in his account of *Cellula* suggests,
Catholicism's abundant materiality continues to be haunted by theological preferences for the spiritual over the fleshly, or the immaterial over the
material.

During *Gravity and Grace*, visitors seemed to find the emphasis placed
on the material particularly disconcerting and generally refused the invitation to engage with the material as a means of accessing something more
immaterial, or spiritual. Instead, visitors critiqued the works as vacuous
and often expressed concerns about the disparity between their true value
and their price. While visitors had asked questions about the costs of all of
the exhibitions, it was during *Gravity and Grace* in particular that concerns
about how much the artists were paid, the value of the art, and the class
distinctions found at the Collège were most frequently expressed. The inaugural years of the Collège (2008–10) were undeniably a moment in which
themes of austerity, waste, and unchecked accumulation were central to
broader discourses in France, Europe, and around the world. As I describe
in the introduction, employees at the Collège felt the constraints of suddenly limited budgets and the uncertainty of the future of corporate and
private funds soon after its opening, which coincided with the beginning
of the global financial crisis. From my vantage point as a mediator, these
constraints were most immediately obvious in the decision to reduce mediators from employees to interns. The broader problem of fiscal tightening,
however, was something to which many employees referred frequently.

Despite the widespread nature of such concerns, there seemed to be
something about *Gravity and Grace* in particular that encouraged visitors
to worry about the value and cost of the exhibit. What are we to make of
the general refusal to dwell with the materiality of *Gravity and Grace* as a
means of arriving at the spiritual? Why did the exhibit seem to so forcefully
bring concerns about value, broadly conceived, to the fore? To my mind, by
asking visitors to pay heed to the surface in a variety of ways, these works
of minimalist abstraction prompted them to ask questions about depth.[1] It
invoked the specter that, rather than the medieval past, what was being celebrated at the Collège was nothing more than the distinctions of the present.
In order to make sense of these responses to *Gravity and Grace*, I argue that,
rather than inhering in the material or immaterial, surface and depth should
instead be mapped onto practices of exclusion and inclusion. I understand

practices of exclusion as those that diminish the complexity and inequality of diverse histories and actors; in contrast practices of inclusion acknowledge this inequality and make space for this complexity and diversity. In what follows, I turn to the critiques made of *Gravity and Grace*, as well as to the writings of the midcentury Marxist mystic Simone Weil, who served as one of the inspirations for the exhibit, and those of St. Bernard and Hannah Arendt in order to demonstrate how *Gravity and Grace* and the Collège in its inaugural years engaged more often in practices of exclusion than those of inclusion.

ABSTRACTION AND EXCLUSION

The art historian Krista Thompson has highlighted how numerous artists in the African diaspora focus on the surface of their work. They do so, however, in order to induce radically distinct effects to those seen in *Gravity and Grace*. According to Thompson, these artists

> present their subjects in ways that call attention to notions of surface—the embellished surface, the reflective surface, the surface of the body, the surface of the photograph or screen, the backdrop and green screen. While modern artists working globally since the early twentieth century have long emphasized the surface of their canvases or sculptures in their artistic practice, these creators who draw on African diasporic practices call attention to what might be described as the surface of the surface—the effect of light reflecting off of surfaces—as the representational space for figuring black subjects. [2015, 35]

The artists Thompson analyzes do so, she argues, in ways that call attention to the limits of vision and that "disaggregate the equation between seeing and knowing" (ibid., 235). Thompson highlights the overlaps between the "shine" or "bling" of African diasporic aesthetic forms and paintings of the sixteenth-century Dutch renaissance. Artists such as Rembrandt, Hans Holbein, and others glorified the wealth of their new patrons, the rising merchant class, by emphasizing the power of their commodified objects through techniques that made them appear to shine. Clothing, jewels, and objects of their interior homes depicted in the paintings popped with color and vibrancy. Numerous art historians, including Hal Foster, have argued that the "'special shellac' of Dutch still life paintings 'endow[ed] them with a pictorial value to match the commercial value they had already acquired on the market'" (quoted in Thompson 2015, 227). In contrast, the white faces and bodies of the subjects were presented without shellac, differentiating their humanity from the commodities that surrounded them. Paintings of black bodies made during the period, however, such as Dirk Valkenburg's (1675–1721) *Slave 'Play' on a Sugar Plantation in Surinam*, painted between 1706 and 1708, represented these bodies with a glistening shine, thereby emphasizing their commodity status.

When modern and contemporary African diaspora artists take up these tactics of surface and shine, Thompson argues, they highlight how "the over-determined surface of black skin prevented many from seeing the humanity and subjectivity of persons of African descent. . . . Observing the surface appearance of things has been an obstacle to certain ways of seeing, a fact of visibility's limits that, historically, people of African descent have long experienced" (ibid., 235–36). Thus, assertions that surface and depth could be distinguished visually have historically contributed to reproducing powerful inequalities and expressions of violence. By demanding viewers pay attention to surface and shine, African diaspora artists encourage questions about the limits of the visible, and the invisible traits that come to be mapped onto it. I also find Thompson's work to be a productive means by which to question the taken-for-granted universality of modernist abstract aesthetics. Modes of abstract modernism that refused the possibility of any form of representation began to exert a powerful influence on the global art market at precisely the moment in the mid-twentieth century when anticolonial movements opened the way for alternative representations of black bodies in works of art. The insistence on a return to representational forms by many contemporary African diaspora artists, such as Jean-Michel Basquiat (1960–1988) and Mickalene Thomas (1971–), addresses the erasures that inhere in abstraction. That the Collège chose to explore questions of spirituality through abstract forms whose presumed universality may also have reiterated the whiteness of the space should not be overlooked.

The curator of the exhibit, de Chassey, was another impressive figure to be brought into the Collège. The director of the renowned Villa Medici in Rome and a specialist in twentieth-century French and American abstraction, de Chassey has published academic texts on the subject and worked as curator for a number of important exhibits over the last few decades. When asked in a Q & A produced with arts staff to explain how the exhibit related to questions or experiences of spirituality, de Chassey pointed to the

"very precise, very fragile, and very difficult to grasp moment when a creation begins to exist; this very precise and very fragile moment where one
passes from nothing at all to something that still isn't defined, something
that still isn't a big thing but is just at the point of tipping." If viewers paid
attention to these tipping points, he explained, they would participate in a
spiritual exercise. "All spiritual traditions emphasize that the foundation of
a spiritual exercise is the ability to feel that moment of passing from nothing
to something."

He elaborated on this idea in the exhibit's accompanying brochure, in
which he explained a concept he saw as central to *Gravity and Grace*: spiri-
tualizing abstraction (*l'abstraction spiritualisante*). "What do these words
mean?" the brochure asked for the viewer:

> This is not, as some would think, spiritual abstraction, in which the con-
> tent would be explicitly spiritual: an artist wishing to represent the invis-
> ible, the metaphysical, the transcendent, etc. No, in this case, the artist's
> first concern is to work with the materials and then only to produce an
> effect on the spectator by giving him access to a spiritual dimension that
> has not been determined in advance, offering the spectator a direction,
> but never providing him or her with an explanation which would counter
> each individual's freedom.

Thus, de Chassey presented the works in the exhibit as modest material
forms that, if looked at with particular kinds of attention, could aid visitors
in approaching spiritual experiences. In the Q & A, when asked how viewers should approach the works, he suggested that "we must accept to put
ourselves in a position of humility or modesty in front of the works, just
as they put themselves in [such] a position in front of the viewer." Despite
de Chassey's framing of the exhibit, most visitors experienced the works as
ostentatious, rather than modest.

On one of the first days of the exhibit, I gave a man a quick tour with
which he was clearly unimpressed. "How many artists are included here?"
he asked. "Five," I responded, hoping this was a sign that he was beginning
to take more interest. "And do we pay them to come here, do we invite them
here, or do they pay for the right to exhibit?" he fired off in short succes-
sion, revealing his interests to be of a very different nature.[2] I explained that
the curator had invited the artists. "Thank you," he said sternly. Gratitude,
however, was not the message he conveyed. Rather, in addition to ending

our conversation, the phrase served to prove his point that the exhibit was indeed as corrupt as it appeared.

At times, the sight of *Gravity and Grace* seemed to inspire visitors to retroactively consider how much earlier exhibits had cost. On one afternoon in mid-May, I struggled to respond to a woman's question as to whether or not "this was all there was to see." She explained that she had visited the previous exhibit but then went on to describe the work by Parmiggiani, rather than *Suite Grünewald* or *Cellula*. She acknowledged that the broken glass had left an impression but shook her head in shock at the memory of the bells "in the shadow" of the sacristy. "And they were from Italy no less!" As I attempted to gauge the nature of her concern about the bells' origins—did she think they ought to have been French?—she offered clarification by lamenting, "Imagine the cost of bringing them all this way, and to do what, just to pile them on the floor? I don't understand!"

The contemporary, classical, and spiritual publics I describe in chapter 4 expressed distinct expectations about and displayed varied responses to *Suite Grünewald* and *Cellula*. During *Gravity and Grace*, however, these publics became harder and harder to distinguish because so many of them tended to both dismiss the exhibit as insignificant and express concerns about its costs. I was surprised in a conversation with one man whom I identified as part of the contemporary public when he impatiently dismissed the exhibit. Having hoped that my conversation with him might prove more positive than so many others in which I had engaged, I asked him what he found so problematic. He explained that he found these kinds of works to be similar to the empty, meaningless works that flood the art market and command far more than they are worth. He saw nothing particularly new or thoughtful in them and suggested they were just like the generic works one would find covering the walls of government offices.

Some visitors even took the exhibit as an opportunity to question the money that had gone into the renovation of the Collège. In early May, I spoke with an elderly couple and another woman. While the trio did not know each other, they joined forces in their desire to commiserate about the exhibit. One woman expressed her frustration by complaining that "they asked for our money to restore this place and then they think they can do whatever they want with it? In a space such as this, this art has no place!" I attempted to offer them pamphlets and information the mediators had put together on the history of abstraction. My efforts seemed only to anger them further. Turning to the works of Innes, the other woman acknowledged that there was, at least, "something to reflect on" in them, that they had "some depth" (*profondeur*). "But this," she exclaimed pointing to Wéry's works, "and this," pointing to the installation by Stoll, "they mean nothing. I feel nothing. It's a disgrace." Here, the critic equated "depth" with works that seemed to exceed the materials that went into them and offered the potential for a representation of something else. Another day in mid-May, two elegantly dressed women made this contrast in more implicit terms, asking how one could buy a painting like one of Van der Meulen's and hang it next to a Caravaggio. (Their mannerisms seemed to suggest that the problem of what to hang next to a Caravaggio was for them familiar.)

The exhibit also seemed to bring feelings of exclusion to the fore. One woman followed up her angry dismissal of the works by asking how long the exhibit would last. I explained that it had opened only the previous week. "I know," she clarified angrily. "We saw all the cars! All the people invited! But we, the donors, and the neighbors, we didn't receive an invitation!" I thought it odd that she was so upset not to have attended the vernissage, given how little she thought of the exhibit, but clearly it seemed to provoke anxiety about who was to be included and excluded from the Collège.

On a quiet afternoon, one pair of visitors asked me about my research. When I explained just how much time I had spent at the Collège over the last two years, they seemed concerned and asked if it was not a "bit of a ghetto." Of the many times I had been forced to pause and wonder at the meaning of the comments offered in this space, this one seemed particularly daunting. Surely they could not be implying that the space was one of poverty? "It is true that you do not see all of Paris here," I acknowledged, wondering how they would respond. "No, no," they agreed. "You don't find the nineteenth, the twentieth [arrondissements], the banlieues." I nodded in agreement. These are the sections of Paris—associated with working-class and racially diverse populations—that I also saw as absent in this elite space. One of the women then explained that she had encouraged a friend to take classes here but that her friend had quit because she was disappointed with how elitist it was. Rather than following up the use of the term "ghetto" and the story of her disaffected friend with a critical analysis of exclusions at the Collège, the woman instead explained that she had admonished her friend for quitting, and she insisted that she and her husband did not come to the Collège for the connections, or for the people they would meet, but for the "richness" of the things they learned there. She lamented how often the Church abuse scandals were mentioned in the media. "We don't talk about that here," she insisted. She then offered a different means of accounting for the isolation of the space of the Collège. "It's our own little bubble," she sighed happily.[3]

It was also during *Gravity and Grace* that I spoke most frequently with the volunteers, employees, and mediators about issues of class—our own and the socioeconomic class of visitors to the Collège. One guide employed a term many at the Collège often used to speak about class differences implicitly rather than explicitly: "culture." He complained that the exhibit was proving more difficult to work into his tours than anticipated. Like many of the mediators, he found it helpful to point to the potential linkage between Cistercian asceticism and the minimalist abstraction in *Gravity and Grace* in order to improve visitors' experience of the exhibit. Unfortunately, this approach rarely proved as productive as we had hoped. The guide insisted, however, that those visitors with the proper "culture" could at least appreciate the ideas behind the exhibit. The group he had just taken through had been both "too old" and lacking in the right culture to get much out of it.[4] He went on to contrast them with a friend for whom all of this is self-evident, if still not exactly to her taste. He returned again to his point that one's ability to appreciate the art was based entirely on the extent of one's culture. "Cultivated" was another term used by guides, volunteers, managers, and employees to make similar critiques. Both terms served as a means of cloaking the class and racial distinctions that were their true object of concern.

Another day, a volunteer named Didier more explicitly acknowledged the problem of elitism at the Collège. He described for me the challenge of having to purchase lunch while volunteering extensively at the Collège, a luxury he could not afford. He knew that if he volunteered for eight-hour days, he was eligible to receive subsidized lunch tickets, but he felt as though there were a general taboo against volunteers' requesting them.[5] While it might seem as though volunteers ought to be key candidates for subsidized lunches, many volunteers who worked at the Collège were wealthy enough to have little need for them. Those of lesser means also felt the pressure to contribute to, rather than take from, the Collège's funds. Didier explained that, unlike many of his colleagues, he did not own his home; he had to pay rent.

Didier's stance became increasingly defensive as he explained that "these women"—pointing to the well-dressed, white, and economically advantaged women who were working to close up the cash registers as the end of the business day approached around us—had no idea where he lived, insisting they had likely never visited it and would perhaps not even consider it to be Paris. Feigning a bit more ignorance than I could reasonably claim after spending a year and a half in this space, I asked Didier where it was that "these women" lived. "In the sixteenth, of course," he replied. "The sixteenth and Versailles," he further explained, referring to the wealthiest arrondisse-ment of Paris and its adjacent western suburb.

Didier went on to explain that his neighborhood—which was located in precisely the arrondissements that the earlier visitors had acknowledged were underrepresented at the Collège and in which I also lived—was rela-tively new for him as well. He, too, had once lived in a wealthier neighbor-hood in the city, but changing life circumstances had forced him to relocate to a different part of the city. "The atmosphere there is very different," he explained. When I asked him to elaborate, he pointed to the characteris-tics many people highlight when they talk about the northeastern parts of the city: its "diversity" and its "immigrants." He described a very "hard" Black population, consuming alcohol and crack, with knife fights breaking out frequently. He acknowledged that it was not a very "Christian" thing to say but suggested that these populations were "cast-offs." He explained that there were also *maghrebins* returning to very "extreme and fanatic notions of identity," including women in full burqa. He described this population as "musulmans, purs et durs." This rhyming phrase, while less poetic in En-glish, remains equally startling: "diehard Muslims." Later, he used the phrase again, this time racializing it as "Arabes, purs et durs."

On another occasion, I watched a woman who had disparaged the exhibit aggressively flick one of Wéry's folded panels before I could stop her. She remarked on how hard it was and on how she had wanted to buy aluminum like this in order print and display the photographs she took. I found the fact that she was an artist surprising; I generally expected artists to have more respect for art objects. She went on to lament the difficulty of finding a place to exhibit her works, looking around the Collège suggestively. While I often offered artists who made similar inquiries the contact information of the arts coordinator at the Collège, I did not do so that afternoon. I asked her about her photographs. She explained that she took photographs of "inter-esting people, cats . . . and tramps (*clochards*). I know we aren't supposed to say that—SDF," she corrected herself in a way I found disturbing. (SDF stands for *sans domicile fixe*, or without fixed address, the more common term for homeless people in France today.) "I found them lying with their heads touching, and I thought it was beautiful, and they were in the Palais Royale [an elite space in Paris]."

In these various moments I have described, numerous privileged—relatively or in more absolute terms—voices demonstrated a limited ability to inhabit the experiences and perspectives of those less privileged. From the woman who shifted her account of the Collège from a "ghetto" to a "bubble" as she dismissed her friend's concerns about the elitism in this space to Didier's abrupt shift from reflecting on his own declining class status to his racist dismissal of those others who "truly" did not belong, to an artist's lament about her own exclusion from exhibiting in the space alongside of her aestheticization of gross inequality, these voices expressed concern about exclusion while simultaneously refusing the possibility of or need for greater inclusion. When employees lamented that the exhibits put at risk the donations they needed to keep the project going, they pointed to some of the material concerns that undergird the elite focus of the Collège. But when visitors critiqued the Collège for paying for art such as that found in *Gravity and Grace*, or in asking for their support to renovate the Collège and then doing "whatever they wanted with it," these elite voices also demonstrated their presumed ownership over the space—the right, that is, to determine who and what belonged in it.

MATERIALITY AND THE LIMITS OF INCLUSION

The title of *Gravity and Grace* is taken from a book of the same name by the mid-twentieth-century Marxist mystic Simone Weil (1909–1943).[6] The book (1988 [1947]) is an ethereal set of reflections on life, work, salvation, Christianity, and death. Collected and published posthumously, the title was extracted by an editor from Weil's writings, largely unpublished at the time of her death. In contrast to her other (numerous) books, *Gravity and Grace* is rather incoherent. While in her other writings, her Marxist leanings are explicitly articulated, the series of thoughts stitched together in *Gravity and Grace* produce a far less systematic ideology.

Weil was born to a wealthy Jewish family in Paris. She "declared herself a Bolshevik at the age of 10" and was among the first women accepted to France's elite institution of higher education, the École Normale Supérieure. While still in her early twenties, Weil worked among and advocated for women factory workers in rural France, debated fiercely with Trotsky while also hosting him at her parents' home, and wrote searing critiques of French colonialism (Weil 2018 [1937], 34). Later in her short life, however, she became disenchanted with the failure of radical politics to flourish in ways that did not devolve into bureaucratic tyranny, and she experienced a series of powerful encounters with Christianity in medieval edifices in

Portugal, Italy, and France. She died of self-starvation and tuberculosis in 1943 at age thirty-four.

The use of Weil's *Gravity and Grace* as an inspiration for the exhibit parallels the role Lustiger's legacy plays at the Collège: the partial incorporation of a particular kind of Judaism that opens onto Christianity. And yet, making use of Weil in this way—not to mention in service of aestheticizing class distinctions—is highly problematic. While many of those who visited the Collège referred to her as a "convert," evidence for such an act is sketchy. The theologian Vincent Lloyd argues that, in fact, she "refus[ed] to consummate her long flirtation with Catholicism" because of the slippery overlap between religious rituals and "patriotic fervor" (Lloyd 2011, 122) so apparent during the 1930s and 1940s in Europe. Similarly, the literary critic Elizabeth Hardwick suggests that these powerful moments of encounter with Christian medieval spaces were "at once an opening to the spirit of Christianity and for her a refusal, the refusal of baptism, the refusal to go through the door of conversion, finally, the refusal of much about the worldly organization of the Catholic church" (1975, 86).

Weil's *Gravity and Grace* is widely known and beloved—and nearly as divergently interpreted—in France, and using its title helped to attract people familiar with Weil to the Collège. It also meant, however, that those who came brought expectations that the exhibit, again and again, seemed unable to meet. Indeed, how Weil's writings related to the exhibit was far from self-evident. De Chassey clarified in the Q & A document that none of the artists had produced their work with Weil's writing in mind. Rather, he brought the title to the exhibit after he had selected the artists who would participate, as he felt that there was something in the work of each that "resonated" with Weil's ideas. He saw the artists as sharing an approach where they brought very little in the way of "pre-existing content" to the realization of their works. "For each, the content is unveiled, opens in the production itself, a production that does not involve know-how but a kind of dispossession, a withdrawal of control in order to stand back so that it is the works themselves that are made, as if they could make themselves." According to the press release produced by the Collège for the exhibit, the connection between Weil's thought and the artists' pieces was located in the fact that "their works, painting, constructing, sculpture, all proceed from the consciousness that grace cannot be reached by a heroic will but by submission to the necessities of gravity. In the words of . . . Weil: 'rising by lowering. It might only be possible for us to rise in this way.'"

This way of presenting Weil's work significantly underplays the critical components of her focus on materiality. In Françoise Meltzer's (2001) reading of Weil, the two seemingly opposite poles of her thinking—her Marxism and her mysticism—are brought together by her theories of work. In an essay entitled "The Mysticism of Work" that serves as the final chapter in the French publication of *Gravity and Grace*, Weil describes labor as central to the human condition in ways similar to Marx: "The secret of the human condition is that there is no equilibrium between man and the surrounding forces of nature, which infinitely exceed him when in inaction; there is only equilibrium in action by which man recreates his own life through work. Man's greatness is always to recreate his life, to recreate what is given to him, to fashion that very thing which he undergoes. Through work he produces his own natural existence. Through science he recreates the universe by means of symbols. Through art he recreates the alliance between his body and his soul" (2003 [1952], 178). At other points in the text, Weil describes the encounter between bodies and art as a means by which to engage in the work of "attention."

As the written materials surrounding the exhibit suggested, Weil dismissed the will as a key factor in human labor. For Weil, labor was a powerful human act because it allowed for the refusal of the will in favor of more humble modes of attention. Lloyd describes how, for Weil, attention to a variety of material forms, including art objects, "*trains* the intelligence, increasing its capacity for discernment. It makes truths appear that were invisible before, but these are worldly truths. They were invisible before not because they were in some spiritual realm but because they were obscured by the social, by enchantment. Put another way, attention is humility. It teaches us that our view of the world is largely wrong, and so prepares us to see the world more clearly" (2011, 125). In ways that overlap with Thompson's account of the emphasis on the surface through shine as a means of calling into question the connection between seeing and knowing, Weil argues that certain enchanting expressions of the social can limit our capacity to see the world fully. Attention to material forms, as products of human labor, however, can open out on to new possibilities that allow for greater access to worldly truths.

As mediators, we tended to frame this concept of attention in ways closer to that of de Chassey than that of Weil. Even when attention was held up as a means of accessing the spiritual, rather than the worldly, however, visitors showed a great deal of reticence about the labor required on the part of the viewer. This reticence became particularly apparent in a new form of labor in which I engaged during the exhibit. Early in the summer, I was asked to assist in a new project initiated by fundraising staff. Those who had given large donations to the space were being offered a new round of privileges, including after-hours guided tours of the art exhibitions. The "aura" of the building and its connections to the medieval past so carefully promoted in the Collège's tours and brochures appeared more accessible when the space was emptied and quiet. While their funds went to support the Collège's varied programming, many donors lamented the presence of any "modern" elements that disrupted their view or experience of the place in its "original" form. The art exhibitions, in particular, provoked the ire of many donors who lamented the very work their donations made possible. By engaging donors with the exhibits as a select few experiencing the space in the darkening hours of the evening, employees at the Collège hoped to improve the contemporary art project in their eyes. In so doing, however, we also amplified their sense of ownership. Such tours, moreover, offered yet another example of the centrality of questions of privilege, inclusion, and exclusion during *Gravity and Grace*.

Along with another mediator, I met the Young Donors Club at the entrance just before nine o'clock in the evening in early May.[7] The group was quiet and they allowed us to make it the entire way through our tour without interruption. Their lack of response signaled to me that there had been few converts. Approaching the end of the tour, I stood among the four paintings by Van der Meulen. I borrowed words from Sylvie, a volunteer guide at the Collège. Sylvie particularly adored these works, and her enthusiasm was infectious. One piece—a blue square topped by a yellow line—reminded her of the famous work by Kazimir Malevich (1879–1935), created in 1915 and entitled *Black Square*. Upon viewing the work by Malevich, Sylvie liked to explain, a Cistercian monk had declared it to be the perfect piece to inspire meditation and prayer. I then referred to discussions I had had with de Chassey about St. Bernard's anxieties around "excessive art." I described how, believing that the Word was the true path to a monk's spiritual formation, St. Bernard had encouraged monks to avoid the sight of fine materials and of images that might distract them from their reflections on the Word of God.

Another of Van der Meulen's paintings included a body-length gray rectangle with a yellow and white X shape painted above (fig. 6.1). On my first few viewings, I had struggled to see any reference to the space of the Collège. Another mediator, however, had helped me to see and experience the painting in a new way. Squaring my body in front of the work one afternoon, he told me to stare straight ahead. The gray rectangle, I finally noticed, func-

FIGURE 6.1. Emmanuel Van der Meulen, Untitled (exhibition view, Paris, Collège des Bernardins), 2010. Acrylic on canvas. Photo courtesy of the artist and Galerie Allen.

tioned as a mirror because, in its emptiness, it turned me back toward my body, standing there before it. My colleague then told me to look up. I did so slowly, and finally noticed how the X mimicked the lines of the vaults above. The effect was remarkable. I felt the enormity of the space enveloping me and demanding my attention through a singular focus on the painting.

After summarizing my experience of the work and the links between the aesthetics of St. Bernard, Malevich, and Van der Meulen to the group of patrons assembled before me, I paused to allow them to ask questions and to stand before Van der Meulen's works themselves. In response, one man simply declared that he was not convinced. Shaking his head, he explained that he could not admire this "as art." He insisted that each person has their "métier" and that the "métier" of an artist is to create something that appears simple but whose complexity or complex techniques can also be identified. Why, he asked, should it be up to viewers to engage in work before his paintings? The group exchanged general nods of agreement as they departed the room. My fellow mediator and I shared sympathetic shrugs of resignation.

To my mind, this patron's objections were significant not only for their conservative response to abstract art but for the assumptions about labor they betrayed, in particular the notion that labor and leisure were two distinct activities. Because the disgruntled patron was at the Collège as part of his nonwork, or leisure time, he should not be expected to do the labor that properly belonged to the artist. In his protest, the disgruntled patron demonstrated how capitalism had shaped his assumptions about time and work. Unbeknownst to him, in so doing he returned to many of the themes found in Weil's text. He took them up, however, in a far less critical vein than she. While de Chassey's desire for potentially spiritual experiences made possible through art objects tended to overlook the particularly capitalist context in which those encounters occur in the present, Weil was well aware of how capitalism transformed humans' encounters with objects, their capacity for attention, and their experiences of time. She worked for a year in a Renault factory in rural France, insisting on the need to submit to the same modes of what she called "affliction" suffered by the majority of workers. Through this firsthand experience, she understood in visceral terms how factory work was "stupefying," arguing that its "production lines, repetitive action, and unskilled labor invariably render attention an impossibility" (Meltzer 2001, 614). In other words, material forms cannot—in and of themselves— transform human attention in ways that lead to something more, whether that be something spiritual, or worldly truths that have shed their ideological enchantments. Certain material-human encounters, particularly under capitalism, Weil argued, will produce conditions of what she called "slavery," rather than liberation. And while few of the visitors at the Collège had likely ever engaged in such monotonous forms of labor, the disgruntled patron's complaints betray how the managerial class, as well as the working class, has been affected by capitalist logics.

Writing some seven hundred years earlier, St. Bernard held a "busy" notion of leisure that Weil might have recognized. The Latin term *otium* describes a highly labored leisure, situated somewhere between the two opposing but equally sinful states of idleness and business. "*Otium* is the major occupation of the monk. It is a very busy leisure," explains Jean Leclerq, Bernard's twentieth-century biographer (1976, 84). A good monk avoids both time spent doing nothing and, unlike patrons of the Collège, time engaged in the making of money. In other words, the medieval monastic setting offered a radically different sense of time, labor, and leisure to that which has come to appear so natural and ubiquitous under capitalism.

The context of the labor of *otium* was also of significant concern to Bernard. While, as I have described, often celebrated for his skepticism and anxieties about material forms, he was by no means an iconoclast. Many have misread Bernard's 1125 *Apologia* as a total refutation of visual art of any form. Some scholars have offered subtler renderings of the risks associated

THE BANALITY OF PRIVILEGE

with art forms found in Bernard's words. The very fact that art and aesthetics were considered "things of greater importance," as Conrad Rudolph argues, points to the significance of art for Bernard. Rather than rejecting art forms entirely, Bernard worried about their place in the monastery, where they might serve as a distraction from those material forms that more productively focused a monk's attention.

> In the cloisters, before the eyes of the brothers while they read—what is that ridiculous monstrosity doing, an amazing kind of deformed beauty and yet a beautiful deformity? What are the filthy apes doing there? The fierce lions? The monstrous centaurs? The creatures, part man and part beast? The striped tigers? The fighting soldiers? . . . Over there an animal has a horse for the front half and a goat for the back; here a creature which is horned in front is equine behind. In short, everywhere so plentiful and astonishing a variety of contradictory forms is seen that one would rather read in the marble than in books, and spend the whole day wondering at every single one of them than in meditating on the law of God. Good God! If one is not ashamed of the absurdity, why is one not at least troubled at the expense? [quoted in Rudolph 1990, 11–12]

This odd list, argues Rudolph, betrays how Bernard's anxieties about art forms were, in fact, quite limited. In the context of the monastery, where a very particular kind of labor was being undertaken and where, in their isolation, the monks might easily find themselves distracted, only images and objects that attuned them to the work of "attention" should be displayed. Bernard may well have preferred the works of Van der Meulen to those of Caravaggio in such a setting.[8]

The experience of *otium*, and the precise kinds of labor it required was, of course, not available to the medieval population at large. It existed as an ideal only in the segregated space of the monastery. In describing the Collège in the present as a resurrection of a medieval monastic project, however, employees do not generally explore how concepts such as *otium* that structured time in a previous incarnation of the space were both limited in their applicability in the thirteenth century and are essentially incoherent under capitalist regimes of leisure and labor in the present.

A number of historians and political economists have described the profound transformations in daily life wrought by the advent of capitalism by focusing on shifts in perceptions of labor and of time. Through the demands placed upon them, workers were carefully disciplined to value time in new ways. As E. P. Thompson (1963) and Max Weber (2009 [1930]) have demonstrated, this transformation took significant social and cultural work, both in getting workers to adhere to the strictures of labor time and in elaborating expectations around leisure time. In the nineteenth century, newly established nation-states invested in the development of sites of leisure to occupy the nonworking time of newly capitalist populations. In Europe, world expositions, museums, concert halls, and parks provided space for workers and employers alike to soberly refresh their spirits and allowed the state to make ample use of material forms to unify the working class with the bourgeoisie as members of a common (white) national body.[9]

The presumed effects of exposure to particular material forms—and particularly to art—shifted over time. According to David Morgan, "in contrast to Romanticism's celebration of folk culture as the repository of the soul, the republican or moral theory of art identified art as a refiner of the popular soul" (2009, 29).[10] Beginning in the eighteenth century, however, museums, art, and carefully curated public spaces were also seen as a means by which to engage both classes in their leisure time in order to reduce possible conflicts during—or over—their labor time. Art was understood to have transformative ends but not in the way that Weil or St. Bernard imagined. Viewing art under conditions of capitalism was imagined as a respite from—rather than a mode of—labor. Moreover, rather than unmasking the limits of the social order, or accessing something spiritual, this respite would help to reproduce the inequalities undergirding the class distinctions that art viewing aimed to downplay.

In the Preface to his critique of the 1846 Salon, the French poet and critic Charles Baudelaire made a plea to the bourgeoisie of Paris that is at once scathing, satirical, and resigned. As "possessors" of the city of the "universal public," declared Baudelaire, the bourgeoisie "must become worthy of this task." And while it was understandable that "when the 7th or 8th hour of your labor sounds, you are inclined to rest your weary head toward the embers of home, and the cushions of your armchair," (1846, 122) the bourgeoisie, Baudelaire argued, must resist the equation of laziness and leisure. Instead, he says, "if two thirds of your day are filled with science, it is only right that the final third should be occupied by sentiment, and it is by this effort that the balance of the forces of your spirit will be constituted" (ibid.). Taking for granted capitalism's permeation into all spheres of life, Baudelaire's satirical mockery of the bourgeoisie, like other moral theories of art, aimed to use the "sensible" to elevate capitalism's elite.

It is the words of Baudelaire, more so than St. Bernard, that one finds most readily echoed in accounts of leisure at the Collège. This is a space where, according to one brochure, "man is explored in all his dimensions: spiritual, intellectual, and emotional." According to one of the mission statements on its website during the time I spent there, the "ambitious path" chosen by the Collège is to "give man the ability to be, at once, free, and anchored in his time, responsible and thoughtful in assuming business as well as heritage." Pamphlets aimed at potential donors explain that "through your gift, you will support the search for meaning." At the Collège, in other words, patrons can transform their capital into "sensible" experiences, not only refreshing their spirits but providing a means by which those lacking capital might do the same.

PATRONAGE AND THE REPRODUCTION
OF INEQUALITY

Given how significant private donations are to the reproduction of the Collège, patrons do not need to worry that the means by which they accumulate that capital—and its very unequal distribution throughout France—will become a point of significant critique. In this medieval space, capitalism serves as a powerful—if typically unseen—mechanism for the Collège's reproduction. This support can come in numerous forms. In brochures that remind patrons of the potential benefits they can accrue from their donations, they are encouraged to make a regular donation (the brochure explains that 66 percent of this donation could be used to reduce their income tax, and up to 75 percent could be used to reduce their solidarity tax on wealth); a one-time legacy donation; or a temporary usufruct donation (in which one can offer the rent gained from an extra property, which would then make that money inaccessible to the solidarity tax on wealth).[11] Patrons are even encouraged to make the Collège the beneficiary on their life insurance. By highlighting how donations to the Collège could benefit those with an extra property, or whose descendants would have no need for their life insurance, or who wanted to avoid the wealth tax, the Collège provided a space in which that wealth could be celebrated and transformed into something more broadly beneficial.

I was surprised, when I returned to the space several years later, to find the brochure describing the various forms of support one could provide to the Collège at the front desk, mixed among advertisements for its programming. But perhaps I should not have been. Nearly all of my scans of those attending any of its events confirmed the fact that a white, wealthy, and elite population served as the base of the Collège's public. In 2009, through a mutual friend, I met a young woman named Anne whose wealthy family had been tapped for donations to the Collège early in the project's imagining. Although we held quite divergent positions on a number of issues, we enjoyed each other's company and often met for lunch at a "classic" French restaurant or to see one of the city's art exhibits. She also offered invaluable insight about this powerfully privileged world to which I—as a foreigner and as someone clearly not from the upper class—could gain only limited access.

For one of our early meetings, I joined Anne at a brasserie near her work. Just next to the entryway was a dark wooden shelf filled with cubbyholes, a single red- and white-checkered cloth napkin inside and a small label next to each. Anne explained that they were for the regulars to put their napkins in, so they could reuse them throughout the week without the staff needing to wash them each time. The place was undeniably an old boys club, with politicians and businessmen hobnobbing over "traditional" French fare. As we looked over the menu, I knowingly engaged in the ordering dance that seemed to be required of white, upper-class French women whenever they ate out in public. Desiring to order a leek tart in a cream sauce—hardly a "slimming" choice—Anne took time to justify her hunger. By lamenting the cold, windy weather, the stress of a new job, and the long hours of work that prevented her from eating, she was able to explain to herself and to me her decision not to order with her figure primarily in mind. (She is a remarkably thin and attractive young woman.) I nodded in support of her decision and chose something equally fattening, a pork and lentil stew.[12]

In learning of my interest in the Collège, Anne explained that she had heard of the project long before it opened. Intrigued, I inquired as to how she was so in the know. She made reference to a woman whose name I had heard around the Collège but never met in person. From this woman—a long-time acquaintance—Anne had received an invitation to hear a presentation about the Collège. Along with a few others, the acquaintance held an evening event that included a slide show filled with images of the medieval space, objects found during the excavations, and what the project would look like once it came to fruition. Anne described the presenters as "coming from these traditional families, and they really strongly believed in the project. After the lecture and slide show, they wouldn't let us leave without signing something explaining how we would help the Collège—it was a bit much."[13]

"When you say 'us,' who are you referring to?" I asked. "Those of us who attended the lecture," she replied. "I don't know how I got the invitation, how they got my email address. They just created this list of people that, you know, were potentially Catholic, friends of friends—people of a very particular social milieu. It's kind of sad, but when I was talking to a priest about his work at the Collège, and I mentioned this group, he said they are exactly the kind of people he doesn't want to attract to the Collège. He wants to have a diversity of people. With these people, there is no debate." I was struck by the explicit manner in which elite support for the Collège had been both cultivated and critiqued from early on in the project.[14] To my eyes, the more critical voices appeared to have been drowned out over the course of the project's implementation.

In allowing for the celebration and arguing for the social utility of privilege, the Collège, in fact, displayed some similarities with its monastic origins. In the tripartite class structure of the feudal period in France, the "warrior" class of the nobility required the distinct efforts of those charged with "praying." It also required the depressed state of the "farmer" classes. Their apparent barbarity could legitimate the elevated living conditions of the nobility, while their poverty allowed for the accumulation of wealth among the few. This poverty also allowed them to become objects of the "charity" in which the nobility needed to engage in order to assure their salvation. The monastic orders were often founded by members of the "war-making aristocracy" who, in the words of one Austrian Cistercian nun living in the twenty-first century,

> were anxious to have people recommend them to God. Their regular program of prayer would mitigate guilt for their earthly sins. This could be salvific in the face of death. For this, they founded a monastery where they would be daily commemorated and their graves would lie as close to the altar as possible. Like other benefactors, they supported their prayer-sites, even holding court there on feast days. It is easy to see how this would contribute to the secularization of the monks. [Pfeifer 2018, 240]

The rising political and economic clout of the monasteries eventually induced a crisis of sorts (Leclerq 1971, Rudolph 1990) and inspired a number of reform movements that aimed to bring monks closer to a strict reading of *The Rule of St. Benedict*. The twelfth century is widely regarded as a moment of extensive reform of monastic life in Europe, largely in response to the potentially corrupting power of wealth. One such group of reformers was the Cistercians, known as the white monks for their insistence on not dying their woolen cloaks black as a reminder of their vow of poverty. Whether robed in black or white, however, during this period numerous groups of monks set out from the often majestic and gilded spaces of their monasteries to found new isolated houses often located far from the centers of power—and certainly far from cities—in the wilderness (Pfeifer 2018, 238–43).

St. Bernard was one of the most influential of the Cistercian reformers (it is for this reason that they are often referred to as the Bernardins). Born to noble parents in 1090 in Burgundy, he led thirty other noblemen into the monastic life in 1113. In 1115, the Cistercian Abbey of Clairvaux in Ville-sous-la-ferté in Aubé, to the east of Paris in northern France, was founded with Bernard as its head.[15] The Cistercians' decision to open the Collège in the center of Paris a century and a half later, however, clearly departed from the desire to isolate monks from the corrupting influences of privilege.[16] The present-day iteration of the Collège similarly struggles to come to terms with the privileges and distinctions at the core of its project.

* * *

I began this text by reflecting on the privilege of banality: the supreme pleasure of occupying the space of the unmarked, of knowing that one's actions, no matter how contradictory, are likely to stand above reproach. I want to conclude it by thinking about the banality of privilege. Hannah Arendt's book *Eichmann in Jerusalem: A Report on the Banality of Evil* was widely despised at the time of its publication and remains controversial. The ambiguity of the concept of banality in the text contributed to the outcry. It seemed the wrong kind of term to apply to the greatest of horrors. The political theorist Corey Robin has argued that it is precisely the notion that we no longer have "an objective or shared foundation for our sense of what is good or right or just" (2015, 20) that makes the banality of evil so threatening. While he does not use the term "secular" to describe this challenge, a loss of shared orientation was certainly a central concern for many committed Catholics I encountered in Paris, and it remains one of the most common critiques of our secular age.

Given this loss of a shared sense of the good, Robin understands contemporary ethics as taking excessive comfort in a presumed ability to identify evil. Even evil proves to be tricky terrain however, as, in order to be recognizable, evil needs to be radical and profound, not banal. Robin cites a letter Arendt wrote to Gershom Scholem in which she defined banality as that which lacks depth: "It is indeed my opinion now that evil is never 'radical,' that it is only extreme, and that it possess neither depth nor any demonic dimension. It can overgrow and lay waste the whole world precisely because it spreads like fungus on the surface. It is 'thought-defying,' as I said, because thought tries to reach some depth, to go to the roots, and the moment it concerns itself with evil, it is frustrated because there is nothing. That is its 'banality.' Only the good has depth and can be radical" (2015, 20).

Without making any explicit or implicit comparisons between privilege and genocide—or even between privilege and evil—I think that banality as thought-defying nothingness may well be the essence of privilege. In an introduction to a collection of her letters (Arendt 2018), Jerome Kohn describes the concept by pointing to how "not only is there no support to hang on to, no root to grasp, but there is also no devil, no corruption, nor even stupidity or madness to blame. There *is* a suffocating ordinariness" (Kohn 2018, xx). Given its occurrence throughout history, there is nothing particularly radical about privilege. It tends to receive attention at those moments—such as the present—when it becomes more extreme, when the gap between those who benefit from privilege and those who are its foil widens. Few scholars who have addressed the power of privilege, furthermore, have done so by identifying its roots or origins. Marx argued that the particular way in which privilege is achieved and protected in any given historical period plays a foundational role in the lived experiences of that social world. Weber insists that its origins and foundations appear inexplicable even to those who benefit from it. One who lives a life of privilege, he argues, is "seldom satisfied with the fact of being fortunate. Beyond this he needs to know that he has a *right* to his good fortune. He wants to be convinced that he 'deserves' it, and above all that he deserves it in comparison with others. He wants to be allowed the belief that the less fortunate also merely experience his due. Good fortune wants to be legitimate fortune" (1946, 271).

Throughout this book, I have approached banality as a means of explaining how actions normally deemed reprehensible come to be legitimated and reproduced. Both Kohn and Robin suggest that, for Arendt, the means by which the unthinkable becomes self-evident is "thoughtlessness." Arendt's portrait of Eichmann as a shallow, and selfish bureaucrat stood in sharp contrast to the demonic masterminds many had imagined in the Nazi high command. Her dismissal of him as "stupid" may have revealed some of her own class prejudices, but it was his inability to view the world from the perspective of others that struck her as shallow. According to Robin, Arendt based her assessment of how banality constrains ethical action on Kant's account of critical aesthetic judgment. "Kantian judgment requires not a deep dive into one's intentions, not a purification of the will, but a willingness to see one's actions as other men and women see them; to depart from oneself; to take on, for a time, the viewpoints of others; 'to imagine,' in the words of Arendt . . . 'what the other person is experiencing'" (Robin 2015, 18).

In other words, humans' responses to objects are informed by and shape their responses to, and ability to empathize with, other humans. For Arendt, "'taste decides not only how the world is to look, but also who belongs together in it'" (Robin 2015, 20). Thus, for Arendt, human-material encounters could produce yet another effect. They could aid in the work of stepping outside of one's own experience and imagining the experiences of others, including how others might conceive of one's actions. Following Arendt's insistence that banality is that which lacks depth, we might understand the exclusion that necessarily accompanies privilege as the refusal to imagine the experience of others and, therefore, to deny the diverse complexity of social worlds. In Kohn's account of Arendt's argument, Eichmann did not need to "believe in" the project of the destruction of European Jews in order to "participate in" it. Similarly, the aestheticization of privilege need not be a specific goal of the project of the Collège in order for those who have shaped it to participate in it.

The distinction between surface and depth, however, is not total. David Graeber has worked to reframe Marx's account of ideology away from an idea of "false consciousness" to one of "partial consciousness." Graeber understands Marx to see the human imagination as full of potential but also of limits. And these limits arise from the ways humans in any given social system are encouraged to or discouraged from imagining the perspectives of others. Capitalism's strict divisions of labor exacerbate the problem of partial consciousness. "It was precisely the fact that people are confined to these partial perspectives that, Marx argued, gave rise to alienation: the 'consolidation of what we ourselves produce into an objective power above us,' the fact that our powers appear to us in strange, external forms" (Graeber 2001, 64–65). Put another way, the limits of the human imagination in any given social system are shaped by processes of banalization. In both the medieval period that reformers like Bernard sought to transform and the present system of capitalism, material processes impose limits on the capacity to empathize with others, in particular those lacking privilege.

Aesthetic judgment considered in light of Arendt's ethics points to how human encounters with objects can contribute to more inclusive or exclusive social worlds. De Chassey insisted that the emphasis on the material surfaces of the abstract works found in *Gravity and Grace* allowed them to offer themselves to viewers from a position of humility. In contrast, viewers most often saw them as ostentatious. In so doing, they displaced concerns about the privilege and exclusivity of the social world that had come to populate the Collège onto the works of abstraction before them. I have argued that, despite the transformative aspirations of many of the artists, abstract works might more easily lend themselves to such acts of deferral. Even more significantly, however, a number of practices underway at the Collège—including curatorial efforts aimed at renaissance, encounter, and (limited) opening, the partial incorporation of certain kinds of difference, the enlivening and aestheticizing of Christian motifs, anxieties surrounding the specter of the fetish, and the refusal of the labor of attention—limit the capacity for the kind of empathy Arendt understood to be necessary to combat banality. Questions of surface and depth have loomed particularly large at the Collège because it is a project that—whether or not such a goal is explicit—celebrates and reproduces France's privileges. At times, its contemporary art exhibits have made space for a different kind of experience— one that, if viewed in a particular way, might open up onto more inclusive encounters, not only with objects but also with others. This possibility, however, is precisely what made them so controversial.

EPILOGUE

ON WARM SUMMER EVENINGS DURING MY fieldwork, I would often meet friends along the banks of the Seine River surrounding the Notre-Dame Cathedral. The structure's awesome presence and enticing shapes—the rounded curve of its apex, its pointed roof, its solid square bell towers, and the finesse of its flying buttresses—made for an extraordinary backdrop to what amounted to a public happy hour. With a bottle of rosé and plastic cups in hand, my friends and I would weave our way through the crowds to find a patch of grass or pavement. The atmosphere was congenial and relaxed and would last well into the evening and night.

At times, however, I found this backdrop more unsettling than idyllic. Through my work at the Collège I was becoming cognizant of how celebrating a certain image of France could also serve to support exclusionary politics. At times, informed by these conversations and with a few glasses of rosé fortifying my courage, I would find myself inspired to approach those around me, enjoying their drinks along the Seine, to ask them why they thought Paris had to look the way that it did. What is it that makes Notre-Dame Cathedral so central to the Parisian landscape? My friends did not always enjoy this portion of the evening—and my rather unusual mode of ethnographic inquiry—but I quickly learned that passions surrounding the cathedral ran deep.

The question I have asked throughout this book is why ostensibly secular Paris still seems to need Catholicism. In other words, why did those I met along the banks of the Seine—most of whom admitted to rarely entering a church—insist upon the centrality of Catholic materiality in their city's skyline? I have argued that these attachments are an expression of the privilege that accompanies the banality of Catholicism in France. While signs of Islam are maligned as excessively religious and, thereby, deemed inappropriate in

the public sphere, Catholic material forms are accepted as cultural, historical, heritage, and even secular. But it is not only the privilege of Catholic
banality that is maintained by the affections expressed toward its material
culture. I have argued that Catholic materiality is also put to the service of
maintaining and reproducing the banality of class privilege in France.

The continued relevance of these questions struck me when, having just
returned from an annual trip to Paris, I watched in shock from a Manhat-
tan doctor's office waiting room as fire ravaged Notre-Dame's pointed roof
and nineteenth-century spire. Reactions to the blaze reiterated many of the
claims I heard throughout my time in Paris, as pundits equated the cathedral
with French culture and European civilization (Beardsley 2019). In order
to understand the full implications of Notre-Dame's symbolic importance
in France, however, I argue that the shocking sums promised to restore the
widely beloved site by the families who own many of France's luxury brands
are even more significant than the unsurprising ease with which commentators fell back on familiar tropes. Among the innumerable references to
Notre-Dame as an "icon" of everything from Paris to civilization itself was
a *New York Times* article published the day following the fire, calling these
wealthy families "another symbol of the country, thanks to names such as
Dior, Louis Vuitton and Saint Laurent" (Friedman 2019). Nations are, of
course, multifaceted, but in the aftermath of the fire it was intriguing to
see how the central symbols of a country widely admired for its Revolution
and its secularism appeared to be medieval Catholicism, luxury brands, and
startling wealth inequality.

François-Henri Pinault, the chairman of luxury brand company Ker-
ing, was the first to announce his support to the tune of €100 million. In
a seemingly purposeful attempt to upstage his rival, Bernard Arnaut, who
chairs the LVMH group, announced the next day that he would provide
€200 million toward efforts to rebuild the cathedral. The *Times* listed the
icons associated with the LVMH group with easy familiarity: "LVMH is the
largest luxury group in the world. Its fashion holdings include Celine, Dior,
Givenchy and Louis Vuitton. The group also owns drink brands including Moët & Chandon, Dom Pérignon and Veuve Clicquot, as well as the
landmark Parisian stores Le Bon Marché and La Samaritaine. The group
reported revenue of €46.8 billion in 2018" (Friedman 2019). Beyond eliciting
admiration for their goodwill and charity, luxury brands have other, more
concrete benefits to glean from the monumental reconstruction of Notre-
Dame. Maintaining the pristine beauty of central Paris does much to help
buttress the connection between the brands held by these families and expe-

riences of luxury. Images of Paris abound in their advertising; they have an interest in maintaining a certain look of Paris. Some of the same families that rushed to contribute to the restoration of Notre-Dame also appear on the wall of patrons found at the Collège. And, like donors to the Collège, those who fund the restoration of Notre-Dame are eligible for certain benefits. In the case of Notre-Dame, some donors could receive a tax cut equivalent to 60 percent of their donation. In response to a public outcry about the hit to public coffers, Arnault explained that his family had already maxed out on deductions. He also complained about the problem of "jealousy" and suggested that, rather than being criticized, "in other countries we'd be congratulated" (Reuters 2019).

These large donations also reflect a vested interest. France's Catholic material forms contribute to reproducing the socioeconomic inequalities that uphold the market in luxury items and experiences. I have argued that the city's innumerable Catholic spaces aid in celebrating and reproducing the inequalities that France failed to overthrow with its Revolution of 1789. The extraordinary distinctions between lives of privilege and wealth and those of labor and poverty in France—not to mention between its citizens of different religious faiths, and between black and white citizens—constantly belie the regime of equality that was supposed to follow from the Revolution. These inequalities were even more amplified in France's colonial empire. Protests held in Overseas France in the past decade have pointed to the immorality of the extravagant profit of a few in the face of the poverty of many (see Bonilla 2015).

Some of France's national inequalities are inscribed in literal terms upon the façade of Notre-Dame itself. In a 2019 visit to the Strasbourg Cathedral museum, I read one of the information panels about the figures of *Synagoga and Ecclessia* that frame the entrance to that medieval edifice. Describing the sculpture as the "Vanquished Synagogue and the Church Triumphant," the museum acknowledged that these had been recognizable Christian symbols since about the eighth century, but it was only in the early thirteenth that they began to adorn the portals of numerous French cathedrals. Describing the Strasbourg Cathedral's version of this sculpture, the museum lauds the beauty of these symbols: "On the left, the Church Triumphant, wearing a crown and holding in her hands a chalice and a banner surmounted by the cross, fixes her self-assured gaze on the Synagogue. The latter, blindfolded and holding a broken lance, averts her head, expressing her inability to recognize the Messiah in the person of Jesus. She appears to let fall the tablet of the Law of Moses, symbolizing the supplanting of the Old Testament. But the extreme humanity and beauty of the young woman's features suggest an awaited revelation rather than the stigma of blindness." In the version that adorns Notre-Dame in Paris, a serpent rather than a piece of cloth blinds the figure of the synagogue, once again demonstrating an interest in the partial incorporation of Judaism through a supersessionist lens.

The apparent viscerality of Notre-Dame and the Collège's medieval forms allow Parisians to imagine they remain materially connected to the medieval past. And yet, the distance between the past and the present is not entirely overcome. Revering and preserving these buildings allows for two contradictory relationships to the past to be mediated by these human-material encounters. First, in encountering a relic of history, visitors are able to note the differences between the past and present and to celebrate the historical inequalities overturned by the Revolution. As appropriately modern subjects, they are able to imagine themselves existing at a remove from this medieval past. Second, however, by encouraging awe and admiration of their forms, Catholic heritage spaces forge a connection to that past and provide an aesthetic ground for the distinctions that remain.

The political work accomplished by the enormous gifts made in support of Notre-Dame becomes all the more evident when one remembers the event that had to be canceled the night of the blaze: President Macron's belated response to the *Gilets Jaunes* (Yellow Vests), the leaderless movement made up of tens of thousands of poor and working-class people who are demanding a more equitable distribution of wealth in France. The president had prerecorded the speech and, instead of airing it as planned at eight o'clock in the evening, simply tweeted "Notre-Dame is beset by flames. The whole nation mourns. Thoughts go out to all Catholics and all French. Like all our compatriots, I am sad tonight to see that part of us burn" (Pietralunga and Faye 2019).

On the day before the fire, Macron had offered a few hints about his Gilets Jaunes speech. According to an article in *Le Monde*, he explained at a government meeting that he hoped to address the Gilets Jaunes "not by multiplying 'categorical or individual' measures," which he described as "an impasse." Instead, he aimed to "redefine" the "national project. The time we are entering is that of redefining the national and European project" (ibid.).

The burning of Notre-Dame, however, offered Macron an opportunity to forgo the far more significant national reconstruction project imagined by the Gilets Jaunes. By Monday night, in front of the dramatic backdrop of a Notre-Dame still aglow Macron emotively explained that another national project now demanded the nation's attention. "And so I say to you tonight, with great solemnity, we will rebuild this Cathedral. Altogether, it is without a doubt a part of the French destiny and the project that we will have for the years to come" ("Notre-Dame de Paris" 2019). In a speech the following evening, the president clarified that now—in a moment when, with remarkable ease, several of France's most profitable companies managed to gather together nearly $1 billion to support Macron's "new" national project—was not the time to ask questions about inequality. "I will return to the subjects with which I was engaged with you in the days to come so that we can act collectively following our Great Debate," Macron glossed.[1] "But today is not the time; tomorrow, politics and its tumults will take back their place, we all know that. But the moment has not yet come." In his brief speech, he even went so far as to suggest that such inequality was necessary to the national project, insisting that "the rich, like those less rich, have given money, each according to what they could give, each in their place, each in their role." Such statements ring of the Catholic theology of personalism, a mode of viewing the human person as a member of a community in which a variety of differences and inequalities are not only acceptable but also desirable (Chappel 2011).

As Macron implicitly acknowledged, the critiques made of his neoliberal government—by far the most committed to a probusiness agenda in France in recent decades—are unlikely to be so easily dismissed. Indeed, the following Saturday the Gilets Jaunes were in the streets again, expressing their disgust that such enormous funds could so easily be accessed to support an ailing building but not a suffering population (Raphelson 2019). And yet, that Macron's attempt to replace the reconstruction of French society along more equitable terms with a national project to reconstruct the cathedral appears even momentarily plausible suggests that material religious forms are never only a means by which to make God present; they are a means by which to make certain fantasies about the past present. As its destruction during the Revolution and massive reconstruction in the nineteenth century reveal, this has been one of the primary functions of the Notre-Dame Cathedral— and many other Catholic spaces throughout Paris—for centuries.

I do not want to argue that the cathedral should not be restored. What will be fascinating to watch in the years to come, however, is the kind of debates its rehabilitation or reconstruction provokes. As the restoration plans develop, we should watch to see if maintaining Notre-Dame as an icon of the medieval period remains a priority. What kind of political will would be necessary for those interested in reconstructing the cathedral to take this opportunity to rethink the inequalities both forged into its stones and maintained by the privilege of its banal place in the Parisian landscape? If such questions were to be posed might they open the way to others? If Notre-Dame is indeed the icon of France, its Kilometer Zero, the use to which the renovation project is put—as a means by which to reproduce or to confront the inequalities and privileges it symbolizes and maintains—may indeed have a great deal to say about the nature of France in the present.[2]

* * *

I have visited the Collège a number of times since leaving France in the fall of 2010, and on each visit I noticed incremental shifts. In January 2016, I took note of how the bookstore seemed to be filled with many Catholic objects. Figurines and magnets depicting saints and angels, children's books exploring Catholic narratives, prayer books, and coffee-table books with images of Paris's churches and historic buildings took up more space than they had in the Collège's opening years. At that time, the emphasis had been on philosophy, history, and art books that one could find at any bookstore or museum in Paris. The bookstore's efforts toward the work of normalization lay in integrating these "secular" texts with books exploring Catholic history, figures, and theology. Such efforts are less apparent in its offerings today. Similarly, when I check in on the Collège on Facebook, I often take note of how notifications of upcoming conferences, concerts, exhibits, and events mingle with celebrations of Catholic saints and holidays. As with the unexpected initiation of noontime masses in the Collège's oratory, I see these small changes as signs that while the participation of the secular state in funding the renovation of the Collège may have incited attempts to maintain certain boundaries in its inaugural years, the apparent absence of the state since has allowed employees to forgo distinctions between sacred and secular that they once saw as necessary.

One change I noticed was subtle, but powerful. While the Collège continues to invite interesting contemporary artists who produce work similar to that they would exhibit elsewhere, the exhibits are no longer held in the nave; they now occur only in the sacristy.[3] This is a space that one may not even notice, let alone enter, during the course of a visit. I heard two explanations for this change. One person hinted that the donors had "won." By managing to do away with the forced encounter between visitors and exhibitions brought about when the latter occupied the nave, "those who wrote the checks" were able to reduce the significance of contemporary art in the project of the Collège. As visitors' responses described throughout this book

reveal, the exhibits brought up a host of uncomfortable questions and possibilities. Those who donated to the Collège particularly disliked the challenge of having to explain them to friends and family when they took them
to enjoy this newest Catholic or heritage space. Shutting the exhibits away
in the sacristy reduced the awkwardness and necessity of these encounters.

The other explanation I heard made no mention of a victory. Instead, the
decision was considered to be primarily economic. The financial struggles
faced by the institution when I worked there had in part been dealt with by
renting the space out to private companies for cocktails, fundraisers, and
events. Demands to rent the space out in the evenings ran so high that the
opportunity costs of mounting exhibitions increased significantly once one
factored in the lost rental income that many would have entailed. Music
concerts, events for which the Collège could charge significantly more than
its other programming, had become another key source of income. They
could fill the nave with chairs, charging €30 or more for each seat, and host
a concert for several evenings. The possibility of limiting those events for an
installation that would bring in no money seemed less and less attractive.

Reducing the space for the contemporary arts exhibits, however, also
served to reduce the space for the potentially critical encounters that they
offered. Glamorous corporate events such as the one held for *Elle* magazine, of which employees posted pictures on Facebook, allowed for the
aestheticization of privilege precisely by suggesting that such events could
be celebrated—rather than critiqued—in a former monastic space. The
human-material encounters at the Collège, in this sense, were put to the
service of reproducing the banality of privilege, rather than calling it into
question. In this way, the rising reliance on corporate rentals and the partial
reduction of the contemporary arts program point to some aspects of continuity, as well as change, at the Collège over the past decade.

One powerful expression of the ongoing limits of the Collège's ouverture occurred on April 9, 2018, when the Conference of French Bishops
invited President Macron to give a speech at the Collège to an audience
filled with bishops, leaders of other religious groups, ministers, parliamentary representatives, and ambassadors.[4] He began by thanking his hosts for
inviting him into "such a particular, such a beautiful space" (Macron 2018).
Turning to the current archbishop of Paris, Monsignor Michel Aupetit, he
acknowledged that, in order for them to be there that evening, they both
had had to brave the skeptics on each side. "And if we succeeded in doing
so," Macron continued, "it is because we vaguely share the feeling that the
connection between the Church and the state has deteriorated, and it is

important for us to repair it" (ibid.). The only solution, he explained, was a truthful "dialogue"—a term long adored at the Collège.

The president noted how the archbishop had referred to the bravery of Colonel Beltrame in his opening speech. On March 23, 2018, Arnaud Beltrame, a lieutenant colonel in the French national army, exchanged himself for one remaining hostage trapped by a man claiming connections to ISIS in a grocery store in Trèbes in southern France. His act of bravery resulted in his death. The president noted how many had attempted to understand the source of such courage. "Some saw the acceptance of sacrifice as anchored in his military vocation, others saw it as the manifestation of his republican loyalty nourished by his Masonic journey; others still, and notably his wife, interpreted his act as the translation of his ardent Catholic faith, which prepared him for the ultimate test of death" (ibid.).

Then Macron went on to make a move quite familiar in the space of the Collège. In his own act of curation, he held up distinctions between the Church and the state, between military valor, republican Masonry, and Catholic faith, and then proceeded to dismantle the distance between them. These various actions, Macron explained, "are so intertwined that it is impossible and useless to disentangle them, because this heroic act is the truth of a man in all of the complexity in which he was raised." Despite widespread suspicion of religion in France, Macron declared, he had not heard anyone contest the evidence, "engraved in the heart of our collective imaginary," of this fact: "When the hour of the greatest intensity arrives, when the demand comes to bring together all of the resources we have in ourselves in the service of France, the part that is citizen and the part that is Catholic burn, in the true believer, with the same flame. I am convinced that the most indestructible connections between the French nation and Catholicism are forged in these moments when the real valor of men and women is put to the test" (ibid.).

The fire of Macron's rhetoric must be understood as political language, first and foremost. Such speeches, aimed at the making of what Roland Barthes (1972) described as "mythologies," cannot be taken too much at their word. And yet, such rhetoric is forged with a purpose in mind. In turning to the actions of Colonel Beltrame, President Macron—without ever having to make the equation explicit—established the Frenchness of Catholicism and the otherness of Islam. Catholic passions forge the nation while supposedly Islamic passions attack it. With such a speech, one might ask whether it is only the benign distance of the state that has allowed the Collège to spend less time downplaying its Catholicism than it did in its early years. Has France's shift ever further to the right and the increasing legibility and popularity of anti-Islamic and anti-immigrant rhetoric made the normalization of Catholicism that many employees desired to achieve at the Collège less than necessary in its second decade of operation? As I have argued, Catholicism's privileged banality resides in its ability, according to the political tide, to either recede into the background or to stand out and be seen. It is the coincidence of rising xenophobia and the willingness for Catholicism to appear in more and more marked ways that I find so unsettling. That Macron chose the Collège as the place to reestablish the privilege of Catholicism and the foreignness of Islam speaks powerfully to how the site encourages exclusionary visions of France. It demonstrates how the decision to create a "cultural" Catholic project in a medieval space is far from neutral. It encourages encounters with the surface of the space, rather than with its complex and varied history, allowing those who enter under these vaults to take them for granted as expressions of the true France. Most significantly, it encourages the kinds of aesthetic judgments that, in Arendt's terms, are banal, limiting the histories that are worthy of empathy, understanding, and inclusion.

ACKNOWLEDGMENTS

A WISE FRIEND ONCE EXPLAINED that there are two schools of thought when it comes to acknowledgments. The first encourages authors to thank everyone. Even if it requires many pages and long lists of names, this is the time to admit that anything we put out into the world is the result of innumerable encounters large and small and, more importantly, of the often invisible support of friends, family, colleagues, partners, and caregivers. The second points to how such a task is doomed to fail, so authors should instead go with something short and sweet, and that way avoid offending anyone who might feel forgotten or overlooked. Given the many years this book and I have spent together and the immense amount of space it has taken up in my various places of work and many homes over that period, what follows is my best attempt at inevitable failure.

I am immensely grateful to the volunteers, mediators, employees, and directors who welcomed me into the Collège des Bernardins for the better part of two years. This acknowledgment is the most necessary and the most difficult as I am aware that many of those who made this research possible may not agree with the critique I offer here. This critique, however, is made with sincere admiration for such an "audacious" project and with the hope that, in the years to come, the practices and ideas that circulate in this space will allow for the broader ouverture many have imagined and desired. The visitors I encountered at the Collège provide most of the voices that animate this book, and I am immensely grateful for our conversations; even when we disagreed I always learned a great deal. Beyond those extraordinary vaults, many Catholics in Paris engaged in thoughtful discussions with me in their homes, in cafés, and in church pews. The remarkable diversity of aspirations articulated in these encounters taught me just how complex and varied Catholicism remains in France today.

Sébastien Greppo, Arnaud Coulembel, Sylvie Grossie, and Arnaud Hédin made the Chicago Center in Paris a warm and convivial place from which to engage in long-term research in Paris. They guided me through France's bureaucratic mazes and patiently explained the obvious to a bumbling ethnographer. Other scholars who I met through the Center—Gerard Cohen-Vrignaud, Michael Dietler, Luis-Manuel García, Julia Langbein, Françoise Meltzer, Erin Thompson, Eli Thorkelson, Jon Ullyot, Erika Vause, and Lily Woodruff—shared their friendship and their own expert knowledge of France and French history. Laurent Pinon made Paris into home, taking me on endless *balades urbaines* to show how the city's boundaries were not so rigid as they might appear. Together with Annie and Jean-Paul Pinon, he filled my time outside of the Collège with fabulous food, engaging debates, and enthusiastic support for the questions I asked.

This book first took shape in the Department of Anthropology at the University of Chicago. Danilyn Rutherford's teaching inspired the questions at the core of the book, and her incisive readings of numerous versions have powerfully influenced its ultimate form. I am immensely grateful for her mentorship and her friendship. Susan Gal has offered an ideal model of generous reading and rigorous scholarship. Her support of this project has continued long past my departure from Chicago as she has continued to share ideas, sources, and insightful discussions about the state of Europe in the present. Jennifer Cole employed me as a research assistant for a number of years. In our many hours together, she taught me a great deal about fieldwork, writing, and collaboration. William Mazzarella offered a powerful critique of my work that I hope I have addressed here. Anne Ch'ien's attention to details rescued me on numerous occasions.

The ideas that shape this book only really began to take concrete form thanks to the extensive efforts of the members of the writing group to which I was lucky enough to belong: Alex Blanchette, Tatiana Chudakova, Kathryn Goldfarb, and Caroline Schuster. Their friendship and support have been key to this book's completion. LaShandra Sullivan kept me afloat during grad school and beyond, and our ongoing conversations have motivated my attempts to think through privilege here. Eli Thorkelson has taught me a great deal about France, and his probing questions pushed this work in numerous ways.

The Social Science Research Council (2008) and New York University's Global Research Initiative (2019) provided funding for this research. Funding to support the writing of this book came from the Department of Anthropology at the University of Chicago (2011), the Cogut Center for the

Humanities at Brown University (2013–15), the Dean of Humanities at NYU
(2018), and a Goddard Fellowship at NYU (2018). Portions of this book have
appeared in earlier forms in book chapters in edited volumes, an online
publication, and a journal article. An earlier version of the final section of
chapter 1 appeared as part of a longer chapter entitled "The Intimate Provo-
cations of Showing Religion in France" in *Showing Off / Showing Up*, edited
by Catherine Schuler, Laurie Frederik Meer, and Kim Marra (Ann Arbor:
University of Michigan Press, 2017). An earlier version of the first half of
chapter 3 appeared as "Circulations of the Sacred: Contemporary Art as
'Cultural' Catholicism in Paris" in *Global Secularisms in a Post-Secular Age*,
edited by Michael Rectenwald, Almeida Rochelle, and George Levine (Ber-
lin: De Gruyters, 2015). An earlier version of chapter 4 appeared as "Beyond
Blasphemy or Devotion: Art, the Secular, and Catholicism in Paris" in the
Journal of the Royal Anthropological Institute 21, no. 2 (2015): 352–73. The first
half of the epilogue appeared as "The Notre Dame Fire and France's National
Reconstruction Project" in *The Revealer*, published online April 26, 2019. I
am grateful to editors and anonymous reviewers for shaping these publications and offering ideas to help push the arguments further.

At New York University, Angela Zito, Adam Becker, Janine Paolucci, and
Kali Handelman kindly opened the remarkable Religious Studies Program
(now Department) to me. Adam and Angela have not only been powerful
mentors and advocates but also delightful friends, who constantly inspire
me to do rigorous work and to build ethical institutions. I have been lucky
enough to have two homes at NYU and have been equally welcomed in the
Department of Anthropology. My colleagues, (the late) Tom Abercrombie,

Jane Anderson, Susan Antón, Shara Bailey, Pam Crabtree, Sonia Das, Arlene Dávila, Todd Disotell, Tejaswini Ganti, Michael Gilsenan, Faye Ginsburg, Bruce Grant, Helena Hansen, Terry Harrison, James Higham, Radu Iovita, Aisha Khan, Sally Merry, Fred Myers, Justin Pargeter, Anne Rademacher, Rayna Rapp, Bambi Schiefflin, Scott Williams, and Amy Zhang have offered encouragement and support. Aisha offered inspiring pep talks as we worked to complete our manuscripts together. Bruce—going far beyond the duties of department chair—read an earlier version of this book in its entirety and provided generous suggestions that powerfully influenced its revision.

A grant from the Dean of Humanities at NYU allowed me to benefit from the judicious and thoughtful readings of an earlier manuscript by Elizabeth Castelli, Omri Elisha, Mayanthi Fernando, Brenna Moore, and Erica Robles-Anderson. While their critiques demonstrated how much more work still needed to be done, their supportive push helped me to articulate my ideas in far more nuanced ways than I had before. My writing group in New York has seen possibilities in these pages that I never would have seen on my own. I am grateful to Elsa Davidson, Maura Finkelstein, Annabella Pitkin, Dani-lyn Rutherford, and Andrea Voyer for their productive feedback on many of these chapters. Michael Ralph helped me open the final two chapters onto far richer terrain. Kali Handelman generously and thoughtfully edited every last page of the manuscript, helping it to take on its final form. Staff at the University of Chicago Press made the publication process seamless and enjoyable. Two anonymous reviewers provided generous insights that improved the book significantly. Priya Nelson gave incisive and thought-ful guidance. Jenni Fry offered judicious editorial suggestions. Dylan Mon-tanari, Tristan Bates, and Kristen Raddatz guided me through steps I had not anticipated, from contract to design and marketing.

Having provided endless support to one another over the years, I look forward to the day when Emily Monks-Leeson, Mary Moreau, Cynthia Shelswell, and I will retire to enjoy our last days together. Scott Clark and Janet Gunn have been important and inspiring cheerleaders throughout this process. My family has withstood my many complaints, worries, and anxieties about this project with patience, loans, and endless favo(u)rs. Dianne Oliphant, Craig Kennedy, and their children have put me up on their couch for the homecomings I needed time and again throughout the years. The love and support of Christopher Oliphant and Ronna Smithrim has been unequivocal and key to this book's completion. My gratitude to Evelyn Patchett for her sacrifices and her limitless love cannot be expressed. Patty and Ken Hepburn have been remarkably enthusiastic supporters and will, no doubt, take us all out for a fabulous meal when these pages finally appear in print.

Peter Hepburn has supported this book from its earliest iterations. He has read endless versions of these chapters (including one final, judicious round of editing), and, despite being a sociologist, has offered critiques and insights that shaped their final form. His willingness to do the errands that needed to be done so that I could keep working is the real reason I have been able to articulate the argument I lay out here. The arrival of our daughter, Amelia, and our son, Coleman, has only increased the sacrifices he made so that I could finish. I am immensely grateful for a love in which we can copyedit each other's marriage vows (and acknowledgments). In their own unique ways, Amelia and Coleman have also encouraged me to get it done. That Amelia is now capable of asking me how the book is going with a raised brow and a bemused grin suggests that it is indeed time to wrap it up and start something new.

NOTES

INTRODUCTION

1. Entrance to the ground floor of the Collège is free of charge. However, in order to gain access to the cellar, one must register for a theology course or purchase a guided visit for €6.

2. I refer to her in this way in part because, as with many people I met at the Collège, our interactions were brief and ephemeral enough to not require proper introductions. Most of the names I use are pseudonyms. Often, and in particular for employees at the Collège, I avoid the use of names altogether and, at times, I have also made changes to their gender, age, and role at the Collège, or created composite characters in order to best hide the identity of those to whom I spoke. However, when citing employees, artists, and speakers as they appear in publications or videos produced by the Collège, I do not mask their identities.

3. I will attend to the names used to refer to the various spaces within the Collège in chapter 1.

4. The vast majority of my research for this project took place in Paris. As a highly centralized republic, a great deal of power and wealth in France is situated in the capital. However, the city cannot serve as a synecdoche for the nation. Public space is differently constituted and public discourse distinctively arrayed in various towns, cities, and regions in what is often referred to as the Hexagon. The term points to the general shape of France as it is found on maps of Europe and is used to distinguish France in Europe from *France d'outre-mer* (Overseas France), as a number of the nation's departments— including Guadeloupe, French Guiana, Réunion, and Martinique—are located outside of Europe in the Caribbean or Indian Ocean. See Yarimar Bonilla (2015) for a powerful analysis of the constrained sovereignty experienced in France's overseas departments. In addition to my ethnographic research in Paris, however, I rely on a number of newspaper articles, novels, surveys, secondary sources, and historical material that engage with France more broadly. I try to distinguish between the Parisian and French public spheres throughout this text accordingly.

5. I borrow the term "Muslim French" from Mayanthi Fernando (2014). Its awkwardness, for Fernando, helps to foreground the way that Muslim and French cannot easily be

imagined together in the early twenty-first century. She also finds the term productive in order to attend to her interlocutors' desire to be both French and Muslim without having to determine which of these identities is primary.

6. All translations from French are my own unless otherwise noted.

7. This contrast between Catholics and Muslims is false. Examples of Catholics in France and elsewhere protesting art and images they deem to be blasphemous abound. In 2011, for example, the director of the Théâtre du Rond-Point located on the Champs-Elysées in Paris received death threats over the mounting of a play entitled "Golgatha Picnic" by Rodrigo García. Police arrested two "fundamentalist" Catholics for attempting to destroy the theater's security system ("'Golgatha Picnic'" 2011).

8. Stéphane Charbonnier was killed along with eleven of his colleagues on January 7, 2015. The gunmen claimed to have attacked the newspaper in response to its depictions of the Prophet Mohammed. The Je Suis Charlie hashtag and slogan were used following his death in marches and online not only to protest the killings but also in order to show broader support for *Charlie Hebdo*'s campaign of blasphemy.

9. See work by Jean Baubérot (2004) and Winnifred Fallers Sullivan (2005), however, for critiques of such distinctions and accounts of how they oversimplify the varied and often contradictory laws and practices found in both traditions.

10. See historian Naomi Davidson's (2012) account of the reduction of Muslims to only religious actors.

11. This term was often incorrectly—and polemically—used to describe what might more accurately be called a *niqab*.

12. Paris is divided into twenty arrondissements, or districts, that are enumerated clockwise in a spiral outward from the center. Each arrondissement has its own mayor's office (called a *mairie*) and elected representatives. Residents of the city also elect a mayor of all twenty arrondissements and make use of its extensive citywide services.

13. For more on these violent acts against bearers of the niqab, see Fernando (2014) and the 2011 Report by the Open Society Foundation.

14. I am not asking here why people continue to be "religious" in a secular age. The secularization thesis that predicted the decline of religious belief in correspondence with the rise of modernity has long ago been dismantled (see, for example, Talal Asad [1993] and José Casanova [1994, 2015 (2012)]). Nor am I asking how the category of the 'secular' needs that of 'religion' (for more on this historical paradox, see Asad [2003] and Masuzawa [2005]). Rather, I am exploring the privileges accrued by allowing particular forms of Catholic materiality to move between the background and the foreground in a secular France that otherwise demands—at least discursively—the purging of religious signs from the public sphere. This is the question induced by banality: how do actions generally considered reprehensible come to appear self-evident?

15. In *The Arcades Project*, Benjamin also pointed to the antirevolutionary potential of "dream images" of the past. Citing the French writer Honoré de Balzac, he acknowledged that "'the ruins of the Church and of the aristocracy, of feudalism, of the Middle Ages are sublime—they fill the wide-eyed victors of today with admiration. But the ruins of the bourgeoisie will be an ignoble detritus of pasteboard, plaster, and coloring'"

(1999, 87). See the Marxist theorist Terry Eagleton (1990 and 2002) for more on the various ideological functions aesthetics have served since the rise of capitalism.

16. Following Julie Byrne's (2016) emphasis on the existence of numerous independent Catholic groups who do not acknowledge the authority of the pope in Rome, I attempt to preface the term Catholic with Roman at numerous points throughout this text to acknowledge that this particular group of Catholics does fall under the authority of the Vatican.

17. This arrondissement in eastern Paris is unusual in the city in that its former industrial spaces have been removed to make way for a host of new construction, including buildings taller than the six-floors (apart from churches) that tend to populate the central arrondissements. It is seen, in other words, as contrasting with the more "classical" Parisian neighborhoods that attract millions of visitors each year.

18. In an interview with one lay woman who assisted in organizing many such events at the church, she expressed her disappointment that although the archbishop, Cardinal-Lustiger, had been an instigator of the project, once the Collège began to take shape he seemed to abandon one cultural project in favor of another, more glamorous one.

19. As far as I know, the project of the Collège is unique within Europe. The presence of the pope at its opening, however, suggests rather high-level approval for and interest in the project within the Vatican.

20. I always prefaced my conversations with employees, volunteers, and mediators at the Collège by explaining that I was there primarily for research. When staff offered to hire me as a mediator for the second contemporary art exhibit, I emphasized that I would continue to use the conversations I had with visitors and my encounters with employees for my research and asked that explicit permission for this practice be included in my employment letter. The arts coordinator—the employee with whom I had the most contact at the Collège—happily complied with this request. While various managers were aware of my presence and I conducted formal interviews with several high-level employees and one of two copresidents, as a low-level employee my interaction with managers, directors, and presidents of the Collège was limited.

21. The French-language website may be found at www.collegedesbernardins.fr.

22. In recent decades, philosophers as diverse as Alain Badiou (2003) and Charles Taylor (2007), historians such as Patrick Geary (2002) and Bruce Holsinger (2005), anthropologists including Douglas Holmes (2000), Paul Rabinow (1989), and Marshall Sahlins (1993), as well as theologians including Pierre de Charentenay (2009), Jean-Luc Marion (2017), and John Milbank (2006 [1990]) have demonstrated how Christian theology informs and backgrounds key conceptual and legal apparatuses within secular modernity. My goal here is different than the genealogies many such scholars have sketched. I am interested in how, broadly speaking, the privilege of Catholicism is potentially reproduced through such intersections.

23. For some of the most significant of these studies, see Hussain Agrama (2012), Talal Asad (2003), Mayanthi Fernando (2014), and Saba Mahmood (2005, 2016).

24. I borrow the term "visual economy" from Deborah Poole's study of colonial imagery in the Andean World. For Poole, "economy" is a useful way of accounting for the mate-

riality of "seeing and viewing" because it "suggests that the field of vision is organized in some systematic way. It also clearly suggests that this organization has as much to do with social relationships, inequality, and power, as with shared meanings and communities" (1997, 8).

25. See Susan Terrio (1999) for an account of the use of this term to describe France in a French presidential election.

26. See Brian Sudlow's (2011, 48-49) detailed account of these two distinct "secularizing" regimes.

27. See Ruth Harris (1999) and David Harvey (2006) for discussions of both the anxieties surrounding and the wide berth given to practices associated with the Marian sighting at Lourdes in 1858 and the Sacred Heart devotional site established at the Sacré-Coeur Basilica in northern Paris in 1873.

28. For Nancy, these examples also prove that civil religion in the way Rousseau imagined is ultimately "impossible," and this failure means that we need to "re-think, from top to bottom, the whole question of the affect according to which we co-exist" (2006, 110).

29. See Jean-Loup Amselle (2003), Cécile Laborde (2008), and Joan Scott (1996) for rich accounts of the paradoxes produced by the effacement of difference in French republicanism.

30. See, for example, anthropologist Paul Silverstein's (2004) account of laïcité as France's "national religion."

31. In the introduction to their edited volume *The Anthropology of Catholicism*, Maya Mayblin, Kristin Norget, and Valentina Napolitano (2017) describe the capacity for Catholicism to appear "invisible" in countries in which it is a majority religion. Catholic materiality may often go unmarked, but it does not suffer from the problem of invisibility, which is more often experienced by minority groups. I use the term "banal" to highlight the tension produced when materiality that has been designed to occupy the public sphere in ways that are monumental are able to move between the background and the foreground.

32. In her study of aesthetic practices in the African diaspora, art historian Krista Thompson cites Ralph Ellison's account of "un-visibility" in the 1981 introduction to his 1952 novel, *Invisible Man*. "He describes blacks in the US as so hypervisible that they have been rendered un-visible. . . . Un-visibility describes the state of not being seen or not being recognized, as well as the 'moral blindness' toward the 'predicament of blacks'" (Thompson 2015, 40).

33. See Tracy Fessenden's (2007) study of religion and American literature for an account of expressions of Catholic abundance in presumably secular artistic forms, in particular in the novel *The Great Gatsby*.

34. Anthropologist Chris Hann, for example, has argued that Eastern Orthodox Christian engagements with materiality cannot be dismissed as "premodern." Many Pentecostal "sensational forms" (Meyer 2015a), moreover, should be seen as "continuations" of what Hann calls the "general 'affectional transposition' . . . of Christianity that flourished in the seventeenth century" (2014, S190) largely through Catholic material practices such as those surrounding the sacred heart. Annalisa Buttici (2016) makes a similar argument about Pentecostalism's "catholicity." Valentino Napolitano argues

that scholars need to pay heed to the "potency that Catholic materialities and affective histories can have in their unfolding within different political imaginaries" (2016, 12–13).

35. For more on the resilience of these myths of Europe, see Anthony Pagden, ed. (2002).

36. In chapter 5, following the work of Engelke (2007) and linguistic anthropologist Webb Keane (2007), I trouble the possibility for unmediated human encounters with God and other intangible forms.

37. The historian of American Catholicism Robert Orsi (2016) sees the tension between presence and absence (or mediated and unmediated human action) as one of the central battles of modernity. However, he insists that it was both Protestant and Catholic reformers and missionaries who fought against the mediation of human encounters with God through objects and often violently dismantled the various "fetishes" and "idols" they encountered at home and in sites of imperial and colonial expansion.

38. The exhibition of contemporary art in medieval spaces in France is, however, far from unprecedented. As just one example, the modernist abstract painter Pierre Soulages contributed stained-glass works to an abbey in Conques in the south of France in the mid-1990s. For an exploration of the exhibition of contemporary art in religious spaces in France, see Lara Blanchy (2004).

39. For a recent, powerful work on the manner in which antiblackness and white supremacy continue to shape representations of black life in the African diaspora, see Sharpe (2016).

40. As I explore in more detail elsewhere (Oliphant [2019]), under the 1905 law separating church and state in France's Third Republic, all religious buildings became the property of the state. Churches tend to be owned by municipalities, while the federal government is responsible for cathedrals and basilicas. Given the high number of Catholic churches in France built prior to this period, one of the unanticipated effect of the laws is a significant subsidization of Catholic practices, as Catholics are given exclusive use of these historic buildings, without carrying the burden of their upkeep.

41. See Stoekl (2006) for more on how many of the political positions held by this "traditionalist" expression of Catholicism share much in common with so-called "fundamentalist" Islam.

42. A general word for suburbs, at the Collège my interlocutors used the term "banlieues" to refer to the underfunded and relatively impoverished neighborhoods and townships to the north, east, and south of the city, separated from the twenty arrondissements by a ring road known as the Periphery.

CHAPTER ONE

1. A video recording of the talk remains available in online collections of the Collège's colloquia. See Barjot (2010).

2. Sciences Po is considered the most liberal of Paris' Grandes Écoles. These institutions are similar to American Ivy League schools in that they are considered superior to

other institutions of higher education in the country. In contrast to the Ivy League, the Grandes Écoles are public institutions. However, they tend to attract an elite population of students who attend both for the reputation of the institutions and the connections they will make while there. Gender studies are not, in fact, obligatory.

3. These demonstrations, known as "*la manif pour tous*" (protest for all), aimed to prevent the passage of a law often referred to as "*le mariage pour tous*" (marriage for all). Camille Robcis has written powerfully on the Catholic influence on theories of gender in France (see Robcis 2015a) and on this law and the Catholic demonstrations against it (see Robcis 2015b).

4. For more on various expressions of the defense of femininity as framed through male desire, see Fernando 2014, 210–14, for an account of how the French feminist group Ni Putes, Ni Soumises (Neither sluts nor doormats) reinforces the "heterosexual norms foundational to secular republican citizenship" (2014, 210).

5. As I will describe in chapter 6, the relationship between Catholicism and capitalism is also forged through far more material means in this space.

6. The organization of the Collège has changed significantly since its opening. It began with one overarching administrative council, known as the sponsoring committee (comité de parrainage). At the time of this writing, it was led by an administrative council and a directors' committee. The former "clarifies and approves" decisions made by the latter and includes a number of French business professionals, but no one who had spent time committed to a monastic life.

7. At times the word "renaissance" was also used during the 1920s to describe what has become more commonly known as the Catholic Renewal (Schloesser 2005, 4). Anthropologist Jennifer Selby's research highlights a community organization aimed at recent Muslim migrants in a Parisian suburb that similarly made use of the term "renaissance," although in this case it was translated into Arabic, "*nahba*." As Selby (2012) powerfully demonstrates, the organization built on stereotypes of oppressed Muslim women to encourage them to take up their liberty through their renaissance in France.

8. Broadly speaking, modernist aesthetics are "dominated by straight lines, clear angles, and simple curves" (Murphy 2015, 44).

9. This interpretation of Bernard's approach to art in the monastery is informed by the work of Conrad Rudolph (1990).

10. The Collège is not the only place in which the Roman Catholic Church has celebrated contemporary architecture. In spring 2018, the Vatican participated in Venice's Architecture Biennale to wide acclaim with a display of similarly minimalist forms. For images of these works see Povoledo (2018).

11. The link between the pope's address at the Collège and his speech at Regensberg has also been identified in a collection of Benedict XVI's thought on "universities, educations, and culture" (see Brown, ed. 2013).

12. Anthropologist David Graeber describes medieval Islam as ripe with "disputes between the Baghdad Aristoteleans and the neo-Pythagoreans in Basra, or Persian Neo-Platonists—essentially, scholars doing the same work [as Christians] of trying to square the revealed religion tradition beginning with Abraham and Moses with the categories of Greek philosophy" (2014 [2011], 271).

13. Having returned to the United States in September 2010, I accessed the colloquium via the Collège's extensive digital archives.

14. In this chapter, I stand by my translation of the term rencontre as "encounter."

15. I gained knowledge of this seminar—as well as access to the transcripts of its proceedings—through the Lustiger Institute, an archive that works to consolidate all of the writings of the cardinal. I discuss this archive further in chapter 2.

16. One research department at the Collège is devoted to exploring another religion besides Catholicism: the Christian Center for Jewish Studies. While rabbis are often present at their colloquia, the center is not explicitly devoted to Jewish-Catholic dialogue. Interfaith goals are tangential rather than central to the project here. On occasion, the Collège does host multifaith dialogues under the auspices of intellectual debates. Interestingly, some employees have pointed to such events as those that affected them the most in their work and suggested to me that their significance was due in part to the fact that they tended to bring in a far more diverse crowd than that they typically encountered at the Collège.

17. In France, the term "Christian" (chrétien) stands in for the unmarked Catholic majority. The term operates in the reverse manner to its use in the majority-Protestant United States. In the US, "Christian" can be used to refer to all Christians and to Protestants in particular. When Catholics in particular are the subjects the specific term Catholic must be used. In France, "Christian" can refer to all Christians or to Catholics in particular, but when Protestants are the subjects, Protestant is used to modify Christian. I try to use Catholic throughout this text whenever I am referring to this particular group, but when quoting my interlocutors I stick to the terms they used.

18. For Bakhtin, double-voiced discourse "serves two speakers at the same time and expresses simultaneously two different intentions" (1981, 324). While its use acknowledges the different needs and agendas potential readers or listeners may bring to a speech act, in certain contexts—particularly in contexts of normalization—double-voicing is most effective when it does not appear as such, when the labor that went into its formation is effaced and it appears the only "natural" way to describe a particular act or event. In Bakhtin's terms, the double-voicing at the Collège is most successful when it appears not as an expression of "heteroglossia," but as an expression of "unitary" language. Unitary language, Bakhtin argues, is never natural and must always be "posited" (1981, 270).

19. The term, in fact, is secular enough to be a source of some confusion. In France today, the term almost exclusively refers to middle schools. A friend who lived around the corner from the Collège for many months once confessed to me that she had never entered it because she presumed that it was a middle school.

20. While the author of this article failed to use the term "Collège," he clearly had picked up on the power of the idea of renaissance and the significance of the encounter between "believers" and "non-believers" to the project.

21. The British sociologist of religion Grace Davie (1994) has described tacit Catholics as those who "believe without belonging." Birgit Meyer (2015a) has called for greater anthropological attention to less-than-committed Christians. The anthropologist of Catholicism Maya Mayblin has similarly argued for attention to "leniency and tacit

accommodation" (2017, 518) in relation to Catholic practice, rather than a singular focus on discipline.

22. Of course, the global calendar in our secular age is also a Christian calendar. Apocalyptic anxieties expressed at the turn of the millennium suggest that a whole host of Christian narratives continue to influence the manner in which we measure the passing of time. Jakobsen and Pellegrini also point to this interconnection between a single religious tradition and global secular power in the Introduction to their edited volume (2008).

23. *Respect de l'autre* (respect of the other) is a phrase generally used by more conservative voices in France than that of Céline to critique Muslim French for their purported incapacity to show respect for others, as demonstrated by the "burqa" and the "Muslim problem" of homophobia. See Fernando (2014, 224–59) for more on this term and the hypocrisy of reducing homophobia to a "Muslim problem."

24. To find your own Saint's Day, see: http://nominis.cef.fr/.

25. The Collège does not currently host any weddings. However, soon after I left, the rental department increased its business significantly and the space is now frequently used for a variety of corporate events, a point to which I will return in chapter 6.

26. Very few voices in Paris expressed much in the way of protest against government support for the renovation of the Collège in the early 2000s. However, as the opening neared, city officials and the archdiocese began debating how, precisely, the space should be made accessible to the public. In yet another example of the distance taken by the state toward Catholicism in France, these debates were ultimately never resolved, allowing the archdiocese to operate the space—like all of the churches built in France prior to 1905—as its own.

27. Such a claim partially contradicts the pope's concern with a present-day crisis. However, these are the words of one employee. Others within the space may have taken more care to align their views with those of the pope. The claim of "moving forward together" is also one that points to the significance of history for the Roman Catholic Church, which authorizes its sacramental and institutional structures through claims that connect them, unbroken, to the time in which Jesus lived.

28. This set-up changed after I left the Collège in 2010. According to one volunteer with whom I spoke in 2016, after a few controversial Bernardins Tuesdays, the Catholic television station began to express resistance to the programming and those at the Collège thought they would have more freedom to engage in the work they wanted to accomplish without worrying about KTO's preferences. The first hour is no longer broadcast on television but is filmed and displayed on the Collège's website. This change further demonstrates the oscillations between evangelization and normalization, and the ongoing tension between catholaïcité and the specter of a secularized Catholicism at the Collège.

29. Labidi-Maïza later served as president of this organization. In 2011, she was elected to the Tunisian Constituent Assembly as the representative for Tunisians living abroad. In 2014, she was elected to the Tunisian Assembly of Representatives and led a Committee for Women, Family, and Children beginning in 2015.

30. In the title of the blog post "Elisabeth Badinter et la laïcité lepénisée," Baubérot (2011) created a new adjective with the word "lepénisée." In modifying laïcité with this term, he is suggesting that Badinter is perverting the concept in a manner similar to that of Marine Le Pen, the leader of France's far-right party. In Badinter's article that was the object of Baubérot's critique, she celebrated Le Pen as the only defender of laïcité in France. If Roy, Barjot, and Kristeva help to incorporate certain forms of French feminism into conservative Catholic thought, Badinter and Le Pen offer similar services to particularly exclusionary visions of laïcité.

CHAPTER TWO

1. Versions of this story also exist in written form. As I note in chapter 1, when announcing the renovation project in 2000, Lustiger had explained to reporters that "in the 1960s, when I was the chaplain of students, I saw the Bernardins monastery occupied by a fire station. I imagined that it could rediscover its original thirteenth-century vocation and be a space of culture and exchange" (Le Mitouard 2000, 1). In the introduction to the publication of a colloquium celebrating Lustiger at the Collège, entitled *Jean-Marie Lustiger: Cardinal républicain,* the editor of the collection describes how, as chaplain of the Sorbonne in the 1950s and 1960s, Lustiger searched the neighborhood for an appropriate space to host the chaplaincy. "It was then that he started to imagine a pastoral future for the Collège des Bernardins, which was still just a fire station" (Rougé 2010, 8). The book by de Feydeau similarly emphasizes the longevity of Lustiger's dream for the Collège. "It was necessary to choose a space with care where we could develop, in the most favorable conditions, a human project that entered into the Creator's design. [Lustiger] had secretly carried this space in his heart for decades: it was the Collège des Bernardins" (de Feydeau 2017, 19).

2. Olivia Harris's (2006) account of indigenous Christian practices in the Bolivian highlands interprets rituals that might be conceived as evidence of a failure to convert as, instead, ritual repetitions of the moment of conversion precisely in order to attend to the impossibility of fully living up to the demands of a good Christian life. By reenacting the moment of conversion, indigenous Christians allow it to remain everpresent as an ideal toward which to strive.

3. See Michel-Rolph Trouillot (1995) for an account of how the erasure of violence is central to the project of the West and its historical narratives more broadly.

4. Some examples of his political acumen to which they pointed included that he had been the first archbishop to receive a formal visit from a French president since the 1905 law separating church and state; that he celebrated masses for opening of the parliamentary sessions; that he participated in the work of the National Commission on the Rights of Man; and that he successfully defended the rights of Catholic schools against government incursion between 1982 and 1984.

5. In the published version of the colloquium, an editor saw fit to correct one of Wolton's

criticisms of Lustiger—that he had paid little attention to the world beyond Europe, especially Africa—by insisting in a footnote that Lustiger had not "neglected Africa," but had merely expressed regret at not going there more often.

6. As I argue throughout this chapter, Catholics are not the only ones who engage in continuity thinking. Asad has pointed to the contrast between the ideal of coherence and the reality of change in his account of the history and ongoing ideological power of liberalism:

> Liberalism has a shifting historical identity. It has changed from being a revolution- ary movement in the seventeenth and eighteenth centuries (when it aimed to cir- cumscribe the privileges of church and monarch) to being socially conservative in the nineteenth and twentieth centuries (when it sought to consolidate elite power and imperial advantage) and, most recently, to being predatory (when it not only accelerated market freedoms but also encouraged the global dominance of finance capital and promoted the growth of inequality). It is the insistence on telling a single, coherent story that allows one to pretend that these radical differences are moments in the historical life of liberalism. [2018, 20]

7. And yet, there is little evidence that the French state has attempted any such thing. Fer- nando offers a rather different account of the relationship between Sarkozy and France's Muslims than that imagined by Lustiger. She recounts the thrill and excitement of many Muslim French when Sarkozy, as minister of the interior, visited the annual conference of the Union des Organisations Islamiques de France (Union of Islamic Organizations of France) on April 19, 2003. Many Muslim French experienced his presence as an unprecedented moment of recognition. And yet, Sarkozy's words while there betrayed the limited nature of this gesture. Fernando describes how "he concluded his speech with the following statement: 'the national community holds out its hand to you. It is watching you. You are from now on accountable for the image of each and every Mus- lim in France. Take this hand held out to you by the republic. Do not disappoint it, for the consequences would be enormous'" (2014, 65).

8. For the final report of this commission, see Bernard Stasi et al. (2003).

9. The debate during this period centered on the potential capaciousness of a secularized Catholicism. The associations cultuelles designation would have allowed the state to vest power over the churches in the parish community, rather than the priests or the diocese. The pope and the French Church hierarchy were concerned that this ambigu- ity would allow groups that fell outside of Catholic orthodoxy to make a claim upon a Catholic church and so they encouraged French Catholics to resist this designation (Larkin 1964). While the 1923 solution to the problem, the creation of a new designa- tion of associations diocésaines (diocesan associations), appeared to resolve this issue, the fears of the Church hierarchy have in some ways been realized by the successful occupation of St. Nicholas du Chardonnet by the excommunicated far-right group St. Pius X for more than thirty years.

10. Here I have in mind the definition used by the historian of the French Revolution David

Bell. Bell describes nationalism as "a program to build a sovereign political community grouping together people who have enough in common . . . to allow them to act as a homogenous, collective person" (2001, 20). Bell's larger argument—that the French Revolution should not be seen as a powerful moment of rupture with the past but as a nationalist program that only became possible through the work of eighteenth-century thinkers who emphasized the continuity of the *patrie* (fatherland) in ways that allowed it to be separated from the monarchy—also informs my argument here.

11. Benedict Anderson's (2000 [1993]) seminal work on nationalism, *Imagined Communities*, for example, cites Renan's argument on page 199.

12. For an example of an account of the baptism of Clovis as the moment of the birth of France see Chauni and Mension-Rigau (1996).

13. Lustiger's oblique reference to Renan is complicated somewhat by another project for which Renan is remembered in France: a "scientific" exploration of the life and legacy of Jesus (1974 [1863]) that relied upon the expulsion of Jesus's Jewishness in his text *La Vie de Jésus* (The Life of Jesus).

14. The joke references René Samuel Sirat, the Algerian-born rabbi appointed to the position of the chief rabbi of France in 1981, the same year Lustiger became archbishop.

15. Originating in the French settlements in North America in the seventeenth century, the term broadly referred to those with French and Indigenous parentage. Desires for intermarriage among the settler elite hinged on the notion of the unification of two populations, ultimately through the decline of a distinctive Indigenous culture. Now the term refers to a recognized population possessing particular rights in Canada. The use of the term to refer generally to those of "mixed race" both effaces particular populations in Indigenous North America and, in the words of Adam Gaudry and Darryl Leroux "capitalize[s] on settler puzzlement over forms of Indigeneity based on kinship and belonging and replace[s] these forms with an imagined past of racial mixedness leading to supposed societal unification" (2017, 116).

16. For more on Lustiger's entanglements with Paris's elite see Lavergnat (2007).

17. Despite popular notions of immigration as a recent "problem" in France, "by the mid-1920s France had become the most important destination for immigrants in the entire industrialized world. In 1930 three million foreigners resided in France, comprising 7 percent of its total population" (Camiscioli 2009, 1).

18. See David Kertzer (2001) for evidence of the Catholic Church's refusal to acknowledge the horrors of the Holocaust while they were unfolding.

19. His visits to Auschwitz are covered extensively in the biopic. In an example of the director's refusal to fully confront what Lustiger's conversion and leadership implied about France's history of anti-Semitism, he chose to represent the visits as the archbishop's attempt to confront the ongoing anti-Judaism and anti-Semitism found in Poland. While, indeed, Lustiger played an important role in discouraging Polish nuns from setting up a Catholic chapel at Auschwitz, the director does not address whether or not Lustiger similarly confronted the legacy of anti-Semitism and anti-Judaism in France. For more on the challenges of acknowledging the role of France in the Holocaust see Henry Rousso (1991).

20. In contrast to religious studies scholar Gil Anidjar (2014), I do not understand this violence to be inherent to Christianity but as expressions of Christian actors and institutions enacted at various moments throughout history.

21. Jews are not the only group for whom the crucifix or cross might serve as a symbol of violence and oppression. In Latin America, North America, Africa, and elsewhere, the cross, or crucifix, was often very visibly elevated as one of the first signs of the expropriation of land and the "Christianization"—or attempted annihilation—of local cosmologies. See the artist Marvin Bartley's use of the cross as symbol authorizing the death and rape of black bodies in his series "Christianity's Catastrophic Gift" found in the journal *Small Axe* in July 2011.

22. The Latin acronym for Jesus of Nazareth, King of the Jews.

23. When I visited the Lustiger Institute in the summer of 2010, it was still early on in the archive's existence and I did not view the documents in typical archival fashion—labeled in pre-organized boxes. Rather, the archivist provided me with a thick folder of documents he had photocopied for me and then allowed me to peruse another set of documents of which he did not want me to make photocopies or take pictures. I was not forbidden, however, from quoting from them. The documents that inform the narrative below are a mixture of documents that were photocopied for me and that I carefully read through and wrote down quotes from while at the Lustiger Institute. Given that the archives were still in formation at the time, other relevant documents may since have been added to the repository.

24. This story is recounted in a similar way in de Feydeau's book. The Collège plays a central role in this text, and its nave, along with a picture of Lustiger, is displayed on the front cover.

CHAPTER THREE

1. See the historian Elizabeth Emery's work (2000, 2001) for more on the powerful influence of the medieval in nineteenth-century French architectural and artistic forms. See Erwin Panofsky (1951) for a rich account of the layered rituals built into medieval gothic forms.

2. Unlike many of its subsequent iterations, Braudel's use of the term was decidedly Marxist. He wanted to escape the limitations of approaching history as a series of events, while also refusing the structuralist approach that made little space for changes of any kind. However, he did not understand the longue durée to be without limits. According to Braudel, "the genius of Marx, the secret of his lasting power, is that he was the first to invent real social models, and starting on the historical *longue durée*" (Braudel 1958, 752). The time scale he had in mind when he used this term emphasized how "the fundamental structures of the longue durée world in which we live, the modern-world system, or capitalist world-economy, emerged in Europe at the beginning of the 'long sixteenth century'" (Lee 2018, 71).

3. I do not use the term "nostalgia" to describe these desires, in part because its negative

valences would risk dismissing the emotions people brought to the Collège. See Svetlana Boym (2001) for a powerful discussion of the significance of materiality for the formation and reproduction of experiences of nostalgia, and anthropologist Andrew Gilbert (2019) for an articulation of why nostalgia may prove insufficient in accounting for the myriad emotions surrounding desires for the past.

4. "Arte povera" refers to an artistic method initiated in the 1960s that made use of simple, brute materials in the creation of artworks.

5. The fact that those with such long roots in France are still known as "immigrants" speaks volumes to how Muslims are presented as something other than French.

6. The Norwegian terrorist Anders Behring Breivik's manifesto, for example, both celebrated Europe's medieval past and insisted that the rising "threat" of Islam made the medieval a model period on which to base present-day Europe's necessary self-defense. For more on the significance of the medieval in Europe's far right see Holmes (2000) and Wollenberg (2014).

7. "Sea of glass" and "library of shadows" were terms used by mediators and in brochures that accompanied the exhibition.

8. Years later, a (by then) former employee of the Collège described the deep anxiety he had felt when charged with supervising this act, given the risks involved and just how recently the space had opened. For this employee, the excessive responsibility he shouldered during this experience demonstrated how ill equipped the employees at the Collège were in those early years to play host to the vagaries of contemporary art display.

9. Sociologists of religion in France have, in part, formed their discipline by charting numerous expressions of the diminution of Catholic institutions, practices, and rituals. These assessments have often taken the form of "counting" both the departing Catholics and those who remain. The Catholic activities quantified by French sociologists include the number of priests (Martine Severgrand 2004) and parishioners (Fernand Boulard and Gabriel Le Bras 1952; Paul Mercator 1997, Colette Muller and Jean-René Bertrand 2002); their charitable activities (Olivier Landron 2004, Jean-Claude Lavigne 1996); their donations to the Church (Dorothée Elineau 2000); their sacramental practices, such as baptism, catechism, and marriage (Alfred Dittgen 1993, Elineau 1997); and the newspapers they read (Lucien Guissard 1998, Muller 1990).

10. *Culte* in French simply translates as religion. The word *secte* is used to refer to the smaller organizations whose legitimacy as "religions" are questioned (and are referred to as "cults" in English).

11. For this first exhibit, I did not work as a mediator but observed it almost daily.

12. In referencing the destruction of the Library of Alexandria, Parmiggiani was repeating a widely held notion that this ancient library was destroyed in a fire during Caesar's Alexandrian war. However, little evidence of the actual occurrence of this event exists, leading scholars to declare it a "falsification" (Heller-Roazen 2002, 148), with some pointing to evidence for its continued existence beyond the war (Hemmerdinger 1985). The library may have simply declined in importance over time, fading away slowly rather than burning up in flames, which would make for a rather different account of history than that offered in Parmiggiani's installation.

13. See historian Alain Corbin (1994) for an analysis of how church bells played a powerful role in linking quotidian life to attachment to a locale in nineteenth-century France.

14. This quote is taken from an interview with Grenier that appeared in the archdiocese's weekly magazine, *Paris Notre-Dame*. A picture of the broken glass in the nave appears on the cover with the words "Parmiggiani Collège des Bernardins EXPOSE," taking advantage of the similar appearance of the term to exhibit (*exposer*) and to explode (*exploser*). The controversial nature of the exhibit for many committed Catholics is revealed in a side panel in which the cultural director at the time, Vincent Aucante, answers the question "Why Parmiggiani at the Bernardins?" In his response he points to how Parmiggiani is an "internationally renowned artist" chosen following advice they received from "professionals in the art world." He also takes the time to point out that Parmiggiani has worked with the Catholic Church in the past, creating a work for the Episcopal Italian Church, for which "he was received . . . by Benedict XVI" (Folscheid 2008, 7).

15. Historian Ellis Hanson describes decadence as the French "fin de siècle fascination with cultural degeneration, the persistent and highly influential myth that religion, sexuality, art, and even language itself, had fallen at last into decay" (1997, 2). Moreover, he points to how Huysmans defined his "conversion" to decadence from realism "as an essentially Roman Catholic revolt against the materialism of the age" (1997, 5).

16. Gauchet served as the Collège's second "research chair," leading research programming at the Collège on the subject of "Transmitting-Learning" from 2010–11.

17. The fact that such labors are necessary speaks to the well-established problem of the whiteness of museums. This whiteness refers both to the majority of the visitors who enter into these spaces and the tendency for collections, labels, and layouts of museums to reproduce racist ideologies.

18. In the video recorded at the Collège, Parmiggiani goes so far as to describe Mantegna as one of his "contemporaries."

CHAPTER FOUR

1. One could argue that Parmiggiani's bells and—given the Church's historical propensity to destroy texts deemed heretical, including copies of the Jewish Torah—burned books might also be seen as Christian motifs. The Christian motifs included in *Suite Grünewald*, however, hovered close to those one might call iconographic.

2. I return to explore Bernard's view of art and images in more detail in chapters 5 and 6.

3. See, for example, Anya Bernstein (2014), Dario Gamboni (1997), and Jojada Verrips (2008).

4. See, for example, Alexandrova (2017), Elkins (2004), Catherine Grenier (2003), Eleanor Heartney (2018 [2004]), and Jean-Luc Nancy (2005).

5. See, for example, Jérôme Alexandre (2010), Jérôme Cottin (2007), Wassily Kandinsky (1989 [1954]), Jeffrey Kosky (2013), Robert Nelson (2007), and Aidan Nichols (1980).

6. Marianne, in contrast, generally refers to a more precise icon of a woman in a red Phyrgian cap, first painted by Jean-Michel Moreau (1741-1814) in 1775.

7. While visitors lamented that the Collège had not endeavored to bring the Isenheim Altarpiece to be exhibited alongside of *Suite Grünewald*, the altarpiece cannot, in fact, leave the museum in which it is currently housed. Alsace, the region that contains the museum, was annexed by Germany during the Franco-Prussian War of 1870–71. It remained part of Germany until after World War I. The Treaty of Versailles included a provision that Germany would return the altarpiece to France. During the Second World War, however, the Isenheim Altarpiece once again found its way to Germany. After its return to France after that war, the two nations agreed to never move it again. See Stieglitz (1993) for more on this history.

8. For more on these pieces and the numerous connections between Grünewald and modern and contemporary works of art, see Apostolos-Cappadona (1992), Jerry Meyer (1997), and Keith Moxey (2004).

9. Interestingly, Grosz was charged with "blasphemy and defamation of the German military" by the secular German state in 1928 for a series of drawings that included *Shut Up and Do Your Duty!*

10. David Nirenberg points to the term "Judaizing" used as an accusation between Christians to describe "erroneous orientation of attention away from the spirit and toward the flesh, the letter of scripture, and the material things of this world" (Nirenberg 1995, 13). The term did not refer to actual Jewish practices, nor did it require the presence of Jewish populations. He points to Nolde's polyptych as one example of how Judaizing continued to haunt regimes of visuality and images in Europe through the twentieth century. Although he was not Jewish, Nolde's *The Life of Christ* was the centerpiece of the Nazis' *Degenerate Art* exhibition, in which abstraction was depicted as the result of Jewish influence in European art (ibid., 74).

11. The line is attributed to John the Baptist in John 3:30 when describing Jesus's followers in comparison to his own. It is generally translated into English as "He must increase, but I must decrease."

12. For a particularly powerful lament of the loss of aura entailed in the movement of Catholic materiality from churches and monasteries into museums in the late eighteenth century, see the writings (in particular, 1989) of Quatremère de Quincy. For a comparison of Quatremère de Quincy's views with those of Walter Benjamin, see Daniel Sherman (1994).

13. On occasion, however, members of the contemporary public would raise their eyebrows and giggle with one another when perusing some of the pamphlets one could find at the Collège, in particular those advertising the events of the Institut de la Famille (Family Institute), which describes itself as a "space of reflection on questions related to the family, approached through the light of the Gospel." At other times, they appeared bemused by the interests of the spiritual public. In early July, an older man interrupted my conversation with two members of the contemporary public to ask why there was no plaque commemorating the Pope's visit. The two young men with whom I had been speaking snickered as I responded "I don't know" to the older gentleman. Here,

however, the contemporary public expressed concern about the actions of people or practices that appeared exceedingly religious, rather than with the space itself.

14. In a different, but equally productive vein, the Louvre held an exhibit on Altarpieces entitled "The First Altarpieces (12th–15th centuries): Staging the Sacred" from April 10–July 6 2009.

15. In so doing, they reminded me of Evans-Pritchard's (1976 [1937]) account of the Azande descriptions of witchcraft.

CHAPTER FIVE

1. Due to the unexpected extension of *Suite Grünewald*, the two exhibits ended up over-lapping for a few months in the early summer. I had been hired to work on *Suite Grünewald* but began working on *Cellula* intermittently until the former closed, at which point I began working full time on *Cellula*.

2. Because of the potential dangers posed by the scaffolding and the addition of a second floor at a significant height, a sign at the entrance requested that adults accompany those under fifteen.

3. There are numerous examples of the distinction between a premodern past in which social and material acts overlapped in meaningful and recognizable ways and the vacu-ous or surface nature of modern life in which social actions are disconnected from any deeper meaning. Durkheim's distinction between mechanical and organic solidar-ity, Weber's account of the differences between *gemeinschaft* and *gesellschaft*, and, in France, Pierre Nora's separation of milieux de mémoire and lieux de mémoire are all examples of this mode of thinking.

4. Recall, for example, Frigide Barjot's celebration of the Collège as a space to celebrate Christian culture and her critique of various "materialist ideologies."

5. If his initial point may have been somewhat acceptable to many of the mediators, his use of Michael Jackson's death as an example of this problem proved more controver-sial. Another mediator and I chuckled at his admonitions later and then both pro-ceeded to describe how, precisely, we had spent the evening of his death. She wondered aloud what had distinguished our late nights of dancing to his music in bars from Catholic pilgrimages to see the relics of saints. The difference, of course, lay in the material practices one saw as lacking a transcendent origin and, therefore, as fetishized: Michael Jackson's music or the adoration of relics.

6. During the iconoclastic violence of the sixteenth-century Protestant Reformation in Germany and Switzerland, Martin Luther warned that the appropriate response to religious images and objects was indifference rather than destruction. While they may appear dangerous, when viewed correctly, Luther argued, one should instead acknowl-edge their powerlessness. Ignoring them would affirm this lack of power. Destroy-ing them, in contrast, would proffer them power. In his 1525 essay "Against the Heav-enly Prophets Concerning Images and Sacraments," he critiqued his fellow reformer

Andreas Karlstadt for his iconoclastic crusades, suggesting that the act of iconoclasm itself became a new false idol.

> For where the heart is instructed that we please God alone through faith, and that in the matter of images nothing that is pleasing to God takes place, but is a fruitless service and effort, people themselves willingly drop it, despise images, and have none made. But where one neglects such instruction and forces the issue, it follows that . . . their idea that they can please God with works becomes a real idol and a false assurance in the heart. [Luther 2015, 55]

Like the manager, Luther found iconoclasm a less than effective means of overcoming idolatry. I use the term fetish over that of idol in part because idolatry carries particularly Christian connotations that fail to account for the varied desires and anxieties surrounding *Cellula*. Pietz offers a definition of idolatry that is very similar to that presumed by Luther, in which it "cover[ed] any religious practice that attended to external forms rather than inner faith" (1987, 29).

7. Given how recent the restoration had been, however, the scaffolding also served as a source of confusion for many visitors who, upon entering the sacristy and encountering the scaffolding, quickly retreated, presuming that the renovations were still ongoing.

8. The ground floor of the building is located a few feet below street level and must be accessed through a wide set of stairs. The floor of the sacristy is located even further below that of the nave. Once inside, those wishing to enter the sacristy must descend a few additional stairs. The presence of these stairs frustrated the artists and many visitors because, in order to increase the accessibility of the space, a lift had also been installed at the entrance to the sacristy. The artists lamented the ugliness of the object, while visitors expressed concern at how it reduced the coherence of the medieval space. A friend who uses a wheelchair complained to me that while the external entrance also has a mechanical device to assist those with limited mobility, the one the architects insisted on using in order not to disrupt the "aesthetic" of the space was not, in fact, made for outdoor use and so quickly stopped functioning after being exposed to rain. An alternative means of access was devised through a side garden, but the prioritization of aesthetics or immediacy over access—by the artists, architects, and visitors alike—speaks volumes about the limits of openness and inclusion here.

9. This attempt to create an exchange with the street that was otherwise inaccessible was effective enough to become a source of consternation for some. Occasionally, neighbors who lived across the street would stop by to complain that the lights from *Cellula* could be seen through their bedroom windows at night.

10. I am grateful to Mayanthi Fernando for pointing out this connection.

11. The addition of the church in the fourteenth century was made possible by the influx of funds to the site by Pope Benedict XII (1285–1342; he was the third Avignon pope). Thus, the inclusion of more architectural flourishes also demonstrates the shifting support given to the space over time.

12. It was not only those seeking visceral immediacy with St. Bernard who found the art-

ists' attempt to emphasize the vagaries of the space problematic. In early September, for example, I encountered two middle-aged women who were reading the exhibit pamphlet in a mocking tone, often breaking into fits of laughter. I offered to walk them through the space and as I finished my account of the installation, one woman interjected to ask why the opportunity to explore the building's varied history should be considered desirable. Perhaps the building's use as a prison and a fire station need not be appreciated or emphasized, she insisted, because these were periods of sacrilege. "And I am not speaking in religious terms," she continued, "but aesthetic ones. These were destructive, sacrilegious periods in this building's *aesthetic* history."

13. This tour was not one of the guided visits provided by volunteers at the Collège. At this point, a year after the Collège's opening, private docents not affiliated with the Collège had begun to integrate the space into their tours of central Paris. Because they were not participating in the broader project of the Collège but were there to celebrate the space alone, they proved particularly reticent in engaging with the exhibits. While they had informed themselves about the Collège's medieval past, most were far less capable of or interested in talking about contemporary art, and so simply ignored the presence of the exhibits, often loudly encouraging their customers to join them in being offended by the sight of such works in a medieval space.

14. The twelfth-century theologian Hugh of St. Victor described the relationship forged between Christ and one who took the Eucharist as that of "incorporation." In his "On the Sacraments of the Christian Faith," composed in 1124, he contrasted this experience with that of digestion. "Elsewhere what is eaten is incorporated. Now when the body of Christ is eaten, not what is eaten, but he who eats is incorporated with Him whom he eats. On this account Christ wished to be eaten by us, that He might incorporate us with Him" (1951, 307).

15. The historian of American Catholicism Robert Orsi has recently described how the incarnation—or, the entrance of the transcendent into the immanent—necessarily produces "excess" that finds expression in a multitude of material practices. However, given modernity's preference for absence, many find such excess disconcerting. He points to the souvenir shops at spaces of pilgrimage as exemplary in this regard:

> Visitors today may be unprepared for the excesses at Lourdes and other shrines to Mary and the saints: the proliferation of souvenir shops overflowing with great heaps of rosaries and statues of the Blessed Mother and other holy figures; the great piles of wax or tin images of body parts that pilgrims buy to place at the Virgin Mary's feet in petition for healing; the stacks of holy cards, alongside umbrellas, playing cards, toys, and crockery ashtrays imprinted with images of Mary. . . . This has offended church officials and Catholic moderns, too, who tell the devout that such tasteless messiness crowds out the real meaning of the sites. These critics fail to see that excess itself is the meaning. [Orsi 2016, 57]

16. See Michael Ralph (2015) for a powerful account of how accusations of the fetish invoked an increasing level of horror in the nineteenth century. In the aftermath of the slave trade and the rise of wage labor, "fetishism came to mark societies struc-

tured through wealth in people (2015, 61). Similar to its sixteenth to eighteenth-century expressions, however, the specter that it was not others but oneself who engaged in such practices made the concept of the fetish particularly fraught.

17. According to McClellan, a number of apocryphal stories accompanied Lenoir's contextualizing exploits. Like the colonial collectors who would bring thousands of objects from Africa and Asia to France's ethnographic museums in the nineteenth and twentieth centuries, myths of his heroic encounters with objects circulated widely. In one case, during an encounter with a vandal at the Sorbonne, "he was stabbed in the hand trying to protect Richelieu's tomb from a vandal's bayonet" (McClellan 1994, 159). A drawing by the artist Pierre-Joseph la Fontaine depicted "Lenoir defending the tomb of Louis XII with his bare hands" (ibid.). He was also reputed to have disguised precious metals when government agents came looking for bronze for canons.

18. Lenoir held a theory that the gothic architecture of the fourteenth century was the result of Arab-influenced design. Returning from the crusades, artists and architects at the time—according to Lenoir—took inspiration from the mosques they had encountered and brought back a new, local, but ultimately hybrid form. Recent studies actually support Lenoir's theory, but he used arabesque flourishes in order to help materially substantiate his claims. Their Arab influence, moreover, could serve as further evidence of their "despotic" rather than liberatory effects.

19. While extremely short-lived (it closed in 1816), the Musée may have had lasting impacts on encounters with objects that appeared to contain the Catholic medieval past in visceral ways in France. Nicole Savy (1995) has called attention to the fact that none other than Victor Hugo lived in an apartment overlooking the garden of the Petits-Augustins at the time of its decommissioning. She suggests that gazing out upon these (mostly) medieval objects may have helped to inspire the formidable role they would come to play in his writing, and in his cultivation of a medieval sensibility in France in the nineteenth century that continues to motor projects such as the Collège today. In a further hint of the power of the Musée for making the Catholic medieval past viscerally proximate in ways that likely would have horrified Lenoir, one of the most important of the medieval revivalist architects in France in the nineteenth century, Viollet-le-Duc, was instrumental in resuscitating the project of the Musée in the late 1880s.

20. In a fascinating and complex argument, Nagel goes on to suggest that the introduction of perspective in painting—generally conceived of as visual evidence of modernity's march of progress—was in fact one of a series of "reactionary" responses to painting that appeared outdated, rather than timeless. The use of perspective shifted the focus away from the details of dress and décor in an attempt to re-establish a painting's proximity to its transcendent origins.

CHAPTER SIX

1. Anthropologist Keith M. Murphy has argued that the modernist aesthetics that undergird abstraction—and, as I described in chapter 1, also find prominent expression in the

design of the Collège—were created with the aim of "advancing a particular political agenda: constructing a new social world made up of 'objective' forms freed from the constraining class markers associated with older styles. According to the logic of modernist design, minimalist forms provoke minimal social distinctions" (2015, 44). And yet, as anyone fooled by the name of the high-end retail chain *Design within Reach* can attest, modernist design has done much more to obscure privilege than to combat it.

2. In our brief and rather fraught conversation, I was unable to ascertain whether he was a donor to the Collège and using the term "we" to suggest that his donations allowed him to presume that he was one of those personally paying for the artists. He may well have used the third-person plural in more general terms, as, perhaps, a Catholic, or simply someone engaged in activities at the Collège. Either way, he articulated a level of ownership that he lacked.

3. I encountered other explicit concerns about the elitism at the Collège in the years following my departure from Paris when I met with those I had worked with at the Collège on return visits to the city. By that point, many had left the space for other opportunities. I was intrigued when, on two different occasions, former employees mentioned that they had occasionally attended mass before working at the Collège but that the association between Catholicism and wealth and privilege had been so strong in this space that they found themselves less inclined to return to mass after working there.

4. He was not the only one to suggest that visitors were "too old" to appreciate abstraction, despite the fact that it has been a powerfully dominant art form in France since the end of the nineteenth century. When I offered an explanation to two older women in late April they mocked me by exclaiming to one another: "it's incredible, she really believes what she is saying. You see the difference between the generations!" When I explained that Wéry was nearly 80 when she died, they flummoxed me by replying, "Thank goodness she did! Imagine if she had just continued on like this!" That I was unable to laugh at their ridiculous statement shows just how difficult mediating the exhibit had become. Strained by the daily work of defending the exhibit, I struggled at times to remain detached and find the humor in these interactions.

5. Boxed lunches brought from home are unusual among middle- and upper-class Parisians. Many large companies include a cafeteria onsite in which substantive, well-made lunches are provided for employees at minimal or no cost. Smaller employers without the space for cafeterias onsite provide booklets of "restaurant tickets," which function essentially as gift certificates of €10 to €12 that almost all restaurants and brasseries in the city accept. Thus, given that employers subsidize lunches so extensively, few people think of bringing their own.

6. The title in French, *La pesanteur et la grâce*, may appear somewhat clumsy in contrast to the smooth alliteration of its English translation. A similar title is available in French as the word *gravité*, rather than *pesanteur*, might also have been used to connote the rules that govern how objects move in space. When I asked friends about the difference between *pesanteur* and *gravité*, they explained that while (as in English) the word gravité can imply an abstract notion of heaviness (for example, the gravity of a situation), the word pesanteur remains tied to something more material (it is related to the verb *peser*, which means to weigh).

7. Formed soon after the opening of the Collège, this group of professionals between the ages of twenty-five and forty-five receives privileged access to a number of events at the Collège. The idea of the group, one fundraiser told me, is that they will amass wealth throughout their lives and that their participation in the Collège in their formative years will help to encourage them to funnel their charitable donations toward the institution in the future. They were also seen as a key source of networking and of expanding the renown of the Collège among elite groups. At the time of the writing of this book, the club included more than three hundred members.

8. For a slightly different perspective on Bernard's asceticism, see the medieval historian Ann Astell who points to "the apparent contradiction between Bernard's outcry against visual ornamentation, one the one hand, and his wonderfully, imagistic, eloquent, and polished sermons, on the other" (2006, 65).

9. For more on class and the history of museums see Tony Bennett (1995) and Howard Becker (1982). For a powerful account of how museums have provided a means for the working class to engage in "civilizing rituals," see Carol Duncan (1995a, 1995b).

10. In Jacques Rancière's terms, "the aesthetic regime of art comes to terms with the ethical regime of images" by "ratif[ying] its basic principle: matters of art are matters of education. As self-education art is . . . a new ethos. . . . The task of 'aesthetic education' . . . is to render ideas sensible by turning them into living images, creating an equivalent of ancient mythology, as the fabric of a common experience shared by the elite and by the common people" (2002, 138).

11. The solidarity tax on wealth—or *impôt de solidarité sur la fortune* (ISF)—was an annual wealth tax ranging from 0.5 to 1.5 percent on those with assets greater that €1.3 million. (Reflecting his neoliberal credentials, President Emmanuel Macron eliminated this tax early on in his tenure.)

12. A few months earlier, an American friend also living in Paris had explained the humiliation she felt when out at a sushi restaurant with wealthy French friends. Thinking that sushi might just be one of those dishes a woman could finish in its entirety without receiving stares, she was mortified when one of her friends—another woman—remarked, upon seeing my friend's empty plate, how hungry she must be, and offered my friend the rest of her plate which she "simply could not finish."

13. This was one of the few relationships I had in Paris in which we spoke entirely in English. Anne spoke at least three languages like a native speaker, and she seemed to appreciate the privacy that speaking in English in public could provide.

14. Within the broader French Church, on such critiques of the fascination with wealth in the archdiocese, see Jean-Louis Schlegel (1998).

15. Despite the Cistercian emphasis on voluntary poverty and the absence of social and economic ties, however, St. Bernard also went on to become the "most influential ecclesiastical politician in Europe" (Rudolph 1990, 5).

16. See Richard Roehl (1969) for more on the distinctions between ideals and reality in Cistercian economic reforms.

EPILOGUE

---

1. In response to the Gilets Jaunes protests, in the early months of 2019 the president held a number of listening sessions throughout the country which he entitled the "Great Debate." The speech was to have included a list of policy and political measures to address the concerns that arose in these sessions.

2. The kilometer markers along all of the highways in France point to the distance from the square in front of the Notre-Dame Cathedral.

3. One exception to this more recent rule occurred for an exhibit in the fall of 2018 celebrating the ten-year anniversary of the Collège.

4. I watched the video on YouTube where the Collège had posted it on April 16, 2018. I was struck at how, over the years, the "B" symbol for the Collège, now recognizable in ways communications staff had hoped for a decade earlier, had been made into a small social media circle so it could appear in legible ways on Facebook, Instagram, and YouTube.

REFERENCES

Agamben, Giorgio. 2005. *The Time That Remains: A Commentary on the Letter to the Romans*. Translated by Patricia Dailey. Stanford, CA: Stanford University Press.
———. 2011. *The Highest Poverty: Monastic Rules and Form-of-Life*. Translated by Adam Kotsko. Stanford. CA: Stanford University Press.
Agrama, Hussein Ali. 2012. *Questioning Secularism: Islam, Sovereignty, and the Rule of Law in Modern Egypt*. Chicago: University of Chicago Press.
Alexandre, Jérôme. 2010. *L'art contemporain: Un vis-à-vis essential pour la Foi*. Paris: Parole et Silence.
Alexandrova, Alena. 2004. "Death in the Image: The Post-Religious Life of Christian Images." In *Religion: Beyond a Concept*, edited by Hent de Vries, 772–87. New York: Fordham University Press.
———. 2017. *Breaking Resemblance: The Role of Religious Motifs in Contemporary Art*. New York: Fordham University Press.
Amselle, Jean-Loup. 2003. *Affirmative Exclusion: Cultural Pluralism and the Role of Custom in France*. Translated by Jane Marie Todd. Ithaca, NY: Cornell University Press.
Anderson, Benedict. 2000 [1993]. *Imagined Communities*. New York: Verso.
Anidjar, Gil. 2014. *Blood: A Critique of Christianity*. New York: Columbia University Press.
Apostolos-Cappadona, Diane. 1992. "The Essence of Agony: Grünewald's Influence on Picasso." *Artibus et Historiae* 13 (26): 31–47.
Arendt, Hannah. 1963. *Eichmann in Jerusalem: A Report on the Banality of Evil*. New York: Penguin.
———. 2018. *Thinking without a Banister: Essays in Understanding, 1953–1975*. New York: Schocken Books.
Arkin, Kimberly A. 2014. *Rhinestones, Religion, and the Republic: Fashioning Jewishness in France*. Stanford, CA: Stanford University Press.
Asad, Talal. 1993. *Genealogies of Religion: Discipline and Reasons of Power in Christianity and Islam*. Baltimore: Johns Hopkins University Press.
———. 1996. "Comments on Conversion." In *Conversion to Modernities: The Globalization of Christianity*, edited by Peter van der Veer, 263–73. New York: Routledge.
———. 2003. *Formations of the Secular: Christianity, Islam, Modernity*. Stanford, CA: Stanford University Press.
———. 2006. "Trying to Understand French Secularism." In *Political Theologies: Public*

Religions in a Post-Secular World, edited by Hent de Vries and Lawrence E. Sullivan, 494–526. New York: Fordham University Press.

———. 2018. *Secular Translations: Nation-State, Modern Self, and Calculative Reason.* New York: Columbia University Press.

Astell, Ann W. 2006. *Eating Beauty: The Eucharist and the Spiritual Arts of the Middle Ages.* Ithaca, NY: Cornell University Press.

Badiou, Alain. 2003. *Saint Paul: The Foundation of Universalism.* Stanford, CA: Stanford University Press.

Bakhtin, Mikhail Mikhailovich. 1981. *The Dialogic Imagination: Four Essays.* Edited by Michael Holquist. Translated by Caryl Emerson and Michael Holquist. Austin: University of Texas Press.

Balibar, Étienne. 2004. "Dissonances within Laïcité." *Constellations* 11 (3): 353–67.

Barjot, Frigide. 2010. "Les Journées des Bernardins: Frigide Barjot." Filmed May 29, 2010, at the Collège des Bernardins, Paris, France. Video, 20:06. https://www.dailymotion.com/video/xdi836.

Barthes, Roland. 1972. *Mythologies.* Translated by Annette Lavers. New York: Hill and Wang.

Bartley, Marvin. 2011. "Christianity's Catastrophic Gift." *Small Axe* 15 2 (35): 85–95.

Baubérot, Jean. 2004. *Laïcité 1905–2005: Entre passion et raison.* Paris: Seuil.

———. 2011. "Elisabeth Badinter et la laïcité lepénisée." Mediapart Blogs. September 30, 2011. https://blogs.mediapart.fr/jean-bauberot/blog/300911/elisabeth-badinter-et-la-laicite-lepenisee.

Baudelaire, Charles. 1846. "Salon de 1846." In *Baudelaire: Salon de 1846*, edited by David Kelley, 121–82. Oxford: Clarendon Press.

Baverel, Philippe. 2007. "D'Aaron à Jean-Marie, la liberté a guidé son existence." *Le Parisien*, August 6, 2007. http://www.leparisien.fr/societe/d-aaron-a-jean-marie-la-liberte-a-guide-son-existence-06-08-2007-2008268761.php.

Beardsley, Eleanor. 2019. "France's President Vows to Rebuild Notre Dame Cathedral." *Morning Edition, National Public Radio.* April 16, 2019. https://www.npr.org/2019/04/16/713809147/frances-president-vows-to-rebuild-notre-dame-cathedral.

Becker, Howard S. 1982. *Art Worlds.* Berkeley: University of California Press.

Bell, David A. 2001. *The Cult of the Nation in France: Inventing Nationalism, 1680–1800.* Cambridge, MA: Harvard University Press.

Bellah, Robert. 1974 [1967]. "Civil Religion in America." In *American Civil Religion.* edited by Russell E. Richey and Donald G. Jones, 40–41. New York: Harper & Row.

Belting, Hans. 1994. *Likeness and Presence: A History of the Image before the Era of Art.* Chicago: University of Chicago Press.

Bender, Courtney. 2010. *The New Metaphysicals: Spirituality and the American Religious Imagination.* Chicago: University of Chicago Press.

Benedict XVI. 2006. "Faith, Reason and the University: Memories and Reflections." The Vatican. Given on September 12, 2006, at University of Regensberg, Germany. Electronic document. https://w2.vatican.va/content/benedict-xvi/en/speeches/2006/september/documents/hf_ben-xvi_spe_20060912_university-regensburg.html.

———. 2008. "Meeting with the Representatives of the World of Culture." The Vatican.

Given September 12, 2008, at the Collège des Bernardins, Paris, France. Electronic document. http://w2.vatican.va/content/benedict-xvi/en/speeches/2008/september /documents/hf_ben-xvi_spe_20080912_parigi-cultura.html.

Benjamin, Walter. 1999. *The Arcades Project*. Translated by Howard Eiland and Kevin McLauglin. Cambridge, MA: Belknap Press of Harvard University Press.

———. 2002 [1936]. "The Work of Art in the Age of Mechanical Reproduction." In *Walter Benjamin: Selected Writings, Vol. 3: 1935–1938*, edited by Howard Eiland and Michael W. Jennings; translated by Edmund Jephcott et al., 101–33. Cambridge, MA: Harvard University Press.

———. 2006 [1940]. "On Some Motifs in Baudelaire." In *Walter Benjamin: Selected Writings, Vol. 4: 1938–1940*, edited by Howard Eiland and Michael W. Jennings; translated by Edmund Jephcott et al., 170–210. Cambridge, MA: Harvard University Press.

Bennett, Jane. 2012. *Vibrant Matter: A Political Ecology of Things*. Durham, NC: Duke University Press.

Bennett, Tony. 1995. *The Birth of the Museum: History, Theory, Politics*. New York: Routledge.

Bensoussan, Georges. 2010. "Éditorial." In *Catholiques et Protestants Français Après la Shoah*, edited by Danielle Delmaire and Georges Bensoussan, 5-21. *Revue d'histoire de la Shoah* 192. Mémorial de la Shoah, Janvier/Juin.

Bernstein, Anya. 2014. "The Post-Soviet Art Wars: Iconoclasm, Secularism, and Ways of Seeing Contemporary Russia." *Public Culture* 26: 419–48.

Blanchy, Lara. 2004. *Les expositions d'art contemporain dans les lieux de culte*. [Exhibitions of Contemporary Art in Religious Spaces.] Paris: Les Éditions Complictés.

Bonilla, Yarimar. 2015. *Non-Sovereign Futures: French Caribbean Politics in the Wake of Disenchantment*. Chicago: University of Chicago Press.

Boucheron, Patrick. 2013. "Religion civique, religion civile, religion séculière: L'ombre d'un doubte." *Revue de synthèse* 134 (2): 161–83.

Boudon, Jacques-Olivier. 2001. *Paris: Capitale religieuse sous le Second Empire*. Paris: Cerf.

Boulard, Fernand, and Gabriel Le Bras. 1952. *Carte religieuse de la France rurale*. Paris: Éditions des Cahiers du clergé rural.

Bourdieu, Pierre. 1977. *Distinction: A Social Critique of the Judgement of Taste*. Translated by Richard Nice. Cambridge, MA: Harvard University Press.

Boym, Svetlana. 2001. *The Future of Nostalgia*. New York: Basic Books.

Braudel, Fernand. 1958. "Histoire et science sociales: La longue durée." *Annales* 13: 725–53.

Brown, Steven, ed. 2013. *Pope Benedict XVI, A Reason Open to God: On Universities, Education, and Culture*. Washington, DC: Catholic University of America Press.

Buck-Morss, Susan. 1986. "The Flaneur, the Sandwichman and the Whore: The Politics of Loitering." *New German Critique* 39 (Autumn): 99–140.

Buttici, Annalisa. 2016. *African Pentecostals in Catholic Europe: The Politics of Presence in the Twenty-First Century*. Cambridge, MA: Harvard University Press.

Byrne, Julie. 2016. *The Other Catholics: Remaking America's Largest Religion*. New York: Columbia University Press.

Calhoun, Craig. 2010. "Rethinking Secularism." *Hedgehog Review* 12 (3): 35–48.

Camiscioli, Elisa. 2009. *Reproducing the French Race: Immigration, Intimacy, and Embodiment in the Early Twentieth Century*. Durham, NC: Duke University Press.

Carruthers, Mary. 2000. *The Craft of Thought: Meditation, Rhetoric, and the Making of Images, 400–1200*. Cambridge: Cambridge University Press.

Casanova, José. 1994. *Public Religions in the Modern World*. Chicago: University of Chicago Press.

———. 2015 [2012]. "Are We Still Secular? Explorations on the Secular and Post-Secular." In *Post-Secular Society*, edited by Peter Nynäs, Mika Lassander, and Terhi Utriainen, 27–47. New Brunswick; London: Transaction Publishers.

Chakrabarty, Dipesh. 1997. "The Time of History and the Times of Gods." In *The Politics of Culture in the Shadow of Capital*, edited by Lisa Lowe and David Lloyd, 35–60. Durham, NC: Duke University Press.

———. 2000. *Provincializing Europe: Postcolonial Thought and Historical Difference*. Princeton, NJ: Princeton University Press.

Chappel, James. 2011. "The Catholic Origins of Totalitarianism Theory in Interwar Europe." *Modern Intellectual History* 8 (3): 561–90.

Chauni, Pierre, and Eric Mension-Rigau. 1996. *Baptême de Clovis, baptême de la France*. Paris: Éditions Balland.

"Claudio Parmiggiani." 2009. *Télérama Sortir* No. 3078. January 7 : 30.

Cohen, Ilan Duran, dir. 2013. *Le Métis de Dieu*. New York: Film Movement.

Connelly, John. 2012. *From Enemy to Brother: The Revolution in Catholic Teaching on the Jews, 1933–1965*. Cambridge, MA: Harvard University Press.

Coomans, Thomas. 2015. "L'order autour du cloître: L'architecture des abbayes et des couvents, entre traditions, réformes et réaffectations." In *Des couvents en héritage: Religious Houses: A Legacy*, edited by Luc Noppen, Thomas Coomans, and Martin Drouin, 13–109. Québec City: Presses de l'Université du Québec.

Corbin, Alain. 1994. *Les cloches de la terre: Paysage sonore et culture sensible dans les campagnes au XIXe siècle*. Paris: Flammarion.

Cottin, Jérôme. 2007. *La mystique de l'art: Art et christianisme de 1900 à nos jours*. Paris: Cerf.

Dagens, Claude. 1996. "Lettre aux catholiques de France: 'Proposer la foi dans la société actuelle.'" Electronic document. Église catholique en France. Conférence des Évêques de France. November 9, 1996. https://ec.cef.fr/wp-content/uploads/sites/2/2014/05/dagens.pdf. Accessed January 16, 2020.

Davidson, Naomi. 2012. *Only Muslim: Embodying Islam in Twentieth-Century France*. Ithaca, NY: Cornell University Press.

Davie, Grace. 1994. *Religion in Britain since 1945: Believing without Belonging*. London: Blackwell.

Davis, Kathleen. 2008. *Periodization and Sovereignty: How Ideas of Feudalism and Secularization Govern the Politics of Time*. Philadelphia: University of Pennsylvania Press.

de Charentenay, Pierre. 2009. *Les nouvelles frontières de la laïcité*. Paris: Desclée de Bouwer.

de Feydeau, Bertrand. 2017. *Au côté du Cardinal Lustiger*. Paris: Cerf.

Delmaire, Danielle and Georges Bensoussan, eds. 2010. *Catholiques et protestants après la Shoah. Revue d'histoire de la Shoah* 192. Mémorial de la Shoah, Janvier/Juin.

de Moulins-Beaufort, Éric. 2010. "Racines chrétiennes de la devise républicaine." In *Jean-Marie Lustiger cardinal républicain*, edited by Matthieu Rougé, 41–69. Paris: Parole et Silence.

Derrida, Jacques. 1995. *Archive Fever: A Freudian Impression.* Translated by Eric Prenowitz. Chicago: University of Chicago Press.

de Souza, Father Raymond J. 2018. "The Benedict XVI Speech That Everyone Missed." *Catholic Education Resource Center.* Web Document. https://www.catholiceducation .org/en/religion-and-philosophy/faith-and-reason/the-benedict-xvi-speech-that -everyone-missed.html. Accessed June 1, 2019.

Dittgen, Alfred. 1993. "Les mariages religieux en France." *La Maison-Dieu* 194: 97–122.

Druckerman, Pamela. 2012. *Bringing Up Bébé: One American Mother Discovers the Wisdom of French Parenting.* New York: Penguin.

Duchesne, Jean, ed. 2010. *Cardinal Jean-Marie Lustiger on Christians and Jews.* New York: Paulist Press.

Duncan, Carol. 1995a. *Civilizing Rituals: Inside Public Art Museums.* New York: Routledge.

———. 1995b. The Art Museum as Ritual. *Art Bulletin* 77: 10–13.

Durkheim, Émile. 1995 [1912]. *The Elementary Forms of Religious Life.* Translated by Karen E. Fields. New York: Free Press.

Eagleton, Terry. 1990. *The Ideology of the Aesthetic.* Oxford: Basil Blackwell.

———. 2002. "Capitalism and Form." *New Left Review* 14 (Mar/Apr): 119–31.

Elineau, Dorothée. 1997. *La catéchèse en Pays-de-la-Loire: Un héritage en voie de disparition? Norois* 44 (174): 306–16.

———. 2000. *Églises, sociétés et térritoires: Paroisses et paroissiens dans les Pays de la Loire.* PhD diss., Le Mans Université.

Elkins, James. 2004. *On the Strange Place of Religion in Contemporary Art.* New York: Routledge.

Ellison, Ralph. 1981 [1952]. "Introduction." In *Invisible Man*, vii–xxiii. New York: Random House.

Emery, Elizabeth. 2000. "The 'Truth' about the Late Middle Ages: *La Revue des Deux Mondes* and Late Nineteenth-Century French Medievalism." *Prose Studies* 23 (2): 99–114.

———. 2001. *Romancing the Cathedral: Gothic Architecture in Fin-de-Siècle French Culture.* New York: State University of New York Press.

Emon, Anver M. 2006. "On the Pope, Cartoons, and Apostates. Shari'a 2006." *Journal of Law and Religion* 22: 303–21.

Engelke, Matthew. 2007. *A Problem of Presence: Beyond Scripture in an African Church.* Berkeley: University of California Press.

———. 2009. "Reading and Time: Two Approaches to the Materiality of Scripture." *Ethnos* 74 (2): 151–74.

———. 2013. *God's Agents: Biblical Publicity in Contemporary England.* Berkeley: University of California Press.

Englund, Steven. 2007. "'*Le Bulldozer*': The Achievement of Cardinal Jean-Marie Lustiger." *Commonweal* 124 (20): 12–14.

———. 2008. "How Catholic Is France? You Might Be Surprised." *Commonweal*, November 7, 2008.

———. 2014. "'What Our Church Has Inflicted on Judaism': An Exchange on Catholic-Jewish Dialogue." *Commonweal*, February 10, 2014. https://www.commonweal magazine.org/what-our-church-has-inflicted-judaism.

Evans-Pritchard, E. E. 1976 [1937]. *Witchcraft, Oracles and Magic among the Azande.* Oxford: Clarendon Press.

"Exposition Claudio Parmiggiani: Dossier de Presse." 2008. Collège des Bernardins. Electronic document. https://www.collegedesbernardins.fr/qui-sommes-nous/exposition -claudio-parmiggiani. Accessed February 4, 2020.

Fabian, Johannes. 2002 [1983]. *Time and the Other: How Anthropology Makes Its Object.* New York: Columbia University Press.

Fanon, Frantz. 1986 [1952]. *Black Skin, White Masks.* Translated by Charles Lam Markman. London: Pluto Press.

Fassin, Éric. 2016. "Gender and the Problem of Universals: Catholic Mobilizations and Sexual Democracy in France." *Religion & Gender* 6 (2): 173–86.

Feldman, Hannah. 2014. *From a Nation Torn: Decolonizing Art and Representation in France, 1945–1962.* Durham, NC: Duke University Press.

Fernando, Mayanthi. 2013. "Save the Muslim Woman, Save the Republic: Ni Putes Ni Soumises and the Ruse of Neoliberal Sovereignty." *Modern and Contemporary France* 21 (2): 147–65.

———. 2014. *The Republic Unsettled: Muslim French and the Contradictions of Secularism.* Durham, NC: Duke University Press.

Fessenden, Tracy. 2007. *Culture and Redemption: Religion, the Secular, and American Literature.* Princeton, NJ: Princeton University Press.

Fredriksen, Paula. 2002. "The Birth of Christianity and the Origins of Christian Anti-Judaism." In *Jesus, Judaism, and Christian Anti-Judaism: Reading the New Testament after the Holocaust*, edited by Paula Fredriksen and Adele Reinharz, 8–30. Westminster: John Knox Press.

Fields, Karen E., and Barbara J. Fields. 2014. *Racecraft: The Soul of Inequality in American Life.* New York: Verso Books.

"Foi et culture chez Benoît XVI". 2013. Collège des Bernardins. Filmed February 26, 2013, at the Collège des Bernardins, Paris, France. Video, 52:19. http://www.collegedes bernardins.fr/fr/evenements-culture/conferences-et-debats/foi-et-culture-chez -benoit-xvi.html.

Folscheid, Claire. 2008. "Quand l'art contemporain rejoint le 'génie d'un lieu." *Paris Notre-Dame* 126 (November 20): 6–8.

Foucault, Michel. 1977. *Discipline and Punish: The Birth of the Prison.* New York: Vintage Random House.

———. 1978. *The History of Sexuality*, Vol. 1: An Introduction. New York: Vintage Random House.

Friedman, Vanessa. 2019. "French Titans' Pledges to Notre-Dame Pass 850 Million

Euros." *New York Times*, April 16, 2019. https://www.nytimes.com/2019/04/16/fashion
/Donations-notre-dame-fire.html.

Gal, Susan. 2002. "A Semiotics of the Public/Private Distinction." *Differences: A Journal of Feminist Cultural Studies* 13 (1): 77-95.

Gamboni, Dario. 1997. *The Destruction of Art: Iconoclasm and Vandalism since the French Revolution*. London: Reaktion Books.

Gauchet, Marcel. 1985. *Le désenchantement du monde: Une histoire politique de la religion*. Paris: Gallimard.

Gaudry, Adam, and Darryl Leroux. 2017. "White Settler Revisionism and Making Métis Everywhere: The Evocation of Métissage in Quebec and Nova Scotia." *Critical Ethnic Studies* 3 (1): 116-42.

Geary, Patrick J. 1991 [1978]. *Furta Sacra: Thefts of Relics in the Central Middle Ages*. Princeton, NJ: Princeton University Press.

———. 1994. *Living with the Dead in the Middle Ages*. Ithaca, NY: Cornell University Press.

———. 2002. *The Myth of Nations: The Medieval Origins of Europe*. Princeton, NJ: Princeton University Press.

"Gérard Titus-Carmel au Collège des Bernardins." 2009. *Collège des Bernardins*. http://www.dailymotion.com/video/xf09bb_gerard-titus-carmel-au-college-des_creation.

Gilbert, Andrew. 2019. "Beyond Nostalgia: Other Historical Emotions." *History and Anthropology*, DOI: 10.1080/02757206.2019.1579089.

Glaeser, Stephanie A. 2004. "Of Revolutions, Republics and Spires: Nineteenth-Century France and the Gothic Cathedral." In *Signs of Change: Transformations of Christian Traditions and Their Representation in the Arts, 1000–2000*, edited by Nils Holger Petersen, Claus Clüver, and Nicolas Bell, 453–74. Amsterdam: Rodopi.

"'Golgotha Picnic': Deux intégristes interpellés au sous-sol du theater du Rond-Point." 2011. Le Point, December 3, 2011. https://www.lepoint.fr/culture/golgotha-picnic
-deux-integristes-interpelles-au-sous-sol-du-theatre-du-rond-point-03-12-2011
-1403456_3.php.

Gombrich, Ernst H. 2008 [1950]. *Histoire de l'art*. Paris: Phaidon.

Graeber, David. 2001. *Toward an Anthropological Theory of Value: The False Coin of Our Own Dreams*. New York: Palgrave MacMillan.

Graeber, David. 2014 [2011]. *Debt: The First 5,000 Years*. Brooklyn; London: Melville House.

Grenier, Catherine. 2003. *L'art contemporain: Est-il chrétien?* Nîmes: Éditions Jacqueline Chambon.

———. 2008. *Claudio Parmiggiani*. Paris: Actes Sud.

Guiliano, Mireille. 2004. *French Women Don't Get Fat*. New York: Knopf.

Guissard, Lucien, ed. 1998. *Le pari de la presse chrétienne*. Paris: Bayard-Le Centurion.

Hann, Chris. 2014. "The Heart of the Matter: Christianity, Materiality, and Modernity." In special issue, "The Anthropology of Christianity: Unity, Diversity, New Directions," *Current Anthropology* 55 (S10): S182–S192.

Hansen, Miriam B. 2012. *Cinema and Experience: Siegfried Kracauer, Walter Benjamin, and Theodor W. Adorno*. Berkeley: University of California Press.

Hanson, Ellis. 1997. *Decadence and Catholicism*. Cambridge, MA: Harvard University Press.

Haraway, Donna. 1985. "A Manifesto for Cyborgs: Science, Technology, and Socialist Feminism for the 1980s." *Socialist Review* 80 (March-April): 65–107.

Hardwick, Elizabeth. 1975. "Reflections on Simone Weil." *Signs* 1 (1): 83–91.

Harris, Olivia. 2006. "The Eternal Return of Conversion: Christianity as Contested Domain in Highland Bolivia." In *The Anthropology of Christianity*, edited by Fenella Cannell, 51–76. Durham, NC: Duke University Press.

Harris, Ruth. 1999. *Lourdes: Body and Spirit in the Secular Age*. New York: Penguin Compass.

Harvey, David. 2006. *Paris, Capital of Modernity*. New York: Routledge.

Hazareesingh, Sudhir. 1988. *From Subject to Citizen: The Second Empire and the Emergence of Modern French Democracy*. Princeton, NJ: Princeton University Press.

Heartney, Eleanor. 2018 [2004]. *Postmodern Heretics: The Catholic Imagination in Contemporary Art*. Second Edition. London: Silver Hollow Press.

Heller-Roazen, Daniel. 2002. "Tradition's Destruction: On the Library of Alexandria." *October* 100: 133–53.

Hemmerdinger, Bertrand. 1985. "Que César n'a pas brulé la bibliothèque d'Alexandre." *Bollettino dei classici* 3 (6): 76–77.

Hervieu-Léger, Danièle. 1996. "'Une Messe Est Possible': Les doubles funérailles du Président" ["A Mass Is Possible": The Double Funerals of the President]. *Le Débat* 4 (91): 23–30.

———. 2001. *Religion as a Chain of Memory*. Translated by Simon Lee. New Brunswick, NJ: Rutgers University Press.

Holmes, Douglas R. 2000. *Integral Europe: Fast-Capitalism, Multiculturalism, Neofascism*. Princeton, NJ: Princeton University Press.

Holsinger, Bruce. 2005. *The Premodern Condition: Medievalism and the Making of Theory*. Chicago: University of Chicago Press.

Houellebecq, Michel. 2015. *Submission: A Novel*. Translated by Lorin Stein. New York: Farrar, Straus and Giroux.

Hugh of St. Victor. 1951. *On the Sacraments of the Christian Faith (De Sacramentis)*. Translated by Roy. J. Deferrari. Book II, Part VIII: On the Sacrament of the Body and Blood of Christ, 304–15. Cambridge, MA: Medieval Academy of America.

"Huit siècles d'histoire." Collège des Bernardins. Electronic document. http://www .collegedesbernardins.fr/fr/le-college/histoire/huit-siecles-d-histoire.html. Accessed March 14, 2016.

Huysmans, Joris-Karl. 1976. *Grünewald. With an Essay by J-K Huysmans*. Translated by Robert Baldick. Oxford: Phaidon.

———. 2013 [1908]. *Trois églises et trois primitifs*. Paris: Hachette Livre-BNF.

"Inauguration du Collège des Bernardins." 2008. Collège des Bernardins. Electronic document. http://www.collegedesbernardins.fr/fr/espace-presse/communiques-et -dossiers/8018-inauguration-du-college-des-bernardins.html. Accessed March 14, 2016.

Jaigu, Charles. 2007. "Sarkozy nationalise l'hommage à Lustiger." *Le Figaro*, August 10: 6.

Jakobsen, Janet R., and Ann Pellegrini. 2008. "Introduction: Times Like These." In *Secularisms*, edited by Janet R. Jakobsen and Ann Pellegrini, 1–35. Durham, NC: Duke University Press.

Kandinsky, Wassily. 1989 [1954]. *Du Spirituel dans l'Art, et dans la peinture en particulier.* Paris: Éditions Denoël.

Keane, Webb. 1997. "Religious Language." *Annual Review of Anthropology* 26: 47–71.

———. 2007. *Christian Moderns: Freedom & Fetish in the Mission Encounter.* Berkeley: University of California Press.

Kempers, Bram. 1987. *Painting, Power, and Patronage: The Rise of the Professional Artist in Renaissance Italy.* London: Penguin Books.

Kertzer, David I. 2001. *The Popes against the Jews: The Vatican's Role in the Rise of Modern Anti-Semitism.* New York: Vintage Books.

Klassen, Pamela E., and John W. Marshall. 2012. "Paul, Badiou, and the Politics of Ritual Repudiation." *History of Religions* 51 (4): 344–63.

Klassen, Pamela E. 2015. "Fantasies of Sovereignty: Civic Secularism in Canada." *Critical Research on Religion* 3 (1): 41–56.

Klassen, Pamela E., and Monique Scheer. 2018. "The Difference That Christmas Makes: Thoughts on Christian Affordances in Multicultural Societies." In *The Public Work of Christmas: Difference and Belonging in Multicultural Societies*, edited by Pamela E. Klassen and Monique Scheer, 3–16. Montreal: McGill-Queen's University Press.

Knausgaard, Karl Ove. 2015. "Michel Houellebecq's 'Submission.'" *New York Times*, November 2, 2015. http://www.nytimes.com/2015/11/08/books/review/michel -houellebecqs-submission.html.

Kohn, Jerome. 2018. "Introduction." In *Thinking without a Banister: Hannah Arendt, Essays in Understanding 1953–1975*, edited by Jerome Kohn, ix–xxx. New York: Schocken Books.

Kosky, Jeffrey. 2013. *Arts of Wonder: Enchanting Secularity—Walter DeMaria, Diller + Scofidio, James Turrell, Andy Goldsworthy.* Chicago: University of Chicago Press.

Kristeva, Julia. 1985 [1977]. "Stabat Mater." Translated by Arthur Goldhammer. *Poetics Today* 6 (1/2): 133–52.

———. 2008. "La parole, cette expérience." In *Chercher Dieu: Discours au monde de la culture*, 35–42. Paris: Parole et Silence.

Laborde, Cécile. 2008. *Critical Republicanism: The Hijab Controversy and Political Philosophy.* Oxford: Oxford University Press.

Lambek, Michael. 2013. "What Is 'Religion' for Anthropology? And What Has Anthropology Brought to 'Religion'?" In *A Companion to the Anthropology of Religion*, edited by Janice Boddy and Michael Lambek, 25–60. Malden, MA: Wiley Blackwell.

Landron, Olivier. 2004. *Les communautés nouvelles: Nouveaux visages du catholicisme français.* Paris: L'Edition du Cerf.

Larkin, Maurice J. M. 1964. "The Vatican, French Catholics, and the Associations Cultuelles." *Journal of Modern History* 36 (3): 298–317.

Lautsi and others v. Italy. Application no. 30814/06. Grand Chamber. European Court of Human Rights. Judgment. Strasbourg: March 18, 2011. http//www.echr.coe.int/echr /resources/hudoc/lautsi_and_others_v_italy.pdf.

Lavergnat, Jean. 2007. "Le Diocèse de Paris après le Cardinal Lustiger: Quelques questions sur les choix de l'Église à Paris." *Esprit* 338 (10): 163–68.

Lavigne, Jean-Claude. 1996. *Petit dictionnaire de la Charité*. Paris: Desclée de Brouwer.

Leclerq, Dom Jean. 1971. "The Monastic Crisis of the Eleventh and Twelfth Centuries." In *Cluniac Monasticism in the Central Middle Ages*, edited by Noreen Hunt, 217–37. London: MacMillan.

———. 1976. *Bernard of Clairvaux and the Cistercian Spirit*. Kalamazoo: Cistercian Publications.

Lee, Richard E. 2018. "Lessons of the Longue Durée: The Legacy of Fernand Braudel." *Historia Critica* 69: 69–77. http://dx.doi.org.proxy.library.nyu.edu/10.7440/histcrit69.2018.04

Le Goff, Jacques. 1983. "Pour un autre moyen âge." *Europe* 654: 19–24.

Le Mitouard, Eric. 2000. "La nouvelle vocation du couvent des Bernardins." *Le Journal de Paris*, December 19, 2000, 1.

Lester, Rebecca J. 2003. "The Immediacy of Eternity: Time and Transformation in a Roman Catholic Convent." *Religion* 33 (3): 201–19.

Lloyd, Vincent. 2011. *The Problem with Grace: Reconfiguring Political Theology*. Stanford, CA: Stanford University Press.

Lofton, Kathryn. 2017. *Consuming Religion*. Chicago: University of Chicago Press.

Lustiger, Jean-Marie. 1987. *Le Choix de Dieu: Entretiens avec Jean-Louis Missika et Dominique Wolton*. Paris: Éditions de Fallois.

———. 2007. "Les 'coups de guele' du cardinal." *Le Monde*, August 11, 2007, 7.

———. 2010. "Notre Laïcité." In *Jean-Marie Lustiger cardinal républicain*, edited by Matthieu Rougé, 155–76. Paris: Parole et Silence.

Luther, Martin. 2015. "Against the Heavenly Prophets in the Matter of Images and Sacraments, 1525." In *The Annotated Luther. Volume 2: Word and Faith*, edited by Kirsi I. Stjerna, Hans J. Hillerband, and Timothy J. Wengert, 39–126. Minneapolis, MN: Augsburg Fortress Press.

Macdonald, Sharon. 2008. "Museum Europe: Negotiating Heritage." *Anthropological Journal of European Cultures* 17 (2): 47–65.

Macron, Emmanuel. "Discours du Président de la République Emmanuel Macron au Collège des Bernardins." 2018. Filmed April 4, 2018, at the Collège des Bernardins, Paris, France. Video, 57:43. https://www.youtube.com/watch?v=S15bhblIQME.

Mahmood, Saba. 2005. *Politics of Piety: The Islamic Revival and the Feminist Subject*. Princeton, NJ: Princeton University Press.

———. 2016. *Religious Difference in a Secular Age: A Minority Report*. Princeton, NJ: Princeton University Press.

Maréchal, Élie. 2000. "La renaissance du couvent des Bernardins." *Le Figaro*, December 16–17, 2000.

Marion, Jean-Luc. 2017. *Brève apologie pour un moment catholique*. Paris: Grasset.

Marshall, Ruth. 2009. *Political Spiritualities: The Pentecostal Revolution in Nigeria*. Chicago: University of Chicago Press.

Martin, David. 2005. *On Secularization: A Revised General Theory*. London: Ashgate.

Masuzawa, Tomoko. 2005. *The Invention of World Religion: Or, How European Universalism Was Preserved in the Language of Pluralism*. Chicago: University of Chicago Press.

Mayblin, Maya. 2017. "The Lapsed and the Laity: Discipline and Leniance in the Study of Religion." *Journal of the Royal Anthropological Institute* 23: 503–22.

Mayblin, Maya, Kristin Norget, and Valentina Napolitano. 2017. "Introduction." In *The Anthropology of Catholicism*, edited by Kristen Norget, Valentina Napolitano, and Maya Mayblin, 1–29. Oakland: University of California Press.

Mazzarella, William. 2003. *Shoveling Smoke: Advertising and Globalization in Contemporary India*. Durham, NC: Duke University Press.

McClellan Andrew. 1994. *Inventing the Louvre: Arts, Politics and the Origins of the Modern Museum in Eighteenth-Century Paris*. Cambridge: Cambridge University Press.

"Médaille d'or pour le Collège des Bernardins." 2009. *Le Figaro*, February 17, 2009.

Meltzer, Françoise. 2001. "The Hands of Simone Weil." *Critical Inquiry* 27 (4): 611–28.

Mercator, Paul. 1997. *La fin des paroisses?* Paris: Desclée de Brouwer.

Meyer, Birgit. 2015a. *Sensational Movies: Video, Vision, and Christianity in Ghana*. Oakland: University of California Press.

———. 2015b. "Picturing the Invisible: Visual Culture and the Study of Religion." *Method and Theory in the Study of Religion* 27: 333–60.

Meyer, Jerry D. 1997. "Profane and Sacred: Religious Imagery and Prophetic Expression in Contemporary Art." *Journal of American Academy of Religion* 65 (1): 19–46.

Milbank, John. 2006 [1990]. *Theology and Social Theory: Beyond Secular Reason*. Second Edition. Malden, MA: Blackwell.

Millet, Catherine. 2002 [2001]. *The Sexual Life of Catherine M*. Translated by Adriana Hunter. New York: Grove Press.

Mitchell, W. J. T. 2005. *What Do Pictures Want? The Lives and Loves of Images*. Chicago: University of Chicago Press.

Moore, Brenna. 2013. *Sacred Dread: Raïssa Maritain, the Allure of Suffering, and the French Catholic Revival (1905–1944)*. Notre Dame, IN: University of Notre Dame Press.

Morgan, David. 2007. *The Lure of Images: A History of Religion and Visual Media in America*. London; New York: Routledge.

Morgan, David. 2009. "Enchantment, Disenchantment, Re-Enchantment." In *Re-Enchantment*, edited by James Elkin and David Morgan. 3–22. New York: Routledge.

Morgan, David. 2012. *The Embodied Eye: Religious Visual Culture and the Social Life of Feeling*. Berkeley: University of California Press.

Moxey, Keith. 2004. "Impossible Distance: Past and Present in the Study of Dürer and Grünewald." *Art Bulletin* 86 (4): 750–63.

Muehlebach, Andrea. 2012. *The Moral Neoliberal: Welfare and Citizenship in Italy*. Chicago: University of Chicago Press.

———. 2013. "The Catholicization of Neoliberalism: On Love and Welfare in Lombardy, Italy." *American Anthropologist* 115 (3): 452–65.

Mukerji, Chandra. 2012. "Space and Political Pedagogy at the Gardens of Versailles." *Public Culture* 24 (3): 509–34.

Muller, Colette. 1990. "La Presse catholique en France." *Atlas Social de Basse-Normandie.* Caen.

Muller, Colette, and Jean-René Bertrand. 2002. *Où sont passés les catholiques?* Paris: Desclée de Brouwer.

Murphy, Keith M. 2015. *Swedish Design: An Ethnography.* Ithaca, NY: Cornell University Press.

Myers, Fred R. 2002. *Painting Culture: The Making of an Aboriginal High Art.* Durham, NC: Duke University Press.

Nagel, Alexander. 2004. "Fashion and the Now-Time of Renaissance Art." *RES: Anthropology and Aesthetics* 46: 32–52.

———. 2012. *Medieval Modern: Art Out of Time.* London: Thames & Hudson.

Nancy, Jean-Luc. 2005. *The Ground of the Image.* Translated by Jeff Fort. New York: Fordham University Press.

———. 2006. "Church, State, Resistance." In *Political Theologies: Public Religions in a Post-Secular World*, edited by Hent de Vries and Lawrence E. Sullivan, 102–12. New York: Fordham University Press.

Napolitano, Valentina. 2016. *Migrant Hearts and the Atlantic Return: Transnationalism and the Roman Catholic Church.* New York: Fordham University Press.

Nelson, Robert. 2007. *Spirit of Secular Art: A History of the Sacramental Roots of Contemporary Artistic Values.* Victoria, Australia: Monah University Press.

Nichols, Aidan. 1980. *The Art of God Incarnate: Theology and Image in the Christian Tradition.* London: Darton, Longman and Todd.

Nirenberg, David. 2013. *Anti-Judaism: The Western Tradition.* New York: W. W. Norton.

———. 2015. *Aesthetic Theology and Its Enemies: Judaism in Christian Painting, Poetry, and Politics.* Waltham, MA: Brandeis University Press.

Nora, Pierre. 1989. "Between Memory and History: *Les Lieux de Mémoire.*" *Representations* 26: 7–24.

"Notre-Dame de Paris: le résumé du discours d'Emmanuel Macron." *Le Monde*, April 16, 2019. https://www.lemonde.fr/societe/video/2019/04/16/notre-dame-de-paris-le -resume-du-discours-d-emmanuel-macron_5451201_3224.html.

Oliphant, Elayne. 2012. "The Crucifix as a Symbol of Secular Europe: The Unlikely Semiotics of the European Court of Human Rights." *Anthropology Today* 28 (2): 16–18.

Oliphant, Elayne 2019. "Christ in the Banlieue: The Passionate Infrastructure of the French Catholic Church." *Exchanges* 48, no. 3: 236-250.

Open Society Foundation. 2011. *Unveiling the Truth: Why 32 Women Wear the Full Face-Veil in France.* An At Home in Europe Project. New York: Open Society Foundation.

Orsi, Robert A. 2012. "Material Children: Making God's Presence Real through Catholic Boys and Girls." In *Religion, Media and Culture: A Reader*, edited by Gordon Lynch, Jolyon Mitchell, and Anna Strhan, 147–58. London: Routledge.

Orsi, Robert A. 2016. *History and Presence.* Cambridge, MA: Belknap Press of Harvard University Press.

O'Sullivan, Noel. 2008. "The Catholic Church in France." Electronic document. Glanmire Parish. October 5, 2008. http://www.glanmireparish.ie/temp/the-catholic-church-in -france-by-fr-noel-osullivan/. Accessed January 16, 2020.

Pagden, Anthony, ed. 2002. *The Idea of Europe: From Antiquity to the European Union.* New York: Cambridge University Press.

Panofsky, Erwin. 1951. *Gothic Architecture and Scholasticism.* Latrobe, PA: St. Vincent Archabby Press.

Pfeifer, Michaela. 2018. "Hot Potatoes of Monastic History—Still Current?" *American Benedictine Review* 69 (3): 237–47.

Pietralunga, Cédric, and Olivier Faye. 2019. "Baisse d'impôt, ENA, proportionnelle . . . Ce qu'Emmanuel Macron devait annoncer aux Français à l'issue du grand débat." *Le Monde,* April 16, 2019. https://www.lemonde.fr/politique/article/2019/04/16/baisse -d-impot-proportionnelle-ce-que-macron-devait-annoncer-aux-francais-a-1-issue -du-grand-debat_5451008_823448.html.

Pietz, William. 1985. "The Problem of the Fetish I." *RES: Anthropology and Aesthetics* 9: 5–17.

———. 1987. "The Problem of the Fetish II: The Origin of the Fetish." *RES: Anthropology and Aesthetics* 13: 23–45.

———. 1988. "The Problem of the Fetish IIIa: Bosman's Guinea and the Enlightenment Theory of Fetishism." *RES: Anthropology and Aesthetics* 16: 105–24.

Pigozzi, Caroline. 2007. "Le Cardinal Lustiger." *Paris Match,* August 9–15, 2007, 43–45.

Pontifical Council for the Family. 2006 [2003]. *Lexicon: Ambiguous and Debatable Terms Regarding Family Life and Ethical Questions.* Front Royal, VA: Human Life International.

Poole, Deborah. 1997. *Vision, Race, and Modernity: A Visual Economy of the Andean Image World.* Princeton, NJ: Princeton University Press.

Portier, Philippe. 2010. "La philosophie du cardinal Lustiger: Éléments d'analyse." In *Jean-Marie Lustiger cardinal républicain,* edited by Matthieu Rougé, 13–31. Paris: Parole et Silence.

Poulot, Dominique. 1994. "L'Élysée du Musée des monuments français: un jardin de la mémoire sous le Premier Empire." *Dalhousie French Studies* 29 (Winter): 159–68.

Povoledo, Elisabetta. 2018. "The Most Surprising Entry in Venice's Biennale? The Vatican's." *New York Times,* May 25, 2018. https://www.nytimes.com/2018/05/25/arts /design/venices-architecture-biennale-the-vatican.html?action=click&module= MoreInSection&pgtype=Article&region=Footer&contentCollection=Arts.

Quatremère de Quincy, Antoine-Chrysostome. 1989. *Lettres à Miranda sur le déplacement des monuments de l'art de l'Italie* [Letters to Miranda on the Displacement of Art Monuments in Italy]. Paris: Persée.

Rabinow, Paul. 1989. *French Modern: Norms and Forms of the Social Environment.* Chicago: University of Chicago Press.

Ralph, Michael. 2015. *Forensics of Capital.* Chicago: University of Chicago Press.

Rancière, Jacques. 2002. "The Aesthetic Revolution and Its Outcomes: Employments of Autonomy and Heteronomy." *New Left Review* 14 (March/April): 133–51.

———. 2004. *The Politics of Aesthetics: The Distribution of the Sensible.* Translated by Gabriel Rockhill. London: Continuum.

Raphelson, Samantha. 2019. "Yellow Vest Protesters Fueled by Anger over Notre Dame Funds March in Paris." *National Public Radio,* April 20, 2019. https://www.npr.org

/2019/04/20/715470174/yellow-vest-protesters-fueled-by-anger-over-notre-dame
-funds-march-in-paris.

Recht, Roland. 2008 [1999]. *Penser le patrimoine: Mise en scène et mise en ordre de l'art.*
Second Edition. Paris: Éditions Hazan.

Renan, Ernest. 1974 [1863]. *Vie de Jésus.* Paris: Gallimard.

———. 2018 [1882]. *What Is a Nation? and Other Political Writings.* Translated by M. F. N.
Giglioli. New York: Columbia University Press.

Reuters. 2019. "LVMH and Arnault Will Not Get Tax Breaks from Notre-Dame Donations." *Business of Fashion,* April 18, 2019. https://www.businessoffashion.com/
articles/news-analysis/lvmh-and-arnault-will-not-get-tax-breaks-from-notre-dame
-donations.

Robbins, Joel. 2003. "What Is a Christian? Notes toward an Anthropology of Christianity." *Religion* 33 (3): 191–99.

———. 2007. "Continuity Thinking and the Problem of Christian Culture: Belief, Time,
and the Anthropology of Christianity." *Current Anthropology* 48 (1): 5–38.

———. 2010. "Anthropology, Pentecostalism, and the New Paul: Conversion, Event, and
Social Transformation." *South Atlantic Quarterly* 109 (4): 633–52.

———. 2012. "Transcendence and the Anthropology of Christianity." *Sumen Antropologi:
Journal of the Finnish Anthropological Society* 37 (2): 5–23.

Robcis, Camille. 2015a. "Catholics, the 'Theory of Gender,' and the Turn to the Human in
France: A New Dreyfus Affair?" *Journal of Modern History* 87 (3): 892–923.

———. 2015b. "Liberté, Egalité, Hétérosexualité: Race and Reproduction in the French
Gay Marriage Debates." *Constellations* 22 (3): 447–61.

Robin, Corey. 2015. "The Trials of Hannah Arendt." *The Nation,* June 1, 2019, 12–25.

Roehl, Richard. 1969. "Plan and Reality in a Medieval Monastic Economy: The Cistercians." *Journal of Economic History* 29 (1): 180–82.

Rouche, Michel. 2008. "La Naissance de l'Université de Paris." In *Le Collège des Bernardins,* edited by Vincent Aucante, 37–51. Paris: Association du 18–24 rue de Poissy.

Rougé, Mathieu, 2010. "Introduction." In *Jean-Marie Lustiger cardinal républicain,* edited
by Matthieu Rougé, 5–11. Paris: Parole et Silence.

Rousso, Henry. 1991. *The Vichy Syndrome: History and Memory in France since 1944.*
Translated by Arthur Goldhammer. Cambridge, MA: Harvard University Press.

Rudolph, Conrad. 1990. *The 'Things of Greater Importance': Bernard of Clairvaux's Apologia and the Medieval Attitude toward Art.* Philadelphia: University of Pennsylvania
Press.

Ruprecht, Louis A., Jr. 2014. "Classics at the Dawn of the Museum Era: The Life and
Times of Antoine Chrysostome Quatremère de Quincy (1755–1849)." *Arion: A Journal
of Humanities and the Classics* 22 (1): 133–74.

Sahlins, Marshall. 1993. "The Sadness of Sweetness: The Native Anthropology of Western
Cosmology." *Current Anthropology* 37: 395–428.

Savy, Nicole. 1995. "Victor Hugo et le Musée des Monuments Français: Les effets d'une
Enfance au Musée." *Revue d'histoire littéraire de la France* 95 (1): 13–26.

Schlegel, Jean-Louis. 1998. "Vide éthique et parole de l'Église catholique." *Esprit* 136/137
(3/4): 165–74.

———. 2010. " Adieu au catholicisme en France et en Europe?" *Esprit* 362 (2): 78–93.

Schloesser, Stephen. 2005. *Jazz Age Catholicism: Mystic Modernism in Post-War Paris, 1919–1933*. Toronto: University of Toronto Press.

Schmitt, Carl. 1922 [1987]. *Political Theology: Four Chapters on the Concept of Sovereignty.* Translated by George Schwab. Chicago: University of Chicago Press.

Schneider, Jane. 1990. "Spirits and the Spirit of Capitalism." In *Religious Orthodoxy and Popular Faith in European Society*, edited by Ellen Badone, 24–54. Princeton, NJ: Princeton University Press.

Scott, Joan Wallach. 1996. *Only Paradoxes to Offer: French Feminists and the Rights of Man.* Cambridge, MA: Harvard University Press.

———. 2005. *Parité: Sexual Equality and the Crisis of French Universalism.* Chicago: University of Chicago Press.

———. 2018. *Sex and Secularism.* Princeton, NJ: Princeton University Press.

Selby, Jennifer A. 2012. *Questioning French Secularism: Gender Politics and Islam in a Parisian Suburb.* New York: Palgrave MacMillan.

Severgrand, Martine. 2004. *Vers une église sans prêtres. La crise du clergé séculier en France (1945–1978).* Rennes: Presses Universitaires de Rennes.

Sharpe, Christina. 2016. *In the Wake: On Blackness and Being.* Durham, NC: Duke University Press.

Sheran, Yasmeen. 2016. "France's Disappearing Mosques." *Atlantic*, August 1, 2016. https://www.theatlantic.com/news/archive/2016/08/french-mosques-islam/493919/.

Sherman, Daniel J. 1994. "Quatremère/Benjamin/Marx: Art Museums, Aura, and Commodity Fetishism." In *Museum Culture: Histories, Discourses, Spectacles*, edited by Daniel J. Sherman and Irit Rogoff, 123–43. Minneapolis: University of Minnesota Press.

Shorto, Russell. 2019. "Rembrandt in the Blood: An Obsessive Aristocrat, Rediscovered Paintings, and an Art-World Feud." *New York Times* Magazine, February 27, 2019. https://www.nytimes.com/2019/02/27/magazine/rembrandt-jan-six.html.

Silverstein, Paul. 2004. "Headscarves and the French Tricolor." *Middle East Report Online.* http://www.merip.org/mero/mer0013004.

Smith, John H. 2011. *Dialogues between Faith and Reason: The Death and Return of God in Contemporary Catholic Thought.* Ithaca, NY: Cornell University Press.

Sollers, Philippe. 2009. *Les Voyageurs du Temps.* Paris: Gallimard.

Soulages, Pierre, and Jacques Le Goff. 1995. *De la pertinence de mettre une oeuvre contemporaine dans un lieu chargé d'histoire.* Toulouse: Le péréginateur éditeur.

Spang, Rebecca. 2017. *Stuff and Money in the Time of the French Revolution.* Cambridge, MA: Harvard University Press.

Stasi, Bernard, et al. 2003. *Commission de Réflexion sur l'Application du Principe de Laïcité dans la République: Rapport au Président de la République.* Paris: La documentation française.

Sternberg, Maximillian. 2013. *Cistercian Architecture and Medieval Society.* Leiden, Netherlands: Brill.

Stieglitz, Ann. 1993. "Exorcizing the Devil: A Recontextualization of Grünewald's Isenheim Altar." *Art History* 16 (1): 173–78.

Stoekl, Allan. 2006. "French Catholic Traditionalism and the Specter of Reactionary Politics." *South Central Review* 23 (1): 89–106.

Sudlow, Brian. 2011. *Catholic Literature and Secularisation in France and England, 1880–1914.* Manchester: Manchester University Press.

Sullivan, Winnifred Fallers. 2005. *The Impossibility of Religious Freedom.* Princeton, NJ: Princeton University Press.

Surkis, Judith. 2015. "A Muslim Future to Come?" *Public Books.* November 18. https://www.publicbooks.org/a-muslim-future-to-come/.

Taylor, Charles. 2007. *A Secular Age.* Cambridge, MA: Belknap Press of Harvard University Press.

Ternision, Xavier. 2012. "À 'Charlie Hebdo,' on n'a 'pas l'impression d'égorger quelqu'un avec un feutre.'" *Le Monde,* September 20, 2012. http://www.lemonde.fr/actualite-medias/article/2012/09/20/je-n-ai-pas-1-impression-d-egorger-quelqu-un-avec-un-feutre_1762748_3236.html.

Terrio, Susan J. 1999. "Crucible of the Millennium? The Clovis Affair in Contemporary France." *Society for Comparative Study of Society and History* 41: 438–57.

———. 2009. *Judging Mohammed: Juvenile Delinquency, Immigration and Exclusion at the Paris Palace of Justice.* Stanford, CA: Stanford University Press.

Thompson, E. P. 1963. *The Making of the English Working Class.* New York: Vintage Books.

Thompson, Krista. 2015. *Shine: The Visual Economy of Light in African Diasporic Aesthetic Practice.* Durham, NC: Duke University Press.

Trouillot, Michel-Rolph. 1995. *Silencing the Past: Power and the Production of History.* Boston, MA: Beacon Press.

Verrips, Jojada. 2008. "Offending Art and the Sense of Touch." *Material Religion* 4: 204–25.

Warner, Michael. 1990. *The Letters of the Republic: Publication and the Public Sphere in Eighteenth-Century America.* Cambridge, MA: Harvard University Press.

———. 2002. *Publics and Counterpublics.* New York: Zone Books.

Waugh, Linda R. 1982. "Marked and Unmarked: A Choice between Unequals in Semiotic Structure." *Semiotica* 38 (3–4): 299–318.

Weber, Max. 1946. *The Methodology of the Social Sciences.* Translated and edited by Edward Shils and Henry Finch. New York: Free Press.

———. 2009 [1930]. *The Protestant Ethic and the Spirit of Capitalism, with Other Writings on the Rise of the West.* Translated by Stephen Kalberg. Fourth Edition. New York: Oxford University Press.

Weil, Simone. 1988 [1944]. *La pesanteur et la grâce.* Paris: Libraire Plon.

Weil, Simone. 2003 [1952]. *Gravity and Grace.* London; New York: Routledge.

———. 2018 [1937]. "Mediations on a Corpse." *New Left Review* 111 (May/June): 34–40.

Wollenberg, Daniel. 2014. "The New Knighthood: Terrorism and the Medieval." *Postmedieval: A Journal of Medieval Cultural Studies* 5 (1): 21–33.

Wolton, Dominique. 2010. "Un 'laïc' habité par le soufflé de Dieu." In *Jean-Marie Lustiger cardinal républicain,* edited by Matthieu Rougé, 33–40. Paris: Parole et Silence.

Zemmour, Éric. 2014. *Le suicide français: Ces quarantess années qui on défait la France.* Paris: Albin Michel.

Zito, Angela. 2008. "Can Television Mediate Religious Experience? The Theology of *Joan of Arcadia*." In *Religion: Beyond a Concept*, edited by Hent de Vries, 724–38. New York: Fordham University Press.

Zitzewitz, Karin. 2014. *The Art of Secularism: The Cultural Politics of Modernist Art in Contemporary India*. New York: Oxford University Press.

Zizek, Slavoj. 2003. *The Puppet and the Dwarf: The Perverse Core of Christianity*. Cambridge, MA: MIT Press.

INDEX

Page numbers in bold refer to illustrations.

Maritain, Raïssa, 87–88

marked/unmarked, 5–6, 18, 25, 40, 53, 61, 68–69, 208, 232n31, 235n17

marriage, 36–37, 58–60, 234n3, 236n25, 239n15

Marshall, Ruth, 8

Martin, David, 12

Marxism, 36, 197, 199, 209–10, 240n2

Mary Magdalene, 134, 147

materiality: and affect, 118, 127, 232n34, 240–41n3; banality of (definition), 4–6, 230n14; definition, 4; expression of privilege, 93 (see also elites; privilege [banality of]); and the past, 106–7, 118; Simone Weil on, 199. See also fetishism and fetishization, immateriality, materiality (Catholic)

materiality (Catholic): affect of, 19–20, 30, 118, 232n34; and conversion, 94–95; disrupted and disruptive, 109, 118, 122; and inequality, 20–21, 25–26, 93; in museums, 139; in Paris, 5–7, 131; symbol of France, 131 (see also "Marianne"; Notre-Dame); theologies of, 42, 189; universalism of, 11; visibility and banality of, 6, 11–14, 17–18, 69, 95–96, 112, 122, 140, 213–14, 232n31. See also fetishism and fetishization, icons, images, cathedrals, Collège des Bernardins (space)

McClellan, Andrew, 171, 174–76

mediation, 10, 12, 19, 29, 119, 149, 151, 169–71, 216, 233n37; definition 107–9

mediators at the Collège: description of, 9–11; instruction of, 54, 162–63, 180–81, 182, 186, 200; labor of, 10, 54, 125, 129, 139–40, 142, 144, 150, 189, 199–200, 248n4; perspectives on the Collège and exhibits, 112, 126–27, 138, 140, 165, 195, 244n5; and visitors, 27–28, 30, 114–15, 139–40, 142–47, 158, 181, 193, 201

medieval past: as critique, 68, 162–63; as French genius, 131, 214; desire for, 3, 11, 22, 105–110, 116–19, 125, 179–80, 200, 216, 241n6; denaturalization of, 30, 106, 164, 189; rebirth of, 42, 132, 247n19. See also monasticism

Meyer, Birgitte, 107–8

Millet, Catherine, 147–48

Missika, Jean-Louis, and Dominique Wolton, 91, 94–95

Mitchell, W.J.T., 161–62, 172

Mitterrand, Francois, 79, 105

modern art. See contemporary art

modernity: European myth, 21; ideologies, 36; and objects, 4, 19–20, 244n3, 247n20; and religion, 12, 36, 42, 82, 230n14, 233n37

monasticism, 1, 42, 46–49, 68, 164, 170, 200–203, 207–8; as metaphor, 64

Moore, Breanna, 21, 87

Morgan, David, 204

Mukerji, Chandra, 21–22

Murphy, Keith M., 247n1

museums, 41, 119, 124, 139, 171, 173–77, 179, 204, 242n17; advertisement/branding, 55–56; Centre Pompidou, 116; of Paris, 27; Louvre, 58, 123–25, 139, 145, 171, 173–75, 183, 244n14; Musée des Arts et Métiers, 179–80; Museum of Jewish Art and History, 97–98; Museum of the Memorial of the Shoah, 91–92; Petits-Augustin (Musée National des Monuments Français), 175–77, 247n19; Profane Museum (Vatican), 138–39; Strasbourg Cathedral Museum, 215; Unterlinden Museum, 128, 132, 134, 243n7. See also Collège des Bernardins

Muslims, 3–4, 17, 18, 25, 30, 62, 65–67, 81–82, 111, 120–122, 196, 229n5, 234n7, 236n23, 238n7, 241n5; as vandals, 109, 115, 125–27

mysticism, 87, 180–81, 199

Nagel, Alexander, 172, 177–78, 180, 247n20

Nancy, Jean-Luc, 16, 232n28

Napoleon: concordat on religion, 15–16, 80–81

narcissism, 162–63, 166

nationalism, 13, 16–17, 80, 82–83, 171, 182, 204, 216–17, 238–39n10

niqab. See burqa

Nirenberg, David, 86, 188, 243n10

Nolde, Emil, 133–34, 243n10

Nora, Pierre, 43–44, 68, 244n3

normalization, 29, 38–42, 48, 50, 51, 53–54, 63, 67, 105, 150, 218, 221, 235n18, 236n28

semblance, 149–50

Shudson, Michael, 40

Six, Jan, 107

Smith, John H., 47

Society of St. Pius X, 25, 238n9

Sollers, Philippe, 48–49, 64

Soulages, Pierre, 106, 233n38

Spang, Rebecca, 183

spiritual meaning, 23, 94, 113, 130, 170, 186,
189–92, 202; and evangelism, 38; spiritual
public, 141, 145–49, 181

Stoll, Georges Tony, 187, 194

Submission (novel). *See* Houellebecq, Michel

Suite Grünewald (artwork). *See* Titus-Carmel,
Gérard

surfaces, 30, 170, 188–91, 199, 210–11, 244n2

Surkis, Judith, 122

Taylor, Charles, 12

temporalities: and material forms, 106, 118,
177; periodization, 106, 175–77, 179–80;
Protestant vs. Catholic, 73; rupture and
continuity, 72–74, 76–77, 82–83, 89, 101,
126, 165, 178. *See also* calendar; continuities; holidays

Thomas, Mickalene, 191

Thompson, Krista, 190–91, 199, 232n32

Titus-Carmel, Gérard, 128–38, **135**, **136**, **137**,
140–151, 155, 244n1

tradition: Christian, 52–53, 58, 80, 169, 177–78,
180–81; republican, 17

translation (French-English), 50–52, 61, 235n14,
241n10, 248n6

unmarked (concept). *See* marked/unmarked

Van der Meulen, Emmanuel, 187–88, 200–201,
201

vandalism, 115, 160, 162–63, 169, 179, 247n17;
unintentional 185. *See also under* Muslims

vernissage (exhibit opening), 109, 115, 141, 185–
186, 187, 194

Veronika, 113

Versailles, 22, 124

Vichy, 91–92, 94, 97

Vingt-Trois, Cardinal Andrè, 53, 76

Virgin Mary, 23, 121, 134, 146–147, 170, 177,
232n27, 246n15

visitors. *See* contemporary art (visitor
responses); publics

visitors' book. *See* livre d'or

Warhol, Andy, 23

Warner, Michael, 61, 140

Weber, Max, 20, 26, 170, 204, 209, 244n3

Weil, Simone, 197–99, 202

Wéry, Marthe, 187, 194, 196, 248n4

Wolton, Dominique, 77, 94, 237n5. *See also*
Missika, Jean-Louis, and Dominique
Wolton

youth, 97; Muslim, 30, 115, 120

Zemmour, Éric, 36

Zimbabwe, 170

Zitzewitz, Karin, 22

Zwingli, Huldrych, 19

Lightning Source UK Ltd.
Milton Keynes UK
UKHW022232140421
381997UK00003B/4